Spatiotemporal Image Understanding

Yu-Jin Zhang

Spatiotemporal Image Understanding

Action, Activity and Behavior

Springer

Yu-Jin Zhang
Department of Electronic Engineering
Tsinghua University
Beijing, China

ISBN 978-981-95-7129-1 ISBN 978-981-95-7130-7 (eBook)
https://doi.org/10.1007/978-981-95-7130-7

This Springer imprint is published by the registered company Springer Nature Singapore Pte Ltd.
The registered company address is: 152 Beach Road, #21-01/04 Gateway East, Singapore 189721, Singapore

Preface

Image understanding is at the high level of image engineering, and spatiotemporal image understanding is a relatively new research direction in image understanding. Its goal is to use various spatiotemporal technologies to analyze and make meaningful explanations and judgments on human activities and behaviors in the objective scenes reflected in images.

This book mainly deals with modeling, detection, recognition, reasoning, and interpreting techniques related to various levels of spatiotemporal image understanding, from action primitives, actions, activities, events, to behavior. This book mainly focuses on introducing the principles of these technologies, discussing and analyzing relevant methods combined with research results, and providing a summary of recent research progress.

In addition to Chap. 1 for introduction, this book consists of seven chapters, which, respectively, introduce spatiotemporal point of interest detection, spatiotemporal motion trajectory analysis, classification and recognition of actors and actions, modeling and recognition of subject activities, detection and classification of human-object interaction relationships, behavior analysis and inference based on various networks, and detection and judgment of abnormal events.

This book focuses on introducing different levels of work and recent developments in the field of spatiotemporal image understanding. In Chaps. 2–8, each chapter first introduces the working principle and provides an overview of existing typical technologies, summarizes their characteristics, and classifies them. Then, several specific methods are analyzed in detail (including the overall flowchart, algorithm principle description, specific process steps, experiment and effect examples, related method comparison, *etc.*). Each chapter also introduces the latest developments in related technical fields, summarizes their characteristics, and categorizes them, which can help readers understand some of the latest development trends.

On the one hand, this book can serve as a professional course textbook for senior undergraduate and graduate students in related disciplines/majors, helping them master the basic principles and carry out scientific research activities, complete graduation projects and theses. On the other hand, it is also suitable as a research reference for researchers in related fields.

The book consists of 8 chapters, with 30 sections (sub-headings) and 72 subsections (sub-sub-headings). There are a total of 88 numbered figures, 56 numbered tables, and 191 numbered formulas. The book provides a list of more than 350 references cited (half are published in the 2020s), and more than 300 subject terms used are listed at the end of the book for indexing and for facilitate further accessing to related literatures.

The book contains considerable amounts of contents based on the research results of many students who have obtained their academic degrees in the author's image engineering research laboratory. Many of the images and curves of the experimental results come from their dozens of research papers. I am very fortunate to work with them and to make discussion with them. I would like to thank them for their hard work and dedication to scientific research, and I wish them all the best in their future endeavors to contribute more and better to the development of science and the progress of society.

Finally, I would like to thank my wife Yun He, daughter Heming Zhang, and other family members for their understanding and support in all aspects.

Beijing, China

Yu-Jin Zhang
zhang-yj@tsinghua.edu.cn
https://www.oa.ee.tsinghua.edu.cn/zhangyujin/

Competing Interests The author has no competing interests to declare that are relevant to the content of this manuscript.

Contents

About the Author

Yu-Jin Zhang, received his doctor's degree in Applied Science from the University of Liège in Belgium in 1989. From 1989 to 1993, he successively engaged in postdoctoral research and served as a full-time researcher at Delft University in the Netherlands. Since 1993, he has worked in the Department of Electronic Engineering of Tsinghua University in Beijing, China. He has been a professor since 1997, a Ph.D. supervisor since 1998, and a tenured professor since 2014. During the sabbatical year of 2003, he was a Visiting Professor in the Nanyang Technological University Singapore.

At Tsinghua University, he has offered and taught over 10 undergraduate and graduate courses, including "Image Processing", "Image Analysis", "Image Understanding", and "Content Based Visual Information Retrieval". At Nanyang Technological University, he offered and taught a postgraduate course (in English): "Advanced Image Analysis". More than 50 Chinese and English textbooks have been written and published (with a total of over 400,000 printed copies). More than 30 research papers on educational and teaching topics have been published both domestically and internationally.

His main scientific research fields are image engineering (image processing, image analysis, image understanding, and their technical applications) that he actively advocates. He has published over 550 research papers on image engineering in national and international journal and conferences. He has published the monographs *Image Segmentation* and *Content Based Visual Information Retrieval* (Science Press, China), as well as *Subspace Based Face Recognition* (Tsinghua University Press, China); has written *English Chinese Dictionary of Image Engineering* (1st, 2nd, and 3rd editions; Tsinghua University Press, China); has written the *Selected Works of Image Engineering Technology*, and *Selected Works of Image Engineering Technology (2)* (Tsinghua University Press, China); has translated *Color in Computer Vision: Fundamentals and Applications* (John Wiley & Sons, Inc. USA) and *Computational Geometry, Topology, and Physics of Digital Images with Applications* (Springer Verlag, Germany) into Chinese; has led the compilation of *Advances in Image and Video Segmentation* and *Semantic Based Visual Information*

Retrieval (IRM Press, USA), as well as *Advances in Face Image Analysis: Technologies and Technologies* (IGI Global, USA); has written *Handbook of Image Engineering* (Springer Nature, Singapore); has written *A Selection of Image Processing Techniques, A Selection of Image Analysis Techniques*, and *A Selection of Image Understanding Techniques* (CRC Press, USA); has written *3D Computer Vision: Foundations and Advanced Methodologies* (Springer Nature, Singapore).

He is currently a fellow member and honorary supervisor of the Chinese Society of Image Graphics; a fellow member of the International Society of Optical Engineering (SPIE), for achievements in image engineering; and formerly served as the Chairman of the Program Committee of the 24th International Conference on Image Processing (ICIP'2017).

Chapter 1
Introduction

Images are entities obtained by observing the objective world in different forms and methods, as well as by using various observation systems, which can directly or indirectly make effects on the human eyes and generate visual perception (Zhang 1996a). The human visual system is an observation system, and the image obtained through it is the image formed by the object in the human mind.

Images contain rich information. Scientific research and statistics show that about 75% of the information that humans obtained from the outside world comes from the visual system, that is, from images. Images are our primary source of information. The concept of images here is relatively broad, including photos, drawings, animations, videos, and even documents, etc.

Image technology includes techniques for image acquisition, processing, analysis, understanding, as well as the interpretation, judgment, etc., based on images. The comprehensive integration and engineering application of these techniques constitute the new discipline of image engineering. Among them, the spatiotemporal technology for understanding behavior introduced in this book represents a new branch of image understanding that corresponds to one of the three core levels of image engineering. With the development of research and application of images and image technology, this direction has received widespread attention and attracted many researches in recent years. In the research and application of spatiotemporal technology, the influence of deep learning and neural networks is becoming increasingly significant and has a great driving force.

The sections of this chapter are arranged as follows.

Section 1.1 shows an overview and development of image engineering.

Section 1.2 discusses the various levels of spatiotemporal technology for understanding spatiotemporal action, activity, and behavior.

Section 1.3 introduces some basic concepts of deep learning based on neuron network.

Section 1.4 provides the overall book structure and an introduction to each chapter.

Y.-J. Zhang, *Spatiotemporal Image Understanding*,
https://doi.org/10.1007/978-981-95-7130-7_1

1.1 Image Engineering

To effectively use visual information, it is necessary to collect images. These images must then be processed to enhance quality, extract useful data, support decision-making, and enable practical applications. These tasks require the use of different imaging and image techniques to complete. Image engineering is the overall framework for comprehensive research and integrated application of all image technologies.

1.1.1 Image Technology and Image Engineering

Image technology is a general term for various image related technologies in a broad sense. Nowadays, it mainly refers to computer image technology, including a series of computing tasks and functions performed and completed with computers and other electronic devices, such as.

- Image acquisition, collection, encoding, storage, and transmission
- Image synthesis and generation, display and output
- Image watermark embedding and extraction, image authentication and forensics
- Image transformation, enhancement, restoration, repair, and reconstruction from projection
- Image segmentation, target location, detection, tracking, extraction, representation, and description
- Target feature extraction, description and measurement
- Image classification, representation, and recognition
- Sequence image correction, 3-D scene reconstruction and restoration
- Image database establishment, indexing, querying and retrieval
- Image model establishment and matching, image and scene interpretation and understanding
- Decision-making and action planning based on image understanding.

In addition, image technology can also include hardware design and production techniques to achieve the above tasks and functions.

Due to the great attention and significant progress of image technology in recent years, many new theories, methods, algorithms, means, devices, and applications have emerged. The research and application of comprehensive integration of various image technologies should be carried out within a holistic framework, which is image engineering (Zhang 1996a).

Image Engineering (IE) is a new discipline that comprehensively and systematically studies image theory methods, elucidates the principles of image technology, promotes the application of image technology, and summarizes production practice experience. It has been widely applied in many fields such as biomedical, materials, remote sensing, communication, traffic management, military reconnaissance, document processing, and industrial automation.

1.1.2 Three Levels of Image Engineering

The research content of image engineering is very rich and covers a wide range, which can be divided into three levels (as shown in Fig. 1.1): image processing, image analysis, and image understanding. Each of the three levels has its own characteristics in terms of operational objects and semantic levels, and each level differs from others in terms of data volume and abstraction. In fact, image engineering is an organic combination of image processing, image analysis, and image understanding that are both related and distinct, as well as their engineering applications (technical applications).

Image processing (IP) can be seen as a major category of image technology that emphasizes the transformation between images. Although image processing commonly refers to various image techniques, the main goal of more narrow image processing techniques is to perform various processing on images to improve their visual effects and lay the foundation for automatic target recognition, or to compress and encode images to reduce the space required for image storage or the time required for image transmission (thereby reducing the requirements for transmission pathways). An introduction to image processing can be found in (Zhang 2017b), some recent progresses can be found in (Zhang 2022b).

Image analysis (IA) mainly involves detecting and measuring objects of interest in an image to obtain their objective information and establish a description of the image and the object. If image processing is a process from image to image (image in to image out), then image analysis is a process from image to data (image in to data out). The data here can be the results of measuring the target features, or a symbolic representation based on the measurements. These data (with less data volume than the original images) describe the characteristics and properties of the target in the

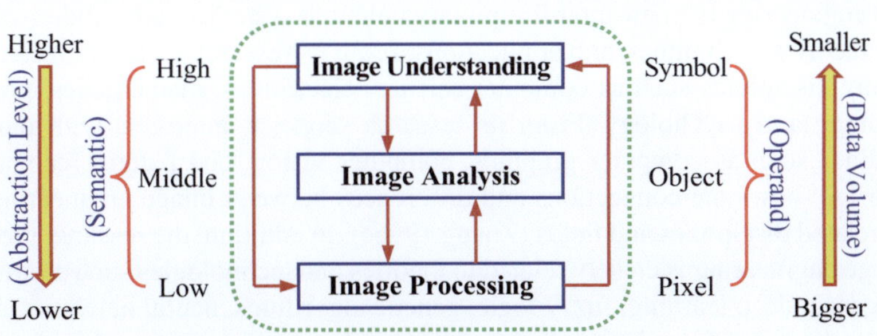

Fig. 1.1 Schematic diagram of three levels of image engineering

image. An introduction to image analysis can be found in (Zhang 2017c), some recent progresses can be found in (Zhang 2023b).

Image Understanding (IU) has the focus on further comprehend the properties of various targets in the image and their interrelationships based on image analysis, and to derive more abstract explanations of the original objective scene through understanding the meaning of the image content, in order to guide and plan actions. If image analysis mainly focuses on the observer to study the objective world (mainly observable things), then image understanding is to some extent centered on the objective world, using knowledge, experience, reasoning, etc. to grasp the entire objective world (including things that are not directly observed). An introduction to image understanding can be found in (Zhang 2017d), some recent progresses can be found in (Zhang 2023c).

As shown in Fig. 1.1, image processing, image analysis, and image understanding are located at three different levels of abstraction and have their own characteristics in terms of data volume. Image processing is a relatively low-level operation that mainly processes at the pixel level of the image, and the amount of data processed is very large. Image analysis has entered the middle level, where segmentation and feature extraction transform images originally described in pixels into more concise non-graphical descriptions. Image understanding is mainly a high-level operation, which involves performing actions on symbols abstracted from descriptions. Its processing and methods have many similarities with human thinking and reasoning. Furthermore, as shown in Fig. 1.1, the amount of data gradually decreases as the level of abstraction increases. Specifically, the original image data undergoes a series of processing steps, and its representation gradually transforms from low-level to high-level, providing more organized and useful information. In this process, on the one hand, semantics are constantly introduced, the operating objects change, and the data volume is compressed; on the other hand, high-level operations have a guiding role in lower level operations and can improve the efficiency of lower level operations.

1.1.3 Disciplines and Fields Related to Image Engineering

Image engineering is a new interdisciplinary field that systematically studies various image theories, techniques, and applications. From its research methods, it can draw on many disciplines such as computer science, electronics, mathematics, physics, physiology and psychology. From its research scope, it intersects with multiple disciplines such as computer graphics, computer vision, and pattern recognition. Figure 1.2 shows the connections and differences between image engineering and some related disciplines and fields (Zhang 1996c). In addition, the research progress of image engineering is closely related to theories and technologies such as artificial intelligence, deep learning, fuzzy logic, genetic algorithms, neural networks, etc.

It can be seen, from Fig. 1.2, that the three levels of image engineering have different input–output contents and they have various relationships with related disciplines such as computer graphics, computer vision, and pattern recognition.

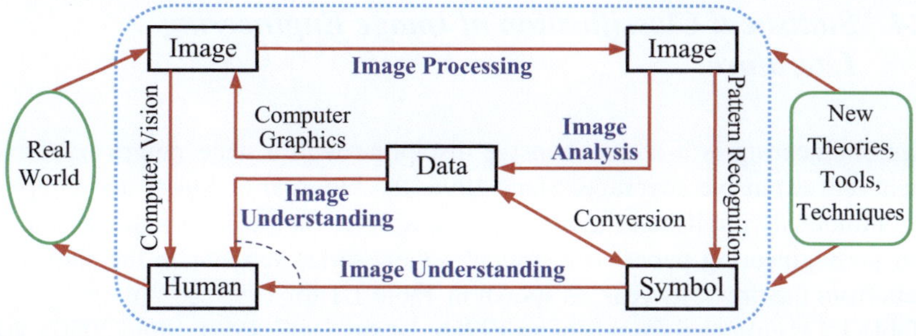

Fig. 1.2 The relationship and differences between image engineering and related disciplines and fields

Graphics originally referred to the science of expressing data information in the form of **graphs**, **charts**, and **drawings**, while **Computer Graphics** (CG) studies how to use computer technology to generate these forms. If compared with image analysis, the processing objects and output results of the two are exactly reversed. Computer graphics attempts to generate (realistic) images from non-visual data descriptions. **Pattern Recognition** (PR) and image analysis are quite related, but the former attempts to decompose images into categories that can be described abstractly with symbols. They have the same input, and their different output results can be easily converted. As for **Computer Vision** (CV), it mainly emphasizes the use of computers to achieve human visual functions, which actually involves many techniques from the three levels of image engineering. However, the current research content is mainly shared with image understanding.

From this description, the above disciplines are interrelated and have certain overlapping coverage. In fact, these names/nouns are often used interchangeably, and there is no absolute boundary between them conceptually or practically. In many occasions and situations, they are just different terms commonly used by people with different professions and backgrounds. Although each of them has its own focus separately, together they often complement each other. In addition, all of the above disciplines have received support from new theories, tools and technologies such as **Artificial Intelligence** (AI), neural networks, genetic algorithms, fuzzy logic, machine learning, and **deep learning** (as shown in Fig. 1.2), and have made significant progress in recent years. Overall, image engineering can effectively integrate many similar disciplines and further emphasize the application of image technology. Here, image engineering can be used to refer to the entire field of image technology and its related research and applications.

1.1.4 Statistical Classification of Image Engineering Literature

Image engineering is a comprehensive discipline with a wide ranges of research content and extensive coverage. Since 1996, the "Journal of Image and Graphics" has continuously published literature review articles on the statistical classification of image engineering papers (the annual review series summarize the statistics of papers from the previous year, as shown in Table 1.1 for 1995–2024).

Table 1.1 is collected from (Zhang 1996b, 1996c, 1997, 1998, 1999, 2000a, 2001, 2002a, 2003, 2004, 2005, 2006, 2007a, 2008, 2009a, 2010, 2011a, 2012, 2013a, 2014a, 2015a, 2016, 2017a, 2018a, 2019, 2020, 2021a, 2022a, 2023a, 2024, 2025). They document the progress of image engineering research and applications. In addition, one can also refer to some stage summaries, including (Zhang 2000b, 2002b, 2007b, 2011b, 2014b, 2021b); as well as relevant literature such as (Zhang 1996a, 2002c, 2009b, 2015b, 2018b, 2018c).

Table 1.1 provides an overview of the statistical classification of image engineering papers published in 15 important journals (in alphabetical order, including "Acta Automatica Sinica", "Acta Electronica Sinica", "Acta Geodaetica et Cartographica Sinica", "Chinese Journal of Biomedical Engineering", "Chinese Journal of Computers", "Chinese Journal of Stereology and Image Analysis", "Computerized Tomography Theory and Applications", "Journal on Communications", "Journal of Data Acquisition and Processing", "Journal of Electronics & Information Technology", "Journal of Electronic Measurement and Instrumentation", "Journal of Image and Graphics", "National Remote Sensing Bulletin", "Pattern Recognition and Artificial Intelligence", "Signal Processing", from 1995 to 2024. In Table 1.1, the total number of papers represents the total number of papers published in the 15 journals for the literature review articles, and the total number of selections is the number of papers selected as they are related to image engineering. The papers are divided into five categories, with the first three categories corresponding to the three research levels of techniques in image engineering. The fourth category includes the technical applications of various image engineering technologies, and the fifth category includes research review papers on cross-category techniques.

In order to see the development of the first four categories over the years more easily and intuitively, Fig. 1.3 depicts the variation curves of the number of papers in these four categories of image processing (IP), image analysis (IA), image understanding (IU), and technical applications (TA) in the paper classification over the past 30 years (the horizontal axis indicates the year, and the vertical axis indicates the percentage of selected literature).

There are several facts worth pointing out from the statistical data in Table 1.1 and Fig. 1.3:

(1) In the first 15 years, both the total number of papers and the total number of selections have been increased year by year. The increase in the total number of papers indicates that these journals have been continuously developing in these years, while the increase in the total number of selections indicates that research

Table 1.1 Statistical table of image engineering literature selection from 1995 to 2024 (Zhang 2025)

Year	Total number of papers	Total number of selections	Selection rate	Number of papers (% of total selected papers in the current year)				
				Image processing	Image analysis	Image understanding	Technology application	Review comments
1995	997	147	14.74	36 (24.5)	51 (34.7)	14 (9.52)	46 (31.3)	–
1996	1205	212	17.59	52 (24.5)	72 (34.0)	30 (14.2)	55 (25.9)	3 (1.42)
1997	1438	280	19.47	104 (37.1)	76 (27.1)	36 (12.9)	60 (21.4)	4 (1.43)
1998	1477	306	20.72	108 (35.3)	96 (31.4)	28 (9.15)	71 (23.2)	3 (0.98)
1999	2048	388	18.95	132 (34.0)	137 (35.3)	42 (10.8)	73 (18.8)	4 (1.03)
2000	2117	464	21.92	165 (35.6)	122 (26.3)	68 (14.7)	103 (22.2)	6 (1.29)
2001	2297	481	20.94	161 (33.5)	123 (25.6)	78 (16.2)	115 (23.9)	4 (0.83)
2002	2426	545	22.46	178 (32.7)	150 (27.5)	77 (14.3)	135 (24.8)	5 (0.92)
2003	2341	577	24.65	194 (33.6)	153 (26.5)	104 (18.0)	119 (20.6)	7 (1.21)
2004	2473	632	25.60	235 (37.2)	176 (27.8)	76 (12.0)	142 (22.5)	3 (0.47)
2005	2734	656	23.99	221 (33.7)	188 (28.7)	112 (17.1)	131 (20.0)	4 (0.61)
2006	3013	711	23.60	239 (33.6)	206 (29.0)	116 (16.3)	143 (20.1)	7 (0.98)
2007	3312	895	27.02	315 (35.2)	237 (26.5)	142 (15.9)	194 (21.7)	7 (0.78)
2008	3359	915	27.24	269 (29.4)	311 (34.0)	130 (14.2)	196 (21.4)	9 (0.98)
2009	3604	1008	27.97	312 (31.0)	335 (33.2)	139 (13.8)	214 (21.2)	8 (0.79)
2010	3251	782	24.05	239 (30.6)	257 (32.9)	136 (17.4)	146 (18.7)	4 (0.51)
2011	3214	797	24.80	245 (30.7)	270 (33.9)	118 (14.8)	161 (20.2)	3 (0.38)
2012	3083	792	25.69	249 (31.4)	272 (34.3)	111 (14.0)	151 (19.1)	9 (1.14)
2013	2986	716	23.98	209 (29.2)	232 (32.4)	124 (17.3)	146 (20.4)	5 (0.70)
2014	3103	822	26.49	260 (31.6)	261 (31.8)	121 (17.7)	175 (21.3)	5 (0.61)

(continued)

Table 1.1 (continued)

Year	Total number of papers	Total number of selections	Selection rate	Number of papers (% of total selected papers in the current year)				
				Image processing	Image analysis	Image understanding	Technology application	Review comments
2015	2975	723	24.30	199 (27.5)	294 (40.7)	103 (14.2)	119 (16.5)	8 (1.11)
2016	2938	728	24.78	174 (23.9)	266 (36.5)	105 (14.4)	172 (23.6)	11 (1.51)
2017	2932	771	26.30	204 (26.5)	248 (32.2)	127 (16.5)	186 (24.1)	6 (0.78)
2018	2863	747	26.09	206 (27.6)	275 (36.8)	100 (13.4)	155 (20.7)	11 (1.47)
2019	2854	761	26.66	165 (21.7)	272 (35.7)	136 (17.9)	183 (24.0)	5 (0.66)
2020	2785	813	29.19	153 (18.8)	300 (36.9)	134 (16.5)	217(26.7)	9 (1.11)
2021	2958	833	28.16	171 (20.5)	312 (37.5)	130 (15.6)	210(25.2)	10 (1.20)
2022	3096	908	29.33	220 (24.2)	284 (31.3)	129 (14.2)	267 (29.4)	8 (0.88)
2023	2989	865	28.94	161 (18.61)	289 (33.41)	112 (12.95)	294 (33.99)	9 (1.04)
2024	2892	889	30.74	203 (22.83)	217 (24.41)	139 (15.64)	326 (36.67)	4 (0.45)
subtotal	**79760**	**20164**	—	**5779 (28.61)**	**6482 (32.1)**	**3017 (14.94)**	**4705 (23.33)**	**181 (0.90)**
average	**2659**	**672**	**25.28**	**193**	**216**	**101**	**157**	**6**

Note "—" indicates no data available

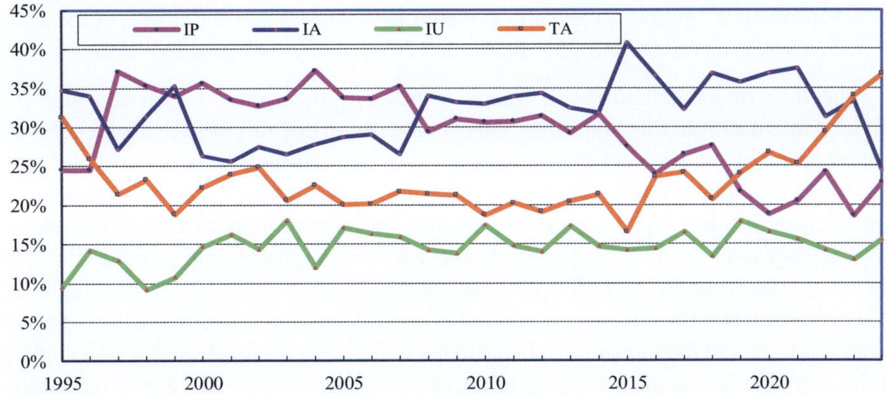

Fig. 1.3 Variation curve of major categories in image engineering papers for 30-year (Zhang 2025)

and applications in image engineering are becoming increasingly widespread, and are developing more rapidly compared to other related disciplines. In the following 15 years, this trend gets slowing down in somewhat, partly due to an increase of the average length on journal papers in these years, with the whole quantity remaining relatively stable. This trend and situation should continue for a certain period of time.

(2) The paper selection rate reflects the importance of image engineering in the professional scope covered by these journals. The paper selection rate in the first 15 years was basically monotone increasing, and the papers on image engineering have been continuously increasing in multiple academic and professional journals, accounting for a considerable proportion. This fully demonstrates that image technology has been widely valued and applied. The paper selection rate for the next 10 years is relatively stable, basically maintaining a high level. The paper selection rate has increased significantly in the past 5 years, compared to the previous 5 years, it has increased by 1.14 times. In 2024, the selection rate exceeded 30%, this is the highest in history.

(3) Looking at the three research levels, the total number of papers related to image processing in the first 15 years was generally higher than that of other major categories. In the past 15 years, the total number of papers related to image analysis has increased rapidly, occupying the first place. This indicates that the focus of image engineering is gradually developing towards higher levels. In addition, the total number of papers in the categories of image understanding is relatively small compared to the categories of image processing and image analysis. It can be seen that on the one hand, research on image understanding still needs to be strengthened; on the other hand, there is still great potential for research on image understanding.

(4) Finally, looking at the application category of image technology, in the first two years, the percentage of in the total number of papers exceeded 25%. In the

following 23 years, it basically hovered between 20 and 25%, and in the past 5 years, it has exceeded 25% again. By 2024, it is even exceeded 36%.

The four major categories of image technology mentioned above can also be divided into multiple subcategories. This approach can not only help to have a general appreciating of the content of image engineering and various image technologies, but also reveal the historical development and current research and application hotspots and focuses. Table 1.2 provides a detailed classification of literature related to image engineering over the past 30 years. At present, image processing is divided into 6 subcategories (referred to as A1–A6), image analysis is divided into 5 subcategories (referred to as B1–B5), image understanding is divided into 5 subcategories (referred to as C1–C5), and technology application is divided into 6 subcategories (referred to as D1–D6). In fact, at the beginning of the review series (year 1996), these four major categories were only divided into 17 subcategories. With the progress of research and application, three subcategories A5, B5, and C4 have been added since 2000 (the number of papers is based on statistical data from 2000 and onwards). Since 2005, two subcategories A6 and C5 (the latter being the category focused on in this book) have been added, with the statistical data from 2005 and onwards. At present, these four major categories are divided into 22 subcategories. It should be pointed out that although the names of these subcategories have been revised and improved year by year, the main content remains basically consistent (Zhang 2025). The definitions of each item in the subcategory names and contents of Table 1.2 can be found in (Zhang 2021c).

The results of counting the number of papers for the 23 subcategories mentioned above for 2024 are shown in Fig. 1.4 (Zhang 2025).

Combining Table 1.2 and Fig. 1.4, it can be seen that the number of papers in each subcategory has undergone significant changes over the years, with some continuously increasing and maintaining a leading position, while others gradually decreasing and falling to the bottom. This reflects the different levels of attention and work engagement in different research directions. This book will focus on the C5 subcategory of image understanding: spatiotemporal technology and behavioral understanding.

1.2 Spatiotemporal Image Understanding

Spatiotemporal technology is a technology aimed at **understanding spatiotemporal behavior**, and is one of five subcategories in image understanding that is at the highest level of image engineering. The position of spatiotemporal technology in image engineering, according to Table 1.2, is shown in Fig. 1.5.

Spatiotemporal technology is a relatively new research field (Zhang 2012, 2013b). Currently, research work is being carried out at different directions and stages, and the following is an overview.

Table 1.2 Classification of Image Engineering Literature from 1995 to 2024 (Zhang 2025)

Category name	Subcategory name and content	Total number	Annually average
Image processing	A1: Image acquisition (various imaging modalities, image acquisition, representation and storage, camera calibration, etc.)	1116	38
	A2: Image projection reconstruction (reconstructing images from projections, indirect imaging, etc.)	526	18
	A3: Image enhancement/restoration (transformation, filtering, restoration, patching, permutation, correction, visual quality evaluation, etc.)	1758	59
	A4: Image/video compression and encoding (algorithm research, relevant international standards, etc.)	1037	36
	A5: Image information security (digital watermarking, information hiding, image authentication and evidence collection, etc.)	977	39
	A6: Image multi-resolution processing (super-resolution reconstruction, image decomposition and interpolation, resolution conversion, etc.)	365	18
Image analysis	B1: Image segmentation and primitive detection (edges, corners, control points, points of interest, etc.)	2220	74
	B2: Object representation, description, measurement (and binary image morphology analysis, etc.)	315	11
	B3: Object feature extraction and analysis (color, texture, shape, space, structure, motion, saliency, attributes, etc.)	636	21
	B4: Object detection, classification and recognition (2-D object localization, tracking, extraction, identification, and categorization, etc.)	1879	63
	B5: Extraction and verification of human biometric features (detection, localization, classification, and recognition of human bodies, faces, organs, etc.)	1432	57
Image understanding	C1: Image matching and fusion (registration, alignment, stitching, inlaying, etc. of stereo and sequence images)	1424	48
	C2: Object reconstruction and scene restoration (3-D scene modeling, refactoring or reconstruction, representation, description, etc.)	427	14

(continued)

Table 1.2 (continued)

Category name	Subcategory name and content	Total number	Annually average
	C3: Image perception and scene interpretation (semantic understanding, scene modeling, machine learning, cognitive reasoning, etc.)	178	6
	C4: Content based image/video retrieval (corresponding annotation, semantic description, modal transformation, scene classification, etc.)	600	24
	C5: Spatiotemporal technology and behavior understanding (high-dimensional motion analysis, 3-D object pose detection, spatiotemporal tracking, and behavior judgment, etc.)	396	20
Technology application	D1: Hardware, systems, devices, and fast, parallel algorithms	532	18
	D2: Communication, video transmission and playback (television, internet, radio, etc.)	394	13
	D3: Documents, text (words, numbers, symbols, etc.)	341	11
	D4: Biology, medicine (physiology, hygiene, health, etc.)	863	29
	D5: Remote sensing, radar, sonar, surveying, etc	1724	58
	D6: Other application domains (technology applications not directly/explicitly included in the above subcategories)	851	28
Review comments	E1: Cross category review (covering image processing/analysis/understanding, or involving comprehensive new technologies)	181	6

1.2.1 Development of Spatiotemporal Technology

The image engineering review series mentioned in Sect. 1.1.4 has been ongoing for 30 years since the literature review started for 1995 (Zhang 2025). In the beginning of the second decade of this review series (starting from the literature in 2005), with the emergence of new hotspots in image engineering research and application, a new subcategory C5 was added to the image understanding category: spatiotemporal techniques and behavior understanding (high-dimensional motion analysis, 3-D object pose detection, spatiotemporal tracking, and behavior judgment, etc.) (Zhang 2006), emphasizing the comprehensive utilization of various information in images/videos to make corresponding judgments and interpretations of the dynamic situation of scenes and objects therein.

In the past 20 years, a total number of 396 papers in the C5 subcategory were collected in the image engineering review series, and the distribution of each year is shown by the histogram bins in Fig. 1.6 (Zhang 2025). This figure also shows the

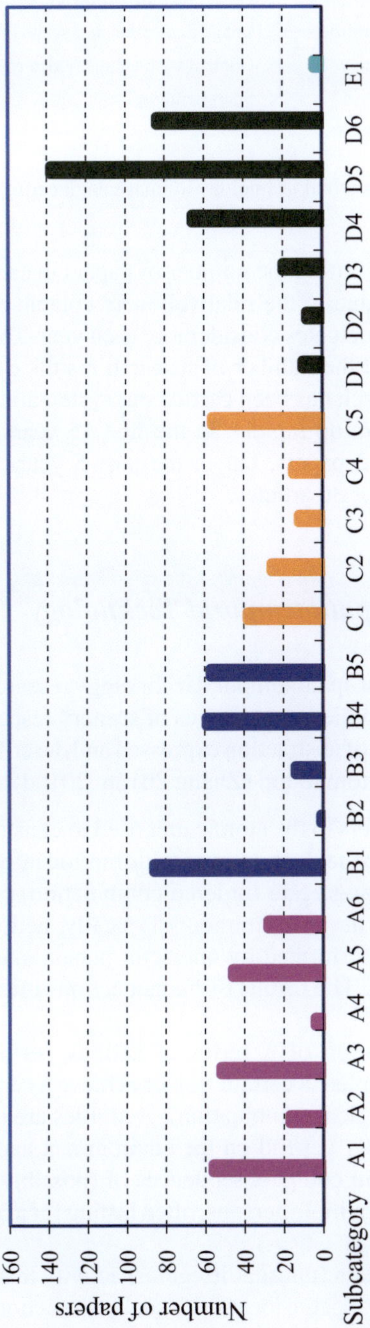

Fig. 1.4 Statistical results of the number of 23 subcategories of papers in 2024 (Zhang 2025)

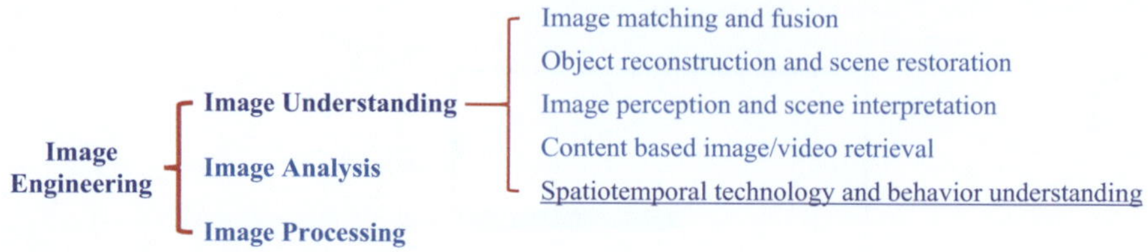

Fig. 1.5 The position of spatiotemporal technology in image engineering

trend of changes obtained by fitting the number of papers in each year using a third-order polynomial. Overall, due to the relatively new content at the beginning, the number of research results fluctuates considerably each year. The mid-term attention has gradually increased, and the number of research results each year is relatively stable. In recent years, research has been carried out systematically, and the number of research results has grown up rapidly. In the first 15 years, the average annual publication was less than 12 papers, but in the past 5 years, the average annual publication has tripled to over 36 articles.

1.2.2 Five Levels of Spatiotemporal Technology

At present, the main objects of spatiotemporal technology research are moving people or objects, as well as the activities and changes of scenery (especially people) in the scene. According to the level of abstraction expressed and described, it can be divided into multiple levels from bottom to top (Zhang 2013b, 2018d):

(1) **Action primitive**: It refers to the atomic unit used to construct an action, which generally corresponds to the short-term specific motion information in the scene.
(2) **Action**: A meaningful aggregate (ordered combination) composed of a series of action primitives of the actor/initiator. Typically, actions represent simple motion patterns, often performed by one actor/person, and typically only last on the order of seconds. The results of human actions often lead to changes in human posture.
(3) **Activity**: The combination of a series of actions performed by the actor/initiator in order to complete a certain task or achieve a certain goal or function (mainly emphasizing logical combination). Activities are relatively large-scale movements that generally depend on the environment and interacting people. Activities often represent complex sequences of (possibly interacting) actions performed by single or multiple persons, often lasting for a relative longer period of time.
(4) **Event**: It refers to a certain (unusual/irregular) activity that occurs in a specific time period and a specific spatial location. Usually, the actions in it are performed by multiple actors/initiators (group activity). Detection of specific events is often associated with significant and/or abnormal activity or behavior.

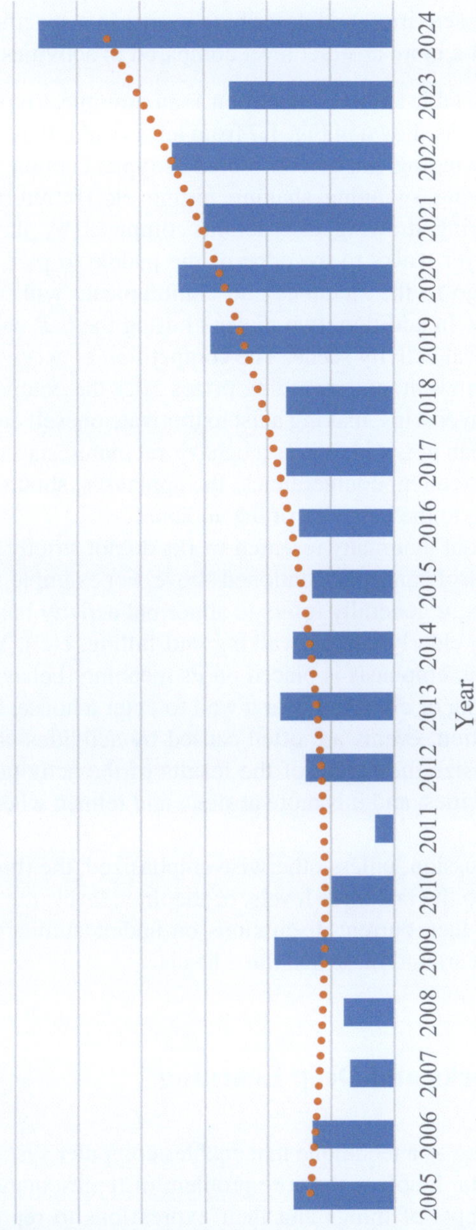

Fig. 1.6 Numbers and trend of changes of spatiotemporal technical papers in the past 20 years (Zhang 2025)

(5) **Behavior**: The actor/initiator mainly refers to people (can be animals), emphasizing that the actor/initiator is dominated by certain thoughts and is changing the actions, continuing activities, and describing events in a specific environment/context, which is at a more abstract level compared to activities.

Taking the program of table tennis competition as an example, a typical example of each level is given below, as shown in Fig. 1.7 from left to right. Players' movements such as footwork and swinging can be considered as typical action primitives. The serving (including throwing, swinging, shaking, hitting, etc.) or returning (including moving, stretching, flipping, drawing, etc.) actions completed by players are typical actions, but when a player walks to the edge of the paddle to pick up the ball, or applies for a pause to go to the sidelines and communicate with the coach, it is often seen as an activity. In addition, two players hitting the ball back and forth to win points is also a typical activity scene. The competition between sports teams is generally regarded as an event, and awarding prizes after the competition is also a typical event. After a player wins, making a fist to motivate oneself can be seen as an action, but more often than not, it is seen as a behavioral manifestation of the player. After players make an excellent counterattack, the applauses, shouts, and cheers of the audience also belong to the behavior of the audience.

It should be pointed out that many research works do not strictly distinguish the use of the last three levels of concepts mentioned above. For example, when referring to an activity as an event, it generally refers to abnormal activity (such as a dispute between two people, an elderly person walking and falling, etc.). When referring to an activity as behavior, emphasis is placed on its meaning (behavior) and nature (such as the act of stealing or climbing over a wall to enter a house, which is called theft behavior). In addition, events are often caused by activities and are referred to as events that emphasize the nature of the results of the activities. Behavior is manifested through activities, and it is more abstract and refined when referred to as behavior.

In the following discussion, unless otherwise emphasized, the (broad) activity is generally used to refer to the last three levels, or the three levels are mixed without strict differentiation. In fact, current discussions on understanding spatiotemporal behavior mainly revolve around these last three levels.

1.3 Neural Networks and Deep Learning

Deep learning can be seen as a technique that enables computer systems to improve from experience and data. It solves the core problem of representation learning by combining simple concepts of things and their expressions to represent complex concepts of things. It uses multi-layer nonlinear processing units to cascade feature extraction and transformation, achieving multi-level feature representation and concept abstraction learning.

Fig. 1.7 Example screens of various levels in table tennis competition (Zhang 2023c)

In recent years, deep learning has developed rapidly, and deep learning algorithms have achieved excellent results in tasks such as object detection, object tracking, object recognition, semantic segmentation, image classification, video classification, depth estimation, and image/video generation.

Deep learning is based on connectionism from a cognitive perspective. However, the complete theoretical framework of deep learning is still being established and improved. At present, there is still a lack of clear and complete theoretical explanations for how deep neural networks operate and why they could produce high-performance for the learning.

1.3.1 Deep Learning in Image Understanding

Image understanding is the use of computers to automatically interpret the meaning of objective scene images. However, it is difficult for computers to directly understand the meaning of the raw sensor input data. For example, when representing an image as a set of pixels, the process and function of directly mapping the set of pixels to the target category are very complex. Deep learning attempts to decompose the required complex mapping into a series of nested simple mappings, and each mapping is described and implemented through a layer. The layer corresponding to the input is called the **visible layer**, which contains directly visible variables. The following includes a series of **hidden layers** that extract more and more abstract concepts and features from the image, whose values are not directly given in the data. Deep learning models need to determine which concepts are beneficial for explaining the relationships between input data. For example, given a set of pixels, the first hidden layer determines the edges in the image by comparing the brightness differences between adjacent pixels. By utilizing edges, the second hidden layer obtains a set of boundaries and contours through search. Using descriptions of contours and corners, the third hidden layer determines the target region in the image by detecting a specific set of contours and corners. Finally, by analyzing the target regions and their relationships in the image, the target category and characteristics are identified and sent to the **output layer**.

Figure 1.8 compares the traditional computational process, machine learning process, and deep learning process in image understanding.

Deep learning still belongs to the category of machine learning in principle, but compared with normal machine learning methods, deep learning methods reduce the requirements for manually designed features under normal machine learning methods, and demonstrate significant advantages based on the use of big data. Compared to normal machine learning methods, deep learning has the characteristics of being more universal, requiring less prior knowledge and annotated data.

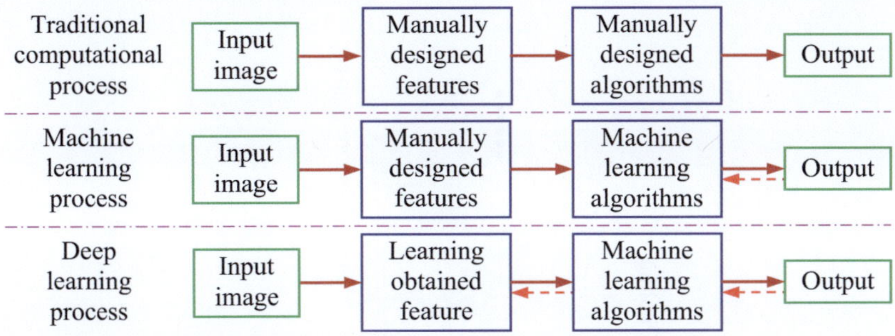

Fig. 1.8 Various types of images understanding processes

1.3.2 Basic Concepts of Convolutional Neural Networks

The current mainstream deep learning methods are based on **Neural Networks** (NN), which have the ability to directly learn pattern features from training data without the need for feature design and extraction, and can easily achieve end-to-end training. The research on neural networks has a long history. In 1989, the universal approximation theorem of **Multi-Layer Perceptron** (MLP) was proved, and one of the basic models of deep learning, **Convolutional Neural Network** (CNN), was also used for handwritten digit recognition. The concept of deep learning was officially proposed in 2006 and sparked extensive researches and applications of deep neural network technology.

1. **Basic Structure of Convolutional Neural Networks**

Convolutional neural networks are developed based on traditional artificial neural networks and have many similarities with Back-Propagation (BP) neural networks. The main input difference is that BP artificial neural networks use 1-D vectors, while convolutional neural networks use 2-D matrices. Convolutional neural networks consist of multiple layers, including input layer, convolutional layer, pooling layer, fully connected layer, batch normalization layer, output layer, etc. In addition, convolutional neural networks also use activation functions (excitation functions), cost functions, and so on.

Figure 1.9 illustrates the basic structure of a typical convolutional neural network.

Convolutional neural networks have four similar points with general fully connected neural networks (multilayer perceptron):

(1) All construct the sum of all products.
(2) All add a bias (see below).
(3) All results are subjected to an activation function (see below).
(4) All will use the activation function value as a single input for the next layer.

Convolutional neural networks have four different points with general fully connected neural networks:

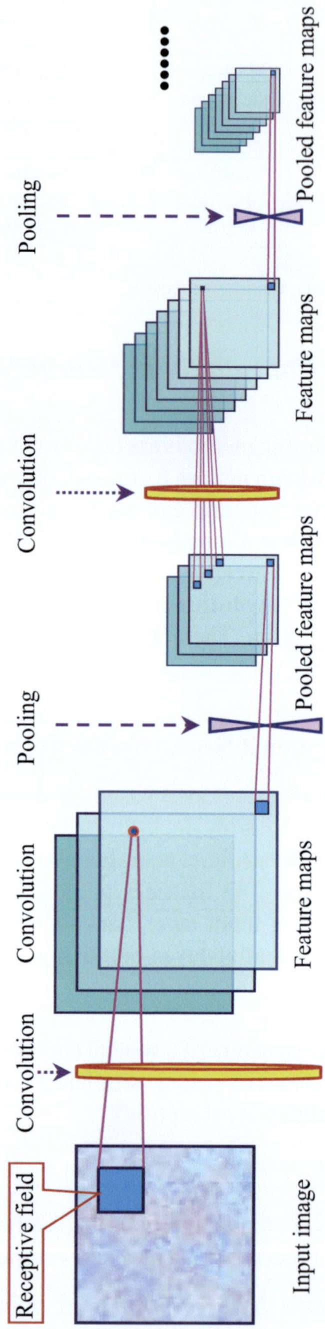

Fig. 1.9 Schematic diagram of the basic structure of a typical convolutional neural network

(1) The input of a convolutional neural network is a 2-D image, while the input of a fully connected neural network is a 1-D vector.
(2) Convolutional neural networks can directly learn 2-D features from raw image data, while fully connected neural networks cannot.
(3) In fully connected neural networks, the outputs of all neurons in a certain layer are directly supplied to each neuron in the next layer, while convolutional neural networks first use convolution operation to combine the outputs of the previous layer's neurons within a spatial neighborhood into a single value, and then supply it to each neuron in the next layer.
(4) In convolutional neural networks, the input 2-D image of the next layer is first subsampled to reduce sensitivity to translation.

Below is a more detailed explanation for the convolutional layers, pooling layers, activation functions, and cost functions.

2. **Convolutional Layer**

Convolutional layers mainly implement convolution operations, and convolutional neural networks are named after convolution operations. At any position in the image, add a **bias** value to the convolution value (sum of products) at that position, and then convert these sums into a single value through an activation function. This value is used as the input for the next layer at that location. If the above operation is performed on all positions of the input image, a set of 2-D values is obtained, which is called a **feature map** (because convolution is to extract features). Different convolutional layers have different numbers of convolutional kernels, which are actually numerical matrices. The commonly used kernel sizes are 1×1, 3×3, 5×5, 7×7, etc. Each convolutional kernel has a constant bias, and all elements in the matrix plus the bias to form the weights of the convolutional layer, which participate in the iterative updates of the network.

The two important concepts in convolution operations are local receptive field and weight sharing (also known as parameter sharing). The size of the local receptive field is the scope of the convolutional kernel operation, and each convolution operation only needs to focus on the information within this range. Weight sharing refers to the process where the values of each convolution kernel remain unchanged during the convolution operation, and only the weights of each iteration are updated. In other words, the same weights and a single bias are used to generate the values of feature maps corresponding to all positions in the receptive field of the input image. In this way, the same features can be detected at all positions in the image. Because each convolution kernel only extracts one or some specific features, the values of different convolution kernels are different.

3. **Pooling Layer**

The operation after convolution and activation is pooling. The **pooling layer** mainly implements dimensionality reduction through down-sampling. This layer is also known as down-sampling layer or subsampling layer. The design of the pooling layer is based on a model of the mammalian visual cortex. This model suggests that the visual cortex includes two types of cells: simple cells and complex cells. Simple cells perform feature extraction, while complex cells combine (merge) these features into a more meaningful ensemble. The pooling layer generally does not have weight updates.

The role of pooling includes reducing the spatial size of the data volume (lowering spatial resolution to achieve translation invariance), reducing the number of parameters and the amount of data to be processed in the network, thereby reducing the cost of computing resources, and effectively controlling overfitting. The **pooling feature map** can be regarded as the result of subsampling (each feature map has a corresponding pooled feature map). In other words, pooling feature maps is a feature map that reduces spatial resolution. Pooling first decomposes the feature map into a set of neighborhoods (small regions), and then replaces all elements within that neighborhood with a single value, this is called **pooling neighborhood**. Here, it can be assumed that pooling neighborhoods are adjacent (non-overlapping).

There are various methods for calculating pooling values, collectively referred to as **pooling methods**. The commonly used pooling methods are as follows:

(1) **Average pooling**: also known as mean pooling, selecting the average of all values in each neighborhood.
(2) **Maximum pooling**: also known as max pooling, selecting the maximum value of all values in each neighborhood.
(3) **L_2-norm pooling**: selecting the square root of the sum of squares of all values in each neighborhood.
(4) **Random value pooling**: selecting corresponding values in each neighborhood that meet certain given criteria.

4. **Activation Functions**

The activation function, also known as the excitation function, selectively activates or inhibits the features of neuronal nodes. It can enhance and activate useful object features, suppress and weaken useless background features, thereby enabling convolutional neural networks to solve nonlinear problems. If nonlinear activation functions are not used in the network model, the network model becomes a linear representation, and the network representation ability would be not strong. Therefore, it is necessary to use nonlinear activation functions to enable the network model to have nonlinear mapping capabilities in the feature space.

The **activation function** must possess some basic characteristics: (i) Monotonicity: a monotonic activation function ensures that the single-layer network model has convex function performance; (ii) Differentiability: it ensures that the model weights can be fine-tuned and updated using error gradients. Some commonly used activation functions are as follows.

(1) **Sigmoid function (Sigmoid)**: It also known as the S-shaped growth function, and has a function curve as shown in Fig. 1.10a.

$$h(z) = \frac{1}{1 + \mathrm{e}^{-z}} \tag{1.1}$$

Its derivative is

$$h'(z) = \frac{\partial h(z)}{\partial z} = h(z)[1 - h(z)] \tag{1.2}$$

(2) Hyperbolic tangent function: It has a function curve as shown in Fig. 1.10b.

$$h(z) = \tanh(z) = \frac{1 - \mathrm{e}^{-2z}}{1 + \mathrm{e}^{-2z}} \tag{1.3}$$

Its derivative is

$$h'(z) = 1 - [h(z)]^2 \tag{1.4}$$

The shape of the hyperbolic tangent function is similar to that of the Sigmoid function, but the hyperbolic tangent function is symmetric about the axis of the function.

(3) Rectifier function: It has a function curve as shown in Fig. 1.10c.

$$h(z) = \max(0, z) \tag{1.5}$$

The name of the rectifier function is derived from the use of units called **Rectifier Linear Units** (ReLU), and their corresponding activation functions are often referred to as **ReLU activation functions**. Its derivative is

$$h'(z) = \begin{cases} 1 & z > 0 \\ 0 & z \leq 0 \end{cases} \tag{1.6}$$

(4) Leaky rectifier function: It is a modification of the rectifier function, named after the adjustment of the rectifier linear unit (ReLU) to become the **leaky Rectifier Linear Unit** (leaky ReLU), which can be expressed as

$$h(z) = \begin{cases} z & z > 0 \\ kz & z \leq 0 \end{cases} \tag{1.7}$$

where k is a very small numerical value. Its derivative is

$$h'(z) = \begin{cases} 1 & z > 0 \\ k & z \leq 0 \end{cases} \tag{1.8}$$

The output of the rectifier function for negative numbers is 0. This can lead to a problem of "neuron death", where the output of certain neurons remains at 0 during the training process, making it impossible to activate these neurons or update their weights. The leaky rectifier function no longer outputs 0 for negative numbers, which

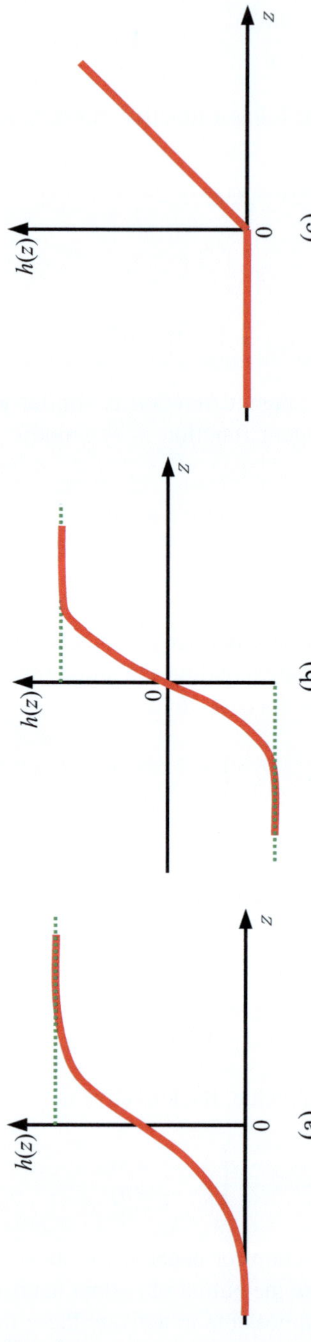

Fig. 1.10 Three commonly used activation functions

can avoid the problem of "neuron death", but it has an additional parameter that needs to be adjusted.

5. **Loss Functions**

The loss function is also known as the cost function. In machine learning tasks, all algorithms have an objective function that needs to be optimized. The direction of optimizing the objective function is to take its maximum or minimum value. When the objective function is minimized under constraints, it becomes the **loss function**. In convolutional neural networks, the loss function is used to drive network training and update network weights.

The most commonly used loss function in training convolutional neural network models is the Softmax loss function, which is the cross entropy loss function of Softmax. Softmax is a commonly used in classifier, expressed as

$$h(\boldsymbol{x}_i) = \frac{\exp\left(\boldsymbol{w}_i^{\mathrm{T}}\boldsymbol{x}_i\right)}{\sum_j^n \exp\left(\boldsymbol{w}_j^{\mathrm{T}}\boldsymbol{x}_i\right)} \tag{1.9}$$

where $\boldsymbol{x}_i$ represents input features; $\boldsymbol{w}_i$ represents the corresponding weight. The Softmax loss function can be expressed as

$$L_s = -\sum_{i=1}^{m} \log h(\boldsymbol{x}_i) = -\sum_{i=1}^{m} \log \frac{\exp\left(\boldsymbol{w}_i^{\mathrm{T}}\boldsymbol{x}_i\right)}{\sum_j^n \exp\left(\boldsymbol{w}_j^{\mathrm{T}}\boldsymbol{x}_i\right)} \tag{1.10}$$

1.3.3 Core Technologies of Deep Learning

The core technologies of deep learning mainly include reinforcement learning, transfer learning, data augmentation, hyper-parameter optimization, network design, etc.

1. **Reinforcement Learning**

The model design based on **reinforcement learning** includes a model generation unit and a model validation unit. The model generation unit first generates a series of sub networks according to a certain random initialization strategy. After training the sub networks on the indicator dataset, the validated accuracy is fed back to the generation unit as a reward. The generation unit updates the design strategy based on the model performance and conducts a new round of attempts. Automated design includes operations such as convolution, pooling, residual, and group convolution, which can be used to micro design the repeated substructures of convolutional networks or macro design the global architecture of the network. The search space contains a large number of neural networks with different structures. By combining decision making reinforcement learning that has decision make ability with deep neural networks, then perception, decision-making, or integrated perception and decision-making can be achieved through end-to-end learning.

2. **Transfer Learning**

Transfer learning refers to a technique that utilizes relevant auxiliary tasks to optimize the current target task, and is suitable for scenarios where the target task has limited annotated data. Generally, the source model is first trained using a source task with rich training samples, and then transfer learning techniques are used to help optimize the model performance of the target task or accelerate training. Transfer learning includes four commonly used methods:

(1) Based on model structure: Deep neural networks exhibit hierarchical characteristics. Taking images as an example, low-level features close to the input represent usual low-level information such as color and texture, while high-level features close to the output represent high-level information such as scenery and semantics. Under the condition of a small number of samples, in order to improve generalization ability, transfer learning often fixes general features and only optimizes high-level features related to the task.
(2) Based on samples: The basic idea is to find a subset in the source task that is closer to the target task sample, and by increasing the weight of this data, change the sample distribution of the source task to make it closer to the target task.
(3) Improved regularization: Compared with general de novo training, transfer learning can improve the prior assumptions of weight distribution by designing more reasonable regularization terms due to the certain correlation between the target task and the source task.
(4) Introducing adapters: Due to the large number of deep network parameters, training directly with limited target data can easily lead to overfitting. Based on the high correlation between the target task and the source task in transfer learning, a larger original network can be fixed, and adapters with fewer parameters can be introduced for targeted training, making the original network applicable to new tasks.

3. **Data Augmentation**

Deep learning requires a large amount of labeled training data, but in practical tasks, the capacity of training datasets is generally limited. **Data augmentation** is an effective means of addressing the problem of small data volumes. Data augmentation generates a new dataset that is similar to the training dataset through operations such as transformation or synthesis. It can be used to expand the training dataset and improve the model's generalization ability, as well as to enhance the model's robustness by introducing noisy data. The common data augmentation methods mainly include three types:

(1) Traditional data augmentation methods (such as flipping, rotating, scaling, translating, random cropping, adding noise, etc.).

(2) Simple and effective data augmentation methods proposed in recent years, such as image cutout, mixing, sample pairing, random erasure, etc.
(3) Automatic data augmentation methods (reinforcement learning based data augmentation methods), etc.

4. **Hyper-Parameter Optimization**

The design of deep learning models requires data preprocessing, feature selection, model design, model training, and hyper-parameter tuning. Hyper-parameters play an important role in deep learning. Manual parameter tuning requires the experience and skills of machine learning. Automated deep learning for **hyper-parameter optimization** can effectively replace manual tuning. The basic idea is to establish the relationship between the validation set loss function and hyper-parameters, and take the derivative of this function on hyper-parameters, thereby using gradient descent method to optimize hyper-parameters. However, the derivative calculation of hyper-parameters is very complex, with high time and space complexity, and cannot be applied to mainstream large-scale deep models. The current research focus is on finding simplified and approximate calculation methods to apply this technology to mainstream deep models.

5. **Network Design**

Network design is a core competency in deep learning. Various new network structures are constantly being proposed, and some typical network examples are shown in Table 1.3 (arranged in alphabetical order).

The content of this list is still constantly expanding. For example, in semantic segmentation, there have been recent developments such as **U-Net**, **dilated convolution**, DeepLab series, and PSRNet for **Pyramid Scene Parsing Network**. In video classification, there are various networks such as **dual stream convolutional networks**, **Boundary Sensitive Networks** (BSN), **attention cluster networks**, and **generalized compact non local networks**. In object detection, there have been networks such as **Deep Supervised Object Detector** (DSOD) and **Receptive Field Block** (RFB) networks. A **Single View Stereo Matching** (SVSM) model was proposed for depth estimation based on monocular data. In image/video generation, there have been some developments such as **Variation Auto Encoders** (VAEs).

1.4 The Book Structure and Chapter Introduction

The spatiotemporal behavior understanding has become a research hotspot in image understanding technology in recent years. This book attempts to comprehensively and systematically introduce the main concepts, basic principles, typical methods, practical techniques, as well as some new achievements and trends in international research related to spatiotemporal behavior understanding, in order to further promote the development of research and application in this field.

Table 1.3 Typical network examples

Network	Explanation
Auto-encoder	An artificial neural network composed of an encoder that converts raw input data and a decoder that restores raw input data
Capsule network (CapsNet)	Multiple capsule layers have been added between the convolutional and fully connected layers of the classical convolutional neural network
Convolutional neural networks (CNN)	A type of feedforward neural network with convolutional computation and deep structure
Deep belief network	A probability generation model composed of stacked restricted Boltzmann machines
Deep residual network (ResNet)	Improvement of Convolutional Neural Networks by introducing identity mapping connections (jumping connections)
Fully convolutional networks (FCN)	Composed of a classical convolutional neural network followed by an upsampling deconvolution network
Generative adversarial networks (GAN)	An artificial neural network composed of a generation model based on capturing the distribution of sample data and a discrimination model that determines whether the input is real data or generated samples
Graph convolutional networks (GCN)	Artificial neural network for convolving graph data
Long short-term memory (LSTM)	A time recurrent neural network that can achieve long-term retention of memory
Multi-layer perceptron (MLP)	A feedforward model that maps multiple input datasets to a single output dataset
Recurrent neural network (RNN)	Obtained by replacing the hidden layers in classical convolutional neural networks with their own closed-loop connected hidden layers
Recursive neural network (RNN)	A dynamic neural network with a tree like hierarchical structure, where nodes loop through input information in the order that they are connected
Siamese neural network (SNN)	A coupling architecture formed by concatenating two neural networks with the same structure and shared weights
Transformer	The network structure that replaces RNN with self-attention structure, which essentially has an encoding–decoding architecture

Considering that spatiotemporal behavior understanding involves multiple disciplines and a wide range of techniques, this book selects some distinctive technical methods for introduction in a hierarchical manner (see Sect. 1.2.2), and provides vivid examples based on scientific research achievements. It is hoped that this book can not only reflect the overall research advancements in this field well, but also provide some inspiration for readers to conduct related research and exploit potential applications. The explanations of many related basic concepts mentioned in the book can be found in (Zhang 2021c).

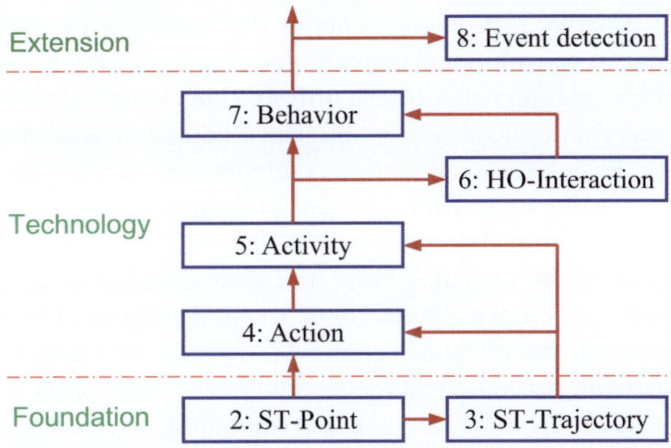

Fig. 1.11 The book structure

The whole book consists of eight chapters. Apart from this introductory chapter, other chapters are organized as shown in Fig. 1.11, which gives the book structure.

Chapters 2 and 3 provide some basic foundations. Chapter 2 starts from spatiotemporal points, and introduces the detection of spatial and spatiotemporal interest points, the detection of 2-D human key-point based on images and videos, and the detection of 3-D human key-point based on multi-view and hierarchical clustering, all of which are closely related to action primitives.

Chapter 3 connects spatiotemporal points to form spatiotemporal trajectory, and analyzes the trajectories obtained by connecting/combining point information, which can be used to characterize the behavior of moving objects. The basic methods of trajectory modeling and learning for activity analysis were first discussed, and then the method of using trajectory feature clustering trees to analyze motion trajectories and achieve motion classification recognition were introduced.

Chapters 4–7 consist of main technologies for spatiotemporal image understanding. Chapter 4 discusses the classification and recognition of various actions. Firstly, the basic methods of action classification and recognition in various activities were outlined, as well as common networks for action recognition. Then, the combination of posture and context information for action classification, as well as the attention based classification and recognition were discussed in detail.

Chapter 5 analyzes several modeling methods for actions and activities, with a focus on the issue of joint modeling of actors and actions. It also specifically introduces graph convolutional networks for activity recognition using human skeletons.

Chapter 6 discusses the detection of human-object interaction. Both two-stage and single-stage methods, as well as transformer-based methods were discussed. Then, several typical techniques with their characteristics were specifically analyzed. Finally, some databases for detecting human-object interaction relationships and several evaluation indicators for judging the performance of related methods were introduced.

Chapter 7 discusses a number of networks for recognizing behavior. The dual stream convolutional network that combines motion and context, and the sequential segmentation network that utilizes video temporal structure information were separately introduced. The graph convolutional network for behavior recognition based on the description of various skeleton models were also analyzed.

Finally, Chap. 8 provides one of the applications of spatiotemporal behavior understanding, the abnormal event detection. Based on the above discussed techniques, many tasks, including event detection, could be accomplished. After presenting the basic detection methods based on neural networks, the sparse denoising auto-encoder network that integrates gradient difference information and the LSTM auto-encoder network based on feature trajectory smoothing were analyzed separately. The deep generation models for temporal smoothing in feature space and scene content adaptation were introduced. Finally, a strategy for integrating main and auxiliary recognizers was introduced.

References

Zhang Y-J, Vincent T. Spatial-temporal behavior understanding. Proc. ICECC, 2012b.

Zhang Y-J. Image engineering and bibliography in China. Technical Digest of International Symposium on Information Science and Technology, 158–160, 1996a.

Zhang Y-J. Image engineering in China: 1995. Journal of Image and Graphics, 1(1): 78–83, 1996b.

Zhang Y-J. Image engineering in China: 1995 (Supplement). Journal of Image and Graphics, 1(2): 170–174, 1996c.

Zhang Y-J. Image engineering in China: 1996. Journal of Image and Graphics, 2(5): 336–344, 1997.

Zhang Y-J. Image engineering in China: 1997. Journal of Image and Graphics, 3(5): 404–414, 1998.

Zhang Y-J. Image engineering in China: 1998. Journal of Image and Graphics, 4(5): 427–438, 1999.

Zhang Y-J. Image engineering in China: 1999. Journal of Image and Graphics, 5A(5): 359–373, 2000a.

Zhang Y-J. Image engineering and its developments and status in China. Strategic Study of Chinese Academic Engineering, 2(8): 91–94, 2000b.

Zhang Y-J. Image engineering in China: 2000. Journal of Image and Graphics, 6A(5): 409–424, 2001.

Zhang Y-J. Image engineering in China: 2001. Journal of Image and Graphics, 7A(5): 417–433, 2002a.

Zhang Y-J. Image engineering in China and some current research focuses. Journal of Computer-Aided Design & Computer Graphics, 14(6): 489–500, 2002b.

Zhang Y-J. Image engineering and related publications. International Journal of Image and Graphics, 2(3): 441–452, 2002c.

Zhang Y-J. Image engineering in China: 2002. Journal of Image and Graphics, 8A(5): 481–498, 2003.

Zhang Y-J. Image engineering in China: 2003. Journal of Image and Graphics, 9(5): 513–531, 2004.

Zhang Y-J. Image engineering in China: 2004. Journal of Image and Graphics, 10(5): 537–560, 2005.

Zhang Y-J. Image engineering in China: 2005. Journal of Image and Graphics, 11(5): 601–623, 2006.

Zhang Y-J. Image engineering in China: 2006. Journal of Image and Graphics, 12(5): 753–775, 2007a.

Zhang Y-J. Research, teaching, and academic exchange in image engineering. Strategic Study of Chinese Academic Engineering, 9(11): 11, 2007b.
Zhang Y-J. Image engineering in China: 2007. Journal of Image and Graphics, 13(5): 825–852, 2008.
Zhang Y-J. Image engineering in China: 2008. Journal of Image and Graphics, 14(5): 809–837, 2009a.
Zhang Y-J. A study of image engineering. Encyclopedia of Information Science and Technology, 2nd Edition, Vol. VII: Chapter 575 (3608–3615), 2009b.
Zhang Y-J. Image engineering in China: 2009. Journal of Image and Graphics, 15(5): 689–722, 2010.
Zhang Y-J. Image engineering in China: 2010. Journal of Image and Graphics, 16(5): 693–702, 2011a.
Zhang Y-J. Fifteen years of image engineering in China. Journal of Harbin Engineering University, 32(9): 1238–1243, 2011b.
Zhang Y-J. Image engineering in China: 2011. Journal of Image and Graphics, 17(5): 603–612, 2012a.
Zhang Y-J. Image engineering in China: 2012. Journal of Image and Graphics, 18(5): 483–492, 2013a.
Zhang Y-J. Understanding Spatial-Temporal Behaviors. Journal of Image and Graphics, 18(2): 141–151, 2013b.
Zhang Y-J. Image engineering in China: 2013. Journal of Image and Graphics, 19(5): 649–658, 2014a.
Zhang Y-J. The current status of image engineering. Machine Vision, (3): 15–22, 2014b.
Zhang Y-J. Image engineering in China: 2014. Journal of Image and Graphics, 20(5): 585–598, 2015a.
Zhang Y-J. Statistics on image engineering literatures. Encyclopedia of Information Science and Technology, 3rd Edition, Chapter 595 (6030–6040), 2015b.
Zhang Y-J. Image engineering in China: 2015. Journal of Image and Graphics, 21(5): 533–543, 2016.
Zhang Y-J. Image engineering in China: 2016. Journal of Image and Graphics, 22(5): 563–574, 2017a.
Zhang Y-J. Image Engineering, Vol.1: Image Processing. De Gruyter, Germany, 2017b.
Zhang Y-J. Image Engineering, Vol.2: Image Analysis. De Gruyter, Germany, 2017c.
Zhang Y-J. Image Engineering, Vol.3: Image Understanding. De Gruyter, Germany, 2017d.
Zhang Y-J. Image engineering in China: 2017. Journal of Image and Graphics, 23(5): 617–628, 2018a.
Zhang Y-J. Development of image engineering in the last 20 years. Encyclopedia of Information Science and Technology, 4th Edition, Chapter 113 (1319–1330), 2018b.
Zhang Y-J. An overview of image engineering in recent years. Proc. ICCSE, 119–122, 2018c.
Zhang Y-J. The understanding of spatial-temporal behaviors. Encyclopedia of Information Science and Technology, 4th Edition, Chapter 115 (1344–1354), 2018d.
Zhang Y-J. Image engineering in China: 2018. Journal of Image and Graphics, 24(5): 665–676, 2019.
Zhang Y-J. Image engineering in China: 2019. Journal of Image and Graphics, 25(5): 864–878, 2020.
Zhang Y-J. Image engineering in China: 2020. Journal of Image and Graphics, 26(5): 978–990, 2021a.
Zhang Y-J. Twenty-five years of image engineering in China. Journal of Image and Graphics, 26(10): 2326–2336, 2021b.
Zhang Y-J. Handbook of Image Engineering. Springer Nature, Singapore, 2021c.
Zhang Y-J. Image engineering in China: 2021. Journal of Image and Graphics, 27(4): 1009–1022, 2022a.

Zhang Y-J. A Selection of Image Processing Techniques: From Fundamentals to Research Front. CRC Press, England, 2022b.
Zhang Y-J. Image engineering in China: 2022. Journal of Image and Graphics, 28(4): 879–892, 2023a.
Zhang Y-J. A Selection of Image Analysis Techniques: From Fundamentals to Research Front. CRC Press, England, 2023b.
Zhang Y-J. A Selection of Image Understanding Techniques: From Fundamentals to Research Front. CRC Press, England, 2023c.
Zhang Y-J. Image engineering in China: 2023. Journal of Image and Graphics, 29(5): 1307–1320, 2024.
Zhang Y-J. Image engineering in China: 2024. Journal of Image and Graphics, 30(5): 1346–1363, 2025.

Chapter 2
Spatiotemporal Points

The most basic element in space–time domain is a point, and each spatiotemporal point corresponds to a certain position in space–time domain.

The development and changes in the objective world are not always smooth, and the points of interest in time and space refer to the locations where scenery changes dramatically in time and space. Different spatiotemporal locations can have many different aspects in their impact, meaning, etc. These positions can be expressed using methods such as directional gradient histograms to describe the features of the action of interest, and these features can be classified (or clustered) to categorize and recognize actions, activities, and behaviors.

The changes in the scene stem from the movement of the objects inside, especially acceleration. The accelerated motion of local structures in video images corresponds to the accelerated motion of objects in the scene. Understanding these situations is crucial for grasping the state, changes, and trends of the objects.

Understanding spatiotemporal behavior focuses more on human behavior. The human body is composed of different organs connected by joints. Determining the position and movement of joints on a person's body is essential for understanding its action and behavior, and therefore these joints can also be referred to as human key points. One approach integrates 3-D convolutional neural networks, self-attention mechanisms, and generative adversarial networks for key point detection is described in (Zhu and Ye 2024). These key points (often significant points of spatiotemporal variation) usually have special significance.

The sections of this chapter are arranged as follows.

Section 2.1 introduces spatiotemporal interest points and their detection methods.

Section 2.2 discusses human key points (including joints) and their detection techniques based on images and videos.

Section 2.3 introduces a hierarchical clustering method for 3-D key point detection of multi persons from multiple perspectives.

Y.-J. Zhang, *Spatiotemporal Image Understanding*,
https://doi.org/10.1007/978-981-95-7130-7_2

2.1 Spatiotemporal Points of Interest

Points with significant characteristics in space–time domain are generally referred to as **points of interest** (POI). These points of interest usually correspond to points on the scenery that have specific meanings (such as the spire of a clock tower being the highest point, the intersection point of a distant railway track and the horizon being the convergence point, etc.), and can also correspond to points where the motion state of the scenery changes (such as points where the direction of motion changes, points where acceleration changes, corresponding to positions with unconventional motion values). These points contain information about the forces that cause motion and structural changes in the physical world, which is very helpful for understanding the scene.

Spatiotemporal interest points refer to interest points in the space–time domain, sometimes they can also be just interest points in the time domain or in the spatial domain. By detecting them, a lot of information about the scene and object characteristics, spatiotemporal state, and other aspects of the scenery can be obtained.

2.1.1 *Detecting Spatial Points of Interest*

Firstly, consider detecting points of interest in the XY space of the image coordinates. Here, the image can be modeled using linear scale space representation, which involves convolving the image $f(x, y)$ with a Gaussian convolution kernel with variance σ_z^2:

$$L(x, y; \sigma_z^2) = g(x, y; \sigma_z^2) \otimes f(x, y) \tag{2.1}$$

where the Gaussian kernel with variance σ_z^2 is

$$g(x, y; \sigma_z^2) = \frac{1}{2\pi\sigma_z^2} \exp\left[-(x^2 + y^2)/2\sigma_z^2\right] \tag{2.2}$$

In such a scale space, **Harris point of interest detector** can be used to detect points of interest. The representation matrix of the detector can be defined by the gradients G_x and G_y in horizontal and vertical directions in the local neighborhoods of the image used. A commonly used Harris matrix can be written as:

$$\boldsymbol{H} = \begin{bmatrix} \sum G_x^2 & \sum G_x G_y \\ \sum G_x G_y & \sum G_y^2 \end{bmatrix} \tag{2.3}$$

The idea of detection is to determine the spatial position of $f(x, y)$ that shows significant changes in both directions. For a given observation scale σ_z^2, these positions can be calculated using a matrix expressing the second-order moment obtained by summing in a Gaussian window with variance $\sigma_z{}^2$:

$$\begin{aligned} \boldsymbol{M}(\cdot;\sigma_z^2,\sigma_i^2) &= g(\cdot;\sigma_i^2)\otimes\{[\nabla L(\cdot;\sigma_z^2)][\nabla L(\cdot;\sigma_z^2)]^{\mathrm{T}}\} \\ &= g(\cdot;\sigma_i^2)\otimes\begin{bmatrix}(L_x)^2 & L_xL_y\\ L_xL_y & (L_y)^2\end{bmatrix} \end{aligned} \tag{2.4}$$

where L_x and L_y are Gaussian differentials calculated at the local scale $\sigma_z{}^2$ based on $L_x = \partial_x[g(\bullet;\sigma_z{}^2)\otimes f(\bullet)]$ and $L_y = \partial_y[g(\bullet;\sigma_z{}^2)\otimes f(\bullet)]$.

The second-order moment descriptor in Eq. (2.4) can be regarded as the orientation distribution covariance matrix of a 2-D image in the local neighborhood of a point. Therefore, the eigenvalues λ_1 and λ_2 ($\lambda_1 \le \lambda_2$) of $\boldsymbol{M}$ form descriptors that describe the variation of $f(x, y)$ along two image directions. If the values of λ_1 and λ_2 are both large, this indicates that it is a point of interest. To detect such points, it is necessary to check the positive maximum value of the corner function (k is the weight coefficient) as follows:

$$H = \det(\mathbf{M}) - k\cdot \mathrm{trace}^2(\mathbf{M}) = \lambda_1\lambda_2 - k(\lambda_1+\lambda_2)^2 \tag{2.5}$$

At the point of interest, the ratio of eigenvalues $r = \lambda_2/\lambda_1$ should be very large. According to Eq. (2.5), for the positive local extremum of H, r should satisfy $k \le r/(1 + r)^2$. If $k = 0.25$, the positive maximum value of H will correspond to the ideal isotropic point of interest (where $r = 1$, *i.e.* $\lambda_1 = \lambda_2$). A smaller k value is suitable for detecting sharper points of interest (corresponding to a larger r value). The commonly used k value in literature is $k = 0.04$, corresponding to the detection of interest points with $r < 23$.

2.1.2 Detecting Spatiotemporal Points of Interest

In spatiotemporal scenes, the detection of points of interest (POI) can be extended from space to space–time (Laptev 2005). Extending the detection of points of interest in space to spatiotemporal space, that is, to detect positions in the local spatiotemporal volume that have significant changes in image values along both time and space directions. Points with such properties correspond to spatial points of interest with specific positions in time, which are located within the spatiotemporal neighborhood having abnormal numerical motion.

Detecting spatiotemporal interest points is a means of extracting low-level motion features that does not require background modeling. Here, the given video can be convolved with a 3-D Gaussian kernel at different spatiotemporal scales. Then, the spatiotemporal gradients are calculated at each layer of the scale space representation, and they are combined in the neighborhoods of each point to obtain a stable estimate of the spatiotemporal second-order moment matrix. Finally, local features can be extracted from the matrix.

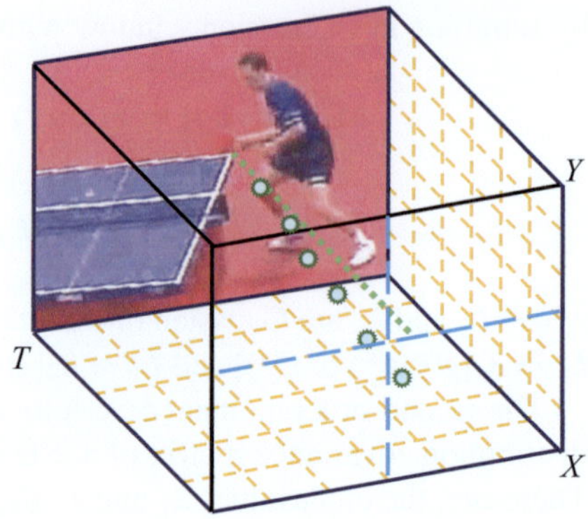

Fig. 2.1 Example of spatiotemporal interest points (Zhang 2023)

Figure 2.1 shows a scene of a player swinging its racket and hitting a ball in a table tennis match, from which several spatiotemporal points of interest are detected. The density of spatiotemporal interest points along the timeline is related to the frequency of the action, while the spatial position of spatiotemporal interest points corresponds to the motion trajectory and amplitude of the beat.

To model spatiotemporal image sequences, the function f: $R^2 \times R \to R$ can be used and its linear scale space expression L: $R^2 \times R \times R_+{}^2 \to R$ can be constructed by convolving f with a non-isotropic Gaussian kernel (with uncorrelated spatial variance $\sigma_z{}^2$ and temporal variance $\tau_z{}^2$):

$$L(\cdot;\sigma_z^2,\tau_z^2) = g(\cdot;\sigma_z^2,\tau_z^2) \otimes f(\cdot) \tag{2.6}$$

where the separable Gaussian kernel for space–time is

$$g(x,y,t;\sigma_z^2,\tau_z^2) = \frac{1}{\sqrt{(2\pi)^3\sigma_z^4\tau_z^2}}\exp\left[-\frac{x^2+y^2}{2\sigma_z^2}-\frac{t^2}{2\tau_z^2}\right] \tag{2.7}$$

It is crucial to use a separate scale parameter for the time domain, as events in the time and space domains are generally independent of each other. In addition, the events detected using the point of interest operator depend on both spatial and temporal observation scales, so the scale parameters $\sigma_z{}^2$ and $\tau_z{}^2$ need to be treated separately.

Similar to the case in spatial domain, consider a matrix that represents second-order moments in the time–space domain. It is a 3×3 matrix consisting of first-order spatial and temporal derivatives convolved with Gaussian weight function $g(\bullet;\sigma_i{}^2, \tau_i{}^2)$:

$$\boldsymbol{M} = g(\cdot;\sigma_i^2,\tau_i^2) \otimes \begin{bmatrix} L_x^2 & L_xL_y & L_xL_t \\ L_xL_y & L_y^2 & L_yL_t \\ L_xL_t & L_yL_t & L_t^2 \end{bmatrix} \tag{2.8}$$

where, the integral scales σ_i^2 and τ_i^2 are related to the local scales σ_z^2 and τ_z^2 according to $\sigma_i^2 = c\sigma_z^2$ and $\tau_i^2 = c\tau_z^2$ (c can be a constant). The definition of first-order differentiation is

$$\begin{aligned} L_x(\cdot; \sigma_z^2, \tau_z^2) &= \partial_x(g \otimes f) \\ L_y(\cdot; \sigma_z^2, \tau_z^2) &= \partial_y(g \otimes f) \\ L_t(\cdot; \sigma_z^2, \tau_z^2) &= \partial_t(g \otimes f) \end{aligned} \tag{2.9}$$

To detect points of interest, it is required to search for regions of $\boldsymbol{M}$ with significant eigenvalues λ_1, λ_2, λ_3 in f. To this end, the Harris corner detection function defined in space domain, *i.e.* Equation (2.5), can be extended to the spatiotemporal domain by combining the determinant and rank of $\boldsymbol{M}$:

$$H = \det(\mathbf{M}) - k \cdot \text{trace}^3(\mathbf{M}) = \lambda_1\lambda_2\lambda_3 - k(\lambda_1 + \lambda_2 + \lambda_3)^3 \tag{2.10}$$

To prove that the positive local extremum of H corresponds to points with large values of λ_1, λ_2 and λ_3 ($\lambda_1 \leq \lambda_2 \leq \lambda_3$), two ratios $a = \lambda_2/\lambda_1$ and $b = \lambda_3/\lambda_1$ are defined, and H is rewritten as:

$$H = \lambda_1^3[ab - k(1 + a + b)^3] \tag{2.11}$$

Because $H \geq 0$, there is $k \leq ab/(1 + a + b)^3$, and k will take its maximum possible value $k = 1/27$ when $a = b = 1$. For significantly larger values of k, the positive local extremum of H corresponds to points with significant changes in both temporal and spatial image values. If a and b take the maximum value of 23 as in space domain, the corresponding k value in Eq. (2.10) will be $k \approx 0.005$. Therefore, the spatiotemporal points of interest in f can be obtained by detecting the positive local spatiotemporal maximum in H.

By detecting the spatiotemporal interest points of actions, it is also possible to extract the spatiotemporal contextual features between frames in the action sequence, and combine them with local action features to form behavioral features, achieving behavioral understanding.

2.2 Key Points of Human Body

To perform **human pose estimation**, it is usually necessary to detect **key points of the human body** (Andriluka 2014). The key points of the human body here refer to the preselected key points detected from the image, including the head, shoulders, wrists, elbows, ankles, etc. Some examples can be found in (Dindorf 2025; Dindorf et al., 2025).

Based on the positions of these key points and combined with human body knowledge, human pose estimation can be performed. This plays an important role in extracting human body information, recording human body posture, analyzing human behavior, and so on. A two-stage network for key point detection based on incremental learning has been introduced (Jiang 2024a).

The types of input images used for the **human key point detection** often include RGB images and depth images, and the output key point coordinates are generally 2-D coordinates in the image coordinate system or 3-D coordinates in the world coordinate system.

2.2.1 2-D Human Body Key Point Detection Based on Image

The detection of 2-D key points on human body is usually based on images, and the common methods can be divided into two categories: traditional methods and deep learning-based methods.

1. **Traditional Methods**

The traditional 2-D key point detection method is mainly based on a graph structure, which takes the key points as nodes in the graph, defines the connections between key points in advance (edges in the graph), and establishes a probability function of the graph structure through *a prior* information and input images. Finally, the coordinates of the key points are obtained by maximizing the posterior probability.

Assuming that the layout of key points on human body (corresponding to human posture) can be represented as $K = \{\boldsymbol{k}_0, \boldsymbol{k}_1, \ldots, \boldsymbol{k}_P\}$. These P nodes form a directed acyclic graph, also known as a motion tree, with the root node k_0 typically defined as the "head" or "torso" of the tree. The *a prior* probability function related to layout is

$$p(K) = p(\boldsymbol{k}_0) \prod_{(i,j)\in E} p(\boldsymbol{k}_i|\boldsymbol{k}_j) \tag{2.12}$$

where E represents all directed edges in the graph. The probability function $p(\boldsymbol{k}_i|\boldsymbol{k}_j)$ between key points can be modeled as a Gaussian distribution.

Assuming the observed image evidence is D, and the image recording the probability of the i-th key point appearing at each position is $\boldsymbol{d}_i$. Assuming $\boldsymbol{d}_i$ only depends on $\boldsymbol{k}_i$, the likelihood function $p(D|K)$ can be simplified as

$$p(D|K) = \prod_{i=0}^{P} p(\boldsymbol{d}_i|K) = \prod_{i=0}^{P} p(\boldsymbol{d}_i|\boldsymbol{k}_i) \tag{2.13}$$

and the posterior probability $p(K|D)$ of posture is

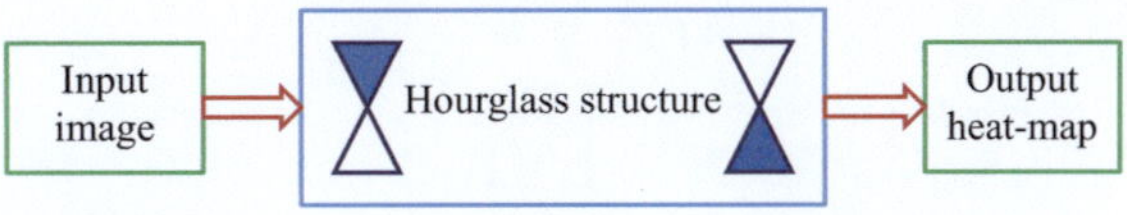

Fig. 2.2 A typical network structure diagram

$$p(K|D) \propto p(\boldsymbol{k}_0)\prod_{i=0}^{P} p(\boldsymbol{d}_i|\boldsymbol{k}_i) \prod_{(i,j)\in E} p(\boldsymbol{k}_i|\boldsymbol{k}_j) \tag{2.14}$$

2. **Deep Learning Methods**

The methods based on deep learning can be mainly divided into two categories: ① Regression-based methods; ② Detection-based methods. The regression-based methods directly regress the coordinates of key points. The detection-based methods indirectly obtain the position of key points by outputting **heat-maps**. On the heat-map, the values at each position represent the likelihood of key points appearing at that position, so key point coordinates can be obtained by detecting extreme values on the heat-map (such as using argmax or softargmax operations).

Among various neural network structures, multi-level structures typically achieve better performance. In this structure, multiple subnetworks are cascaded, with each subnetwork outputting a heat-map and using the heat-map output from the previous level as input to the next level. After multiple refinements, the heat-map will be more accurate. In addition, supervised signals can be introduced in the middle layer of the neural network to assist in training.

The network structure of a typical method is shown in Fig. 2.2 (Newell 2016), which uses cascaded hourglass modules to facilitate and repeat bottom-up and top-down reasoning.

3. **Multi Person 2-D Key Point Detection**

On the basis of single person key point detection, it is possible to detect 2-D key points of multi persons. The methods used here can be mainly divided into two categories: ① Top-down methods; ② Bottom-up methods. The top-down method first detects each person in the image, then separates the image block where each person is located using a **bounding box**, and finally performs individual key point detection on each image block. Typical methods include Mask R-CNN (He 2017) and CPN (Chen 2018). The bottom-up approach first detects all key points of all persons in the image, and then combines or arranges these key points according to different persons. A typical method is Part Affinity Fields (PAF) (Cao 2017).

The **Part Affinity Fields** (PAF) is based on a multi-level structure. It has a feature extractor and multi-level key point detection modules (levels 1–6). The **feature map** output by the feature extractor is the input of the first stage of the key point detection module. After neural network training, the feature map encodes necessary information for inferring the position of key points in the human body, such as appearance information. The feature map output by the feature extractor and the heat-map output by the 6th stage of the detector module have the same resolution. If their size is H

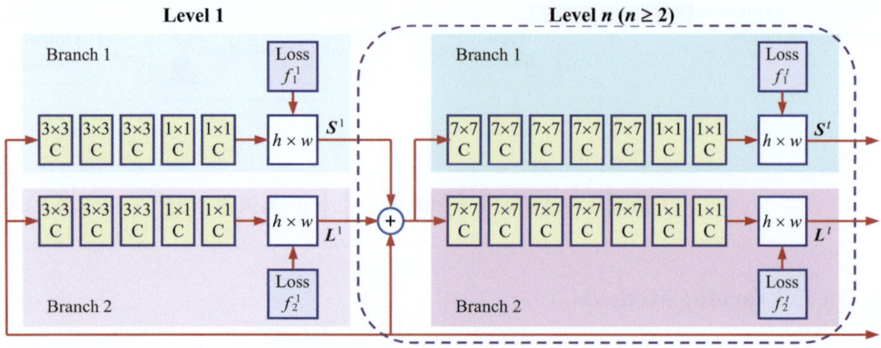

Fig. 2.3 The structure of the PAF key point detection module

$\times$ W, the corresponding input image size is $8H \times 8W$. The structure of the PAF key point detection module can be seen in Fig. 2.3. The 1st stage is shown in the left part of the figure, and the 2nd–6th stages are shown in the right part of the figure.

In Fig. 2.3, each level has two branches. Branch 1 outputs a heat-map indicating the location of each key point; Branch 2 outputs a part affinity field (vector diagram) indicating the direction of limbs (pre-defined key point pairs). Assuming the number of persons in the image is N, the coordinates of the j-th key point of the k-th person are $\boldsymbol{x}^*_{j,k}$, and their contribution to the heat-map is

$$\boldsymbol{B}^*_{j,k}(\boldsymbol{x}) = \exp\left[-\frac{\left\|\boldsymbol{x} - \boldsymbol{x}^*_{j,k}\right\|_2^2}{2\sigma^2}\right] \tag{2.15}$$

where $\boldsymbol{x}$ is any position on the image, and σ is a predefined parameter. Considering all the persons in the image, the heat-map of key point j is

$$\boldsymbol{B}^*_j(\boldsymbol{x}) = \max_k \boldsymbol{B}^*_{j,k} \tag{2.16}$$

If the key points at both ends of the k-th person's limb (z, k) are j_1 and j_2, and their coordinates are $\boldsymbol{x}^*_{j_1,k}$ and $\boldsymbol{x}^*_{j_2,k}$, respectively, then the contribution of limb (z, k) to the affinity field is

$$\boldsymbol{L}^*_{z,k}(\boldsymbol{x}) = \begin{cases} \boldsymbol{v} & \boldsymbol{x} \text{ in region}(z,k) \\ 0 & \text{otherwise} \end{cases} \tag{2.17}$$

where $\boldsymbol{v} = \boldsymbol{l}_{z,k}/\|\boldsymbol{l}_{c,k}\|_2$ represents the unit vector consistent with the limb direction, $\boldsymbol{l}_{z,k} = \boldsymbol{x}^*_{j_1,k} - \boldsymbol{x}^*_{j_2,k}$. The coordinate $\boldsymbol{x}$ located in the region (z, k) needs to meet the following conditions:

$$0 \leq \boldsymbol{v} \cdot \left(\boldsymbol{x} - \boldsymbol{x}_{j_1,k}^*\right) \leq \left\|\boldsymbol{l}_{z,k}\right\|_2 \tag{2.18}$$

$$\left\|\boldsymbol{v}_{\perp} \cdot \left(\boldsymbol{x} - \boldsymbol{x}_{j_1,k}^*\right)\right\| \leq T_l \tag{2.19}$$

where $\boldsymbol{v}_{\perp}$ is the unit vector perpendicular to $\boldsymbol{v}$, and T_l is a predefined parameter. The affinity field of everyone's limbs z is

$$\boldsymbol{L}_z^*(\boldsymbol{x}) = \frac{1}{N_z(\boldsymbol{x})} \sum_k \boldsymbol{L}_{z,k}^*(\boldsymbol{x}) \tag{2.20}$$

where $N_z(\boldsymbol{x})$ represents the total number of non-zero values of $\boldsymbol{L}_{z,k}^*(\boldsymbol{x})$ at position $\boldsymbol{x}$. Because the affinity field is a 2-D vector field, it needs to be represented by two channels in neural networks.

After obtaining the heat-map and affinity field output by the neural network, all key points are first determined, and the affinity strength between all possible paired key points is calculated using path integration. Then, the Hungarian algorithm (a combinatorial optimization algorithm for solving task allocation problems in polynomial time) (Zhang 2010) is used to calculate the optimal match, thereby concatenating key points onto multiple individual persons.

2.2.2 2-D Human Body Key Point Detection Based on Video

Video based human key point detection typically involves modifying or adding structures to image-based key point detection in order to introduce temporal connections. For example, 3-D Mask R-CNN (Girdhar 2018) modified the structure of Mask R-CNN by changing the number of channels in the input layer, transforming the input from a single frame to multiple frames, and allowing the neural network to learn and utilize spatiotemporal information.

The following introduces a video detection algorithm for human key point based on feature similarity between video frames (Li 2019), which adopts a new framework that incorporates temporal information into the detector for 2-D key points of human body. Through feature extraction and related operations, a full image search was conducted on key points, and the information of key point displacement was obtained. The overall framework, main steps, and detection results are presented as the follows.

1. **Overall Framework**

This algorithm uses the **Part Affinity Fields** (PAF) (Cao 2017) network (see Fig. 2.3) as the baseline neural network. The overall flowchart is shown in Fig. 2.4, where C represents **concatenation**, ⊗ represents weighted sum, and ⊗ represents convolution. Consider that the current frame input to the neural network is the Frame t, and the intermediate results output by the neural network when processing the Frame t-1 can help with detection in the current frame. If the feature map and heat-map of

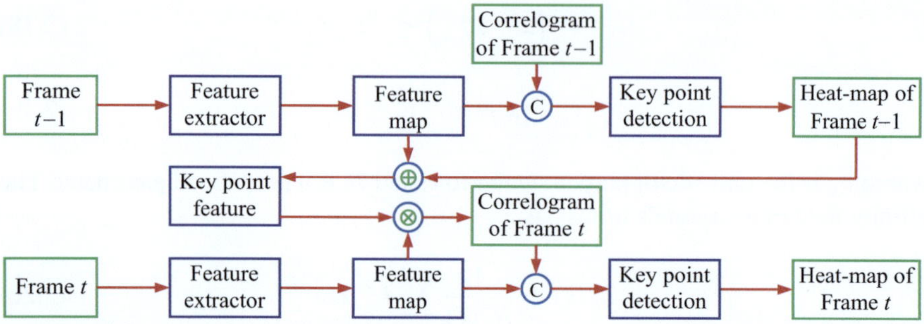

Fig. 2.4 Overall flowchart of the algorithm

Frame *t*-1 are weighted and averaged, the features of each key point can be obtained. For the sake of simplicity, only one key point feature is depicted in the figure. By performing correlation operations between the extracted key point features and the feature map of the Frame *t*, the correlogram (**correlation map**) of the Frame *t* can be obtained, with each key point corresponding to a **correlogram**. Use the correlogram as temporal information, associate it with the feature map, and then input the result into the key point detection module of the neural network, the heat-map of Frame *t* can be obtained.

This framework is not limited to a specific neural network structure, as long as all feature maps and heat-maps in the middle layer have the same size.

2. **Main Steps**

Firstly, extracting the features of each key point from the feature map output in Frame *t*–1, that is, weighting average the feature map in spatial dimension, and using the final output heat-map of the baseline network as the weight of each position on the feature map. In this way, positions with non-zero score values will receive certain weights, and positions near the key points in Frame *t*–1 will be given greater weights. Let the dimension of the feature map be $H \times W \times C$, where H, W, and C are the height, width, and number of channels of the feature map, respectively (*i.e.*, the feature dimension of each key point is C). The dimension of the heat-map is $H \times W \times (M + 1)$, where M is the number of key points, and each of the M channels corresponds to a key point. Additionally, there is a channel that represents the background and does not participate in extracting key point features.

If the feature map is denoted as F_{t-1} and the heat-map corresponding to the p-th key point is denoted as R_p, then the features of key point p can be calculated as follows:

$$\boldsymbol{K}_p(c) = \frac{1}{N_p} \sum_{h,w} \boldsymbol{R}_p(h, w) \boldsymbol{F}_{t-1}(h, w, c) \tag{2.21}$$

where (h, w) corresponds to various spatial positions on the feature map and heat-map, and the normalization coefficient N_p makes the L_2 norm of the key point feature to be 1, in order to eliminate the influence of amplitude changes in the feature map and heat-map.

After extracting the features of the key-point region, the extracted features can be regarded as examples and searched on the feature map of Frame t using template matching (which can solve the problem of key point displacement between frames). If the feature dimensions of key points are expanded and relevant operations are performed at each position of the feature map, the response of the template (corresponding to the correlogram) can be obtained:

$$\mathrm{CorrMap}_p(c) = \sum_c \boldsymbol{K}_p(c)\boldsymbol{F}_t(h, w, c) \tag{2.22}$$

A higher correlation value indicates a higher likelihood of the key point appearing at that location. Because the relevant calculations here are relatively simple, it is possible to perform a full image search with a smaller computational load.

Although the calculated correlogram provides clues for the key point positions in the current frame, it is not yet possible to directly obtain the positions of each key point in the current frame from the correlogram as in template tracking. In template tracking tasks, the search target is artificially given and has a large area, with rich visual characteristics that can distinguish it from other content in the image. Therefore, the correlogram usually contains a more obvious single peak. There are two differences in the relevant images obtained here: firstly, the extraction of key point features uses the previous frame's heat-map, and the correctness of the previous frame's detection results cannot be guaranteed; the second issue is that regions with significant response on the heat-map typically have a scale of only a few pixels, meaning that key point regions are generally smaller. The problem brought by the latter is that it may be confused with other regions in the image that have similar features to the extracted key point area. For this purpose, it is necessary to consider using the correlogram as part of the input for the key point detection module in the current frame, so that the neural network can learn to integrate the information of each key point through training to filter out confusion areas, and ultimately detect key points in the current frame.

In order to make the neural network converge better, a learnable weight and bias scale layer can be added after the correlogram. The correlogram and feature maps from this layer are concatenated together in the channel dimension and input into the key point detection module.

3. **Detection Results**

The algorithm was experimentally compared with other related algorithms using several databases. The compared algorithms include **Part Affinity Fields** (PAF) (Cao 2017), **Thin-Slicing Network** (TSN) (Song 2017), and **Long Short Term Memory Pose Machine** (LSTM-PM) (Luo 2018).

The detection experiments mainly used two databases: the JHMDB database (Jhuang 2013) that removed a subset of incomplete human postures (referred to as sub-JHMDB); Penn Action database (Zhang 2013). Because the specific names and locations of key points in the human body are not exactly the same in various databases, certain normalization adjustments are required. For specific details, please refer to (Li 2019).

The evaluation indicators are all selected as PCK@0.2 (Luo 2018), that is, taking the long side of the human body enclosure (bounding box) as the reference, if the difference between the detected key point coordinates and the true value is less than 0.2 compared to the reference, the detection result will be judged as correct.

The experimental results for these two databases are shown in Tables 2.1 and 2.2 (bold numbers indicates the best), respectively. As can be seen from the two tables, the algorithm introduced above has achieved high accuracy on both sub-JHMDB and Penn Action databases. In order to fairly compare the performances of the baseline network PAF and the improved model, the baseline network was trained separately under the same settings for comparison. The results in the two tables show that introducing temporal information has improved the accuracy of each key point category.

Some examples of correlogram are shown in Fig. 2.5. Among them, Fig. 2.5a, b are the previous frame and the current frame, respectively (with a certain interval in time, and significant displacement of key points can be observed). Figure 2.5c–e correspond to the correlograms of the head, right wrist, and right ankle, respectively. Figure 2.5f–h are the corresponding heat-maps, where red represents large response amplitude and blue represents small response amplitude. From these figures, it can be seen that most of the key points can be correctly located in the correlograms.

Figure 2.6 shows some experimental results, where Figs. 2.6a, b are from the sub-JHMDB database, and Fig. 2.6c, d are from the Penn Action database. The dots of different colors in the figure represent the detected output key points. If multiple candidate points are detected in a certain area, the one with the highest score will be selected. The connections drawn between key points indicate that the affinity field

Table 2.1 Sub-JHMDB database PCK@0.2 (Jhuang 2013)

Method	Head	Shoulder	Elbow	Wrist	Buttocks	Knee	Ankle	Average
PAF (Cao 2017)	96.7	95.8	90.2	86.6	97.1	94.3	90.2	93.0
TSN (Song 2017)	97.1	95.7	87.5	81.6	98.0	92.7	89.8	92.1
LSTM (Luo 2018)	**98.2**	96.5	89.6	86.0	**98.7**	**95.6**	90.0	93.6
TFC (Li 2019)	97.7	**96.6**	**91.5**	**88.1**	97.9	94.9	**91.1**	**94.0**

Table 2.2 Penn action database PCK@0.2 (Zhang 2013)

Method	Head	Shoulder	Elbow	Wrist	Buttocks	Knee	Ankle	Average
PAF (Cao 2017)	98.4	98.2	96.1	95.9	98.5	97.9	97.6	97.5
TSN (Song 2017)	98.0	97.3	95.1	94.7	97.1	97.1	96.9	96.5
LSTM (Luo 2018)	**98.9**	**98.6**	**96.6**	**96.6**	98.2	98.2	97.5	97.7
TFC (Li 2019)	98.8	98.5	**96.6**	**96.6**	**98.8**	**98.3**	**98.2**	**98.0**

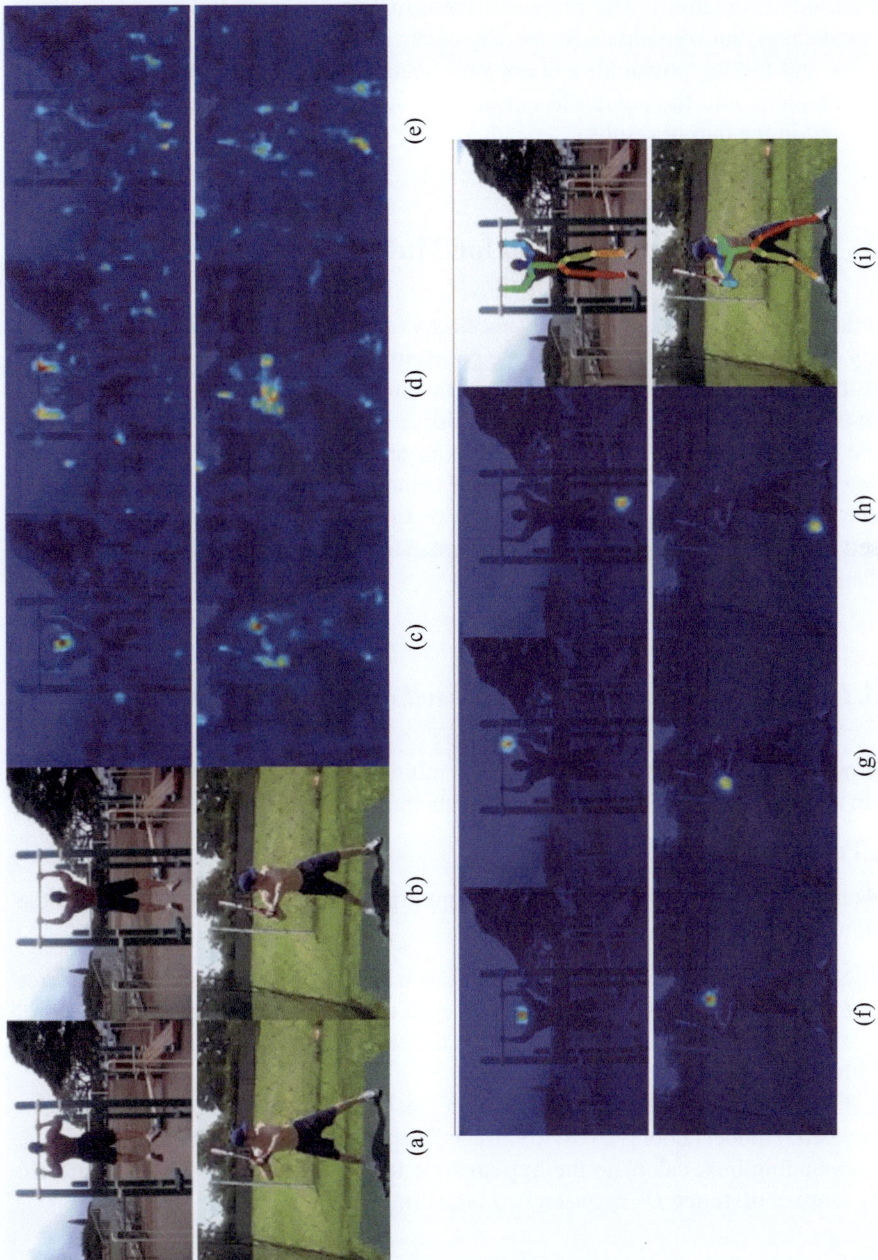

Fig. 2.5 Visualization of correlograms (Li 2019)

has connected them together (Fig. 2.6i shows the result obtained by connecting the key points detected in the corresponding frame sequence, which can be further used for attitude estimation). The presented algorithm can accurately locate key points in most cases, but sometimes errors may occur. For example, the scene in Fig. 2.6b is dark and the leg positioning is not very accurate. The human body in Fig. 2.6d is incomplete, and the ankle did not actually appear, but it was still detected and appeared in the output results.

2.3 3-D Key Point Detection for Multiple Persons

In practical applications, it is usually necessary to obtain the 3-D key points of human body, that is, the 3-D positions of these points in the world coordinate system (Jiang 2024b). If only a single image is used, sufficient information cannot be guaranteed, so it is necessary to consider obtaining multiple images. Here, multiple images need to be obtained from different perspectives in order to have richer information. By using the method of stereo vision, multiple cameras can be used to capture the same scene from different perspectives at the same time, and the obtained images can be fused to obtain the 3-D key points of the human body through geometric calculations (triangulation).

2.3.1 3-D Key Point Detection Based on Multiple Perspectives

Below is an introduction to a fast and robust multi person 3-D pose estimation method from multiple perspectives (Dong 2019), which is based on 3-D key point detection.

1. **Pose Estimation Steps**

This method of estimating 3-D pose from multiple perspectives mainly includes the following four steps:

(1) Single view 2-D key point detection. Use a multi person 2-D key point detector CPN (Chen 2018) to detect persons in each viewpoint image from top to bottom, and then use bounding box calibration to detect 2-D key points in each bounding box.

(2) Calculating the **affinity matrix**. After using the pedestrian re-identification (ReID) model (Zhong 2018) to extract the apparent features f_i of persons in each bounding box, calculate the **appearance feature distance** D^a and **geometric feature distance** D^g between two bounding boxes:

$$D^a(f_i, f_j) = \|f_i - f_j\|_2 \tag{2.23}$$

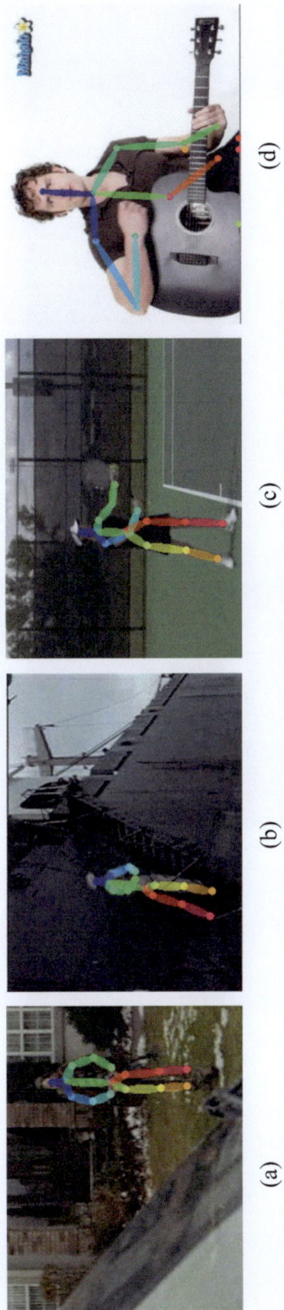

Fig. 2.6 Some examples of experimental results (Li 2019)

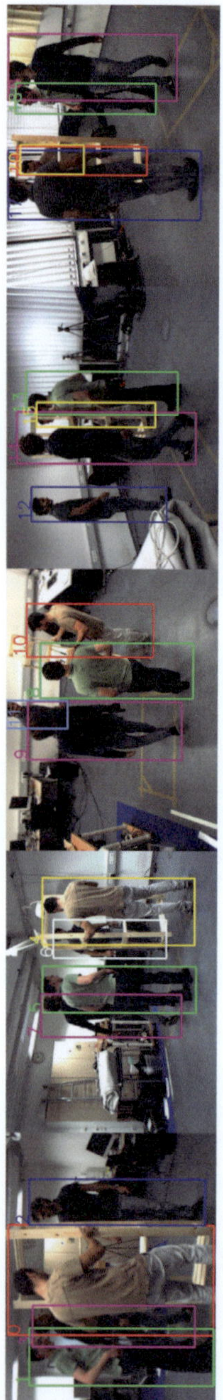

(a) Examples based on matrix optimization

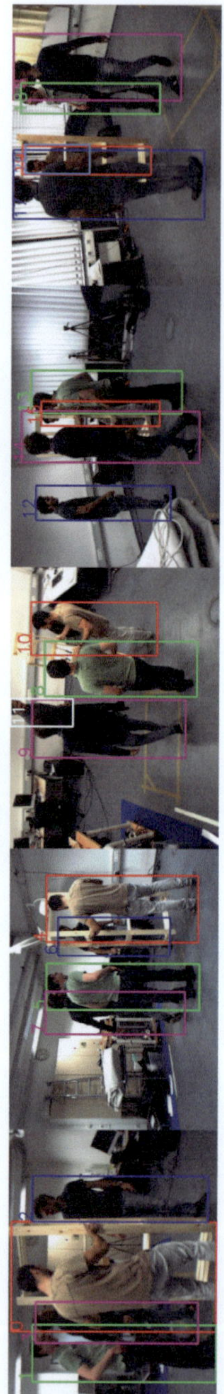

(b) Examples based on hierarchical clustering

Fig. 2.7 Comparison examples of detection on Shelf database (Li 2020)

$$D^g(\boldsymbol{x}_i, \boldsymbol{x}_j) = \frac{1}{2P} \sum_{p=1}^{P} \left\{ d^g\left[\boldsymbol{x}_{p,i}, \boldsymbol{L}_{ij}(\boldsymbol{x}_{p,j})\right] + d^g\left[\boldsymbol{x}_{p,i}, \boldsymbol{L}_{ji}(\boldsymbol{x}_{p,i})\right] \right\} \tag{2.24}$$

where $\boldsymbol{x}_{p,i}$ represent the 2-D coordinates of the p-th key point within the i-th bounding box; $\boldsymbol{L}_{ij}(\boldsymbol{x}_{p,j})$ represents the epi-polar line obtained by geometric transformation of $\boldsymbol{x}_{p,j}$ under the camera corresponding to the i-th bounding box; $d^g(\bullet, l)$ represents the distance from a 2-D point to the epi-polar line l.

By using the apparent feature distance and **geometric pose distance**, the **appearance affinity matrix** $\boldsymbol{A}^a$ and **geometric affinity matrix** $\boldsymbol{A}^g$ can be calculated, and the values of each element in them can be represented as

$$A^a(f_i, f_j) = 1 - \text{Sigmoid}\left[D^a(f_i, f_j)\right] \tag{2.25}$$

$$A^g(\boldsymbol{x}_i, \boldsymbol{x}_j) = 1 - \text{Sigmoid}\left[D^g(\boldsymbol{x}_i, \boldsymbol{x}_j)\right] \tag{2.26}$$

where the Sigmoid function is used to ensure that the values of each element in $\boldsymbol{A}^a$ and $\boldsymbol{A}^g$ fall within the interval [0, 1]. Next, calculate the (total) affinity matrix $\boldsymbol{A}$, where the values of each element are the geometric means of the corresponding apparent affinity matrix values and geometric affinity matrix values:

$$A_{ij} = \sqrt{A^a(f_i, f_j) A^g(\mathbf{x}_i, \mathbf{x}_j)} \tag{2.27}$$

(3) Solving the matching of bounding boxes. That is, to determine which bounding boxes correspond to the same person (see below for details).
(4) Using graph models to determine optimal 3-D coordinates. Taking bounding boxes obtained from the same person with different perspectives, the triangulation is employed to calculate the 3-D candidate coordinates for each key point of that person. Because a 3-D coordinate needs to be derived from at least two 2-D coordinates, multi person 3-D key point detection from multiple perspectives requires determining which 2-D key points correspond to the same point in 3-D space. Here, a graph model can be used to find the optimal candidate. If N bounding boxes match the same person, there are $N(N - 1)/2$ candidate coordinates. If it is determined for each 2-D key point of a person belonging to in these respective perspectives, then the matching problem under multiple perspectives can be solved on a human body basis, thereby establishing the relationship between 2-D key points and ultimately obtaining the optimal 3-D coordinates.

2. **Bounding Box Matching**

When there are multiple persons in the scene, it is necessary to establish a matching relationship between the person detected from different perspectives. Here, it is necessary to utilize the feature similarity of the same person from multiple perspectives. The matching result needs to satisfy **cycle consistency**, that is, if bounding box i matches bounding box j, and bounding box j matches bounding box k, then bounding box k and bounding box i should also match.

In order to achieve matching, it is necessary to optimize and solve the **partial permutation matrix** $\boldsymbol{P} \in \{0, 1\}^{N \times N}$. $\boldsymbol{P}$ should be able to maximize the sum of associations between matching boxes. At the same time, in order to reduce redundant matching results, it should also be possible to minimize the number of persons in the scene.

Given a total of V perspectives, $\boldsymbol{P}$ can be written as a combination of sub-matrixes:

$$\boldsymbol{P} = \begin{bmatrix} \boldsymbol{P}_{11} & \boldsymbol{P}_{12} & \cdots & \boldsymbol{P}_{1V} \\ \boldsymbol{P}_{21} & \boldsymbol{P}_{22} & \cdots & \boldsymbol{P}_{2V} \\ \vdots & \vdots & \ddots & \vdots \\ \boldsymbol{P}_{V1} & \boldsymbol{P}_{V2} & \cdots & \boldsymbol{P}_{VV} \end{bmatrix} \tag{2.28}$$

Assuming that perspectives i and j have N_i and N_j bounding boxes, respectively, the sub-matrixes of the affinity matrix $\boldsymbol{A}$ and permutation matrix $\boldsymbol{P}$ are $\boldsymbol{A}_{ij} \in \mathrm{R}^{Ni \times Nj}$ and $\boldsymbol{P}_{ij} \in \{0, 1\}^{Ni \times Nj}$, respectively. The permutation matrix $\boldsymbol{P}_{ij}$ satisfies a **doubly stochastic constraint**:

$$0 \leq \boldsymbol{P}_{ij}\mathbf{1} \leq 1, \qquad 0 \leq \boldsymbol{P}_{ij}^{\mathrm{T}}\mathbf{1} \leq 1 \tag{2.29}$$

i.e., at most one bounding box corresponds to one bounding box, and $\boldsymbol{P}_{ii}$ in the corresponding equation should be the identity matrix.

It can be proven that if $\boldsymbol{P}$ satisfies cycle consistency, then there must be:

$$\mathrm{rank}(\boldsymbol{P}) \leq M, \qquad \boldsymbol{P} \geq 0 \tag{2.30}$$

where M is the number of persons detected in the scene; $\boldsymbol{P}$ can be decomposed into $\boldsymbol{Y}\boldsymbol{Y}^{\mathrm{T}}$, $\boldsymbol{Y} \in \mathrm{R}^{N \times M}$.

The optimization formula for matching is

$$\min_{\boldsymbol{P}} \left\{ -\sum_{i=1}^{V}\sum_{j=1}^{V} \langle \boldsymbol{A}_{ij}, \boldsymbol{P}_{ij} \rangle + k\,\mathrm{rank}(\boldsymbol{P}) \right\} \tag{2.31}$$

where k is the coefficient of the penalty item. For the convenience of solving the formula, it can be considered to relax the values of elements in $\boldsymbol{P}$ to real numbers within the interval [0, 1], and no longer force $\boldsymbol{P}$ to be a semi-positive definite matrix.

Since the rank of the matrix cannot be directly optimized, Eq. (2.31) can be transformed into

$$\min_{\boldsymbol{P}} \{ -\langle \boldsymbol{A}, \boldsymbol{P} \rangle + k\,||\boldsymbol{P}||_* \} \tag{2.32}$$

where the nuclear norm $||\boldsymbol{P}||_* = \mathrm{tr}(\sqrt{\boldsymbol{P}^{\mathrm{T}}\boldsymbol{P}})$ constrains the low rank of the matrix, which is used to penalize the total number of persons in the scene.

Equation (2.32) represents a convex optimization problem, where $\boldsymbol{P}$ must satisfy certain conditions, namely Eq. (2.29), where $\boldsymbol{P}_{ii}$ is the identity matrix and $\boldsymbol{P}$ is the symmetry matrix. By using the **Alternating Direction Method of Multipliers** (ADMM) and the **augmented Lagrange method of multipliers**, Eq. (2.32) can ultimately be rewritten as

$$L_r(\boldsymbol{P}, \boldsymbol{Q}, \boldsymbol{Y}) = -\langle \boldsymbol{A}, \boldsymbol{P} \rangle + k||\boldsymbol{Q}||_* + \langle \boldsymbol{Y}, \boldsymbol{P} - \boldsymbol{Q} \rangle + \frac{r}{2}||\boldsymbol{P} - \boldsymbol{Q}||_F^2 \tag{2.33}$$

where $\boldsymbol{P}$ is the primary variable; $\boldsymbol{Q}$ is an auxiliary variable; $\boldsymbol{Y}$ is a dual variable; $\boldsymbol{R}$ is the penalty parameter; $||\ldots||_F$ is the Frobenius norm. In the optimization process, it is necessary to update the original variables and dual variables alternately until convergence.

Due to the relaxation of both conditions in Eq. (2.30) during the solving process, the optimization result $\boldsymbol{P}$ may not satisfy cycle consistency. Therefore, it is necessary to obtain the final matching result based on $\boldsymbol{P}$: if $\boldsymbol{P}[i, j] = 1$, or if there exists k such that $\boldsymbol{P}[i, k] = 1$ and $\boldsymbol{P}[j, k] = 1$, then box i and box j match. This result satisfies cycle consistency.

2.3.2 3-D Key Point Detection Based on Hierarchical Clustering

The matrix optimization used in the aforementioned 3-D pose estimation to solve the matching problem of bounding boxes has the following shortcomings:

(1) It cannot be guaranteed that the same camera is mutually exclusive, that is, two bounding boxes detected from the same perspective are matched with the same person. In fact, human detectors rarely have duplicate detections, so different bounding boxes detected from the same perspective generally do not correspond to the same person and should not be matched. Although the iteration of matrix optimization includes processing of camera number information, the final matching result cannot guarantee mutual exclusion with the camera. In addition, even if the human detector experiences duplicate detection, where two bounding boxes from the same perspective correspond to the same person, only one of the bounding boxes needs to be successfully matched to obtain the required 2-D key point information.

(2) There is not a clear threshold, that is, two bounding boxes corresponding to one person will be matched with two persons. Although penalty terms related to the number of persons in the scene are introduced in matrix optimization, the optimal weight of this term varies depending on the scene, and it is not universal. This can lead to situations where, despite the high correlation between certain bounding boxes, they are still not matched, resulting in redundant 3-D results.

(3) The apparent affinity is unstable. In multi person scenes, there are often situations where there is occlusion, the human body exceeds the image boundary, or there is a significant difference in angle between different perspectives, which may lead to low apparent affinity of the same person in different perspectives and easy omission of matching. Due to the fact that the affinity matrix in matrix optimization is the geometric average of apparent and geometric affinities, some geometric affinity information may not be fully utilized.

1. **Hierarchical Clustering**

Given the shortcomings of the matrix optimization mentioned above, a **hierarchical clustering** approach can be used to solve the matching problem (Li 2020). Hierarchical clustering (Johnson 1967) is an unsupervised clustering method. In clustering algorithms, "association" and "distance" are considered reciprocal to each other. Consider having N samples and knowing the distance between each pair of samples. At the beginning of clustering, each sample is a cluster, and after N steps of merging, all samples will be merged into the same cluster. The clustering process is an iterative process. In each iteration, it is necessary to find the two clusters with the closest distance and merge them. To determine whether to merge, a merge threshold can be set. After merging, the distance between clusters needs to be updated. There are different methods for defining the distance between clusters, and one commonly used method is the "farthest distance method", which defines the distance between two clusters as the maximum distance between them when one element is taken from each cluster. This method ensures that the distance between two bounding boxes within the same cluster is not too large, meaning that there is a significant correlation between every two bounding boxes.

Camera mutual exclusion conditions can be added to the process of hierarchical clustering. If there is a conflict in camera numbers between the two clusters selected in the iterative process, they will not be merged. It is worth noting that if merging is not performed and the distance matrix is not updated, it will cause the iteration to enter a dead loop. The solution is to adjust the distance between the two conflicting clusters to infinity, while other elements that are not in these two clusters are completely unaffected. It has been proven that the clustering results naturally satisfy cycle consistency.

2. **Matching Algorithm**

The affinity matrix can integrate information from both apparent and geometric correlations, as they have different characteristics. The apparent correlation is easily affected by factors such as angle, occlusion, and overlap, and its performance is unstable, making it unsuitable for clustering alone. Geometric correlations have better stability than apparent correlations. The experiment found that if two bounding boxes from different perspectives correspond to the same person, even if there are individual errors in the 2-D key point detection results of the two bounding boxes, the geometric correlation between their poses is still high. Because the 2-D key points are constrained by the bounding box and do not deviate too far from the corresponding epi-polar lines in the image space of another camera, so geometric correlations can serve as a supplement to restore omissions caused by low apparent correlations. Therefore, the matching algorithm based on hierarchical clustering considers performing two rounds of clustering, the first using an affinity matrix (which combines appearance and geometric affinity information), and the second using a geometric affinity matrix alone.

In order to facilitate the fusion of multiple hierarchical clustering results, the sequence numbers of the two samples found during each iteration are recorded in order during each clustering process to form a list. Then, the multiple lists obtained from multiple clusters are connected into a new list, and the clusters corresponding to the sequence numbers are merged based on the same camera exclusion criteria according to the new list to obtain a matching result.

In practice, by observing frames outside the testing range in the database, the thresholds T_1 and T_2 for the first and second clustering are selected as 0.9 and 0.95, respectively. Due to the complementary role of geometric affinity, the threshold is relatively high.

3. **Experimental Setup, Results, and Comparison**

The algorithm was experimentally compared with four other algorithms using two databases. The experimental data includes: ① Campus database (Bursnius 2013), all three perspectives with three individuals are selected;② Shelf database (Burenius 2013), all 5 perspectives from 4 individuals are selected;③ Panoptic database (Joo 2015), 143 frames from 6 perspectives with 10 persons using VGA cameras are selected. In Table 2.3 (Li 2020), the experimental results are given for all five compared algorithms and two (Campus and Shelf) databases.

Due to the fact that the specific names and positions of human body key points in different databases are not exactly the same, certain normalization adjustments have been made for evaluation and comparison. For specific details, please refer to (Li 2020).

In multiple perspectives situations, camera parameters need to be calculated based on the data provided by the database. The calculation methods based on different databases are different.

For the Campus database, the camera's internal parameter matrix $\boldsymbol{K}$ is

Table 2.3 Experimental results of detection for five algorithms on two databases (Li 2020)

Algorithms (References)	Campus	Shelf
3-D pictorial structures revisited: Multiple human pose estimation (Belagiannis 2016)	84.5	77.5
Multiple human 3-D pose estimation from multi-view images (Ershadi-Nasab 2018)	90.6	95.1
Multi-person 3-D pose estimation and tracking in sports (Bridgeman 2019)	92.6	96.7
Fast and robust multi-person 3-D pose estimation from multiple views (Dong 2019)	96.3	96.9
3-D pose estimation based on multi-level clustering (Li 2019)	**96.4**	**97.1**

$$K = \begin{bmatrix} \frac{f}{s_x}s & 0 & c_x s \\ 0 & \frac{f}{s_x}s & c_y s \\ 0 & 0 & 1 \end{bmatrix} \tag{2.34}$$

where all parameters are provided by the database; s is the scale and can be omitted.

The camera rotation matrix $\boldsymbol{R} \in \mathrm{R}^{3\times 3}$ is

$$\boldsymbol{R} = \begin{bmatrix} \cos r_y \cos r_z & \cos r_z \sin r_x \sin r_y - \cos r_x \sin r_z & \sin r_x \sin r_z + \cos r_x \cos r_z \sin r_y \\ \cos r_y \sin r_z & \sin r_x \sin r_y \sin r_z + \cos r_x \cos r_z & \cos r_x \sin r_y \sin r_z - \cos r_x \sin r_x \\ -\sin r_y & \cos r_y \sin r_x & \cos r_x \cos r_y \end{bmatrix} \tag{2.35}$$

The external parameter matrix $\boldsymbol{T}$ of the camera is

$$\boldsymbol{T} = \begin{bmatrix} \boldsymbol{R} & \boldsymbol{t} \\ \boldsymbol{0}^{\mathrm{T}} & 1 \end{bmatrix} \tag{2.36}$$

where $\boldsymbol{t}$ is the translation vector.

The projection matrix of the camera is $\boldsymbol{P} = \boldsymbol{KT}$. The projection of 3-D coordinates $[x_{3\mathrm{D}}, y_{3\mathrm{D}}, z_{3\mathrm{D}}]^{\mathrm{T}}$ in the world coordinate system onto the image space can be calculated as follows:

$$\begin{bmatrix} u \\ v \\ w \end{bmatrix} = \boldsymbol{P} \begin{bmatrix} x_{3\mathrm{D}} \\ y_{3\mathrm{D}} \\ z_{3\mathrm{D}} \\ 1 \end{bmatrix} \tag{2.37}$$

where $[u, v, w]^{\mathrm{T}}$ is a homogeneous coordinate, transformed into 2-D coordinates: $x_{2\mathrm{D}} = u/w$, $y_{2\mathrm{D}} = v/w$.

The Shelf database directly provides $\boldsymbol{P}$, $\boldsymbol{K}$, $\boldsymbol{R}$, and $\boldsymbol{t}$.

The value of the camera translation vector $\boldsymbol{t}$ in the Panoptic database (Joo 2015) is measured in centimeters and needs to be scaled when calculating the external parameter $\boldsymbol{T}$:

$$\boldsymbol{T} = \begin{bmatrix} \boldsymbol{R} & \boldsymbol{t}/100 \\ \boldsymbol{0}^{\mathrm{T}} & 1 \end{bmatrix} \tag{2.38}$$

The fundamental matrix $\boldsymbol{F}$ between camera i and camera j (Hartley 2003) is

$$\boldsymbol{F} = \left(\boldsymbol{K}_j^{-1}\right)^{\mathrm{T}} \boldsymbol{R}_j \boldsymbol{R}_i^{\mathrm{T}} \boldsymbol{K}_i^{\mathrm{T}} \boldsymbol{M}_{\mathrm{skew}} \left[\boldsymbol{K}_i \boldsymbol{R}_i \boldsymbol{R}_j^{\mathrm{T}} \left(\boldsymbol{t}_j - \boldsymbol{R}_j \boldsymbol{R}_i^{\mathrm{T}} \boldsymbol{t}_i\right)\right] \tag{2.39}$$

where the skew symmetric matrix $\boldsymbol{M}_{\mathrm{skew}}$ has the following structure:

$$\boldsymbol{M}_{\text{skew}}\left(\begin{bmatrix} a_0 \\ a_1 \\ a_2 \end{bmatrix}\right) = \begin{bmatrix} 0 & -a_2 & a_1 \\ a_2 & 0 & -a_0 \\ -a_1 & a_0 & 0 \end{bmatrix} \tag{2.40}$$

The evaluation indicator is the **Percentage of Correctly estimated Parts** (PCP). First, use the human body as the unit to find the nearest human body in the detection results for each labeled true value, and then compare the coordinates of key points. Compare the two adjacent key points x_i and x_j at both ends of the limb with the annotated truth values $\boldsymbol{x}_i^{\text{gt}}$ and $\boldsymbol{x}_j^{\text{gt}}$, if the following equation is satisfied (with a threshold T of 0.5):

$$\frac{\left\|\boldsymbol{x}_i - \boldsymbol{x}_i^{\text{gt}}\right\|_2 + \left\|\boldsymbol{x}_j - \boldsymbol{x}_j^{\text{gt}}\right\|_2}{2\left\|\boldsymbol{x}_i^{\text{gt}} - \boldsymbol{x}_j^{\text{gt}}\right\|} < T \tag{2.41}$$

then the detection result will be judged as correct.

The algorithm based on hierarchical clustering takes about one-fifth the time of the matching algorithm based on matrix optimization.

As shown in Table 2.3, the algorithm based on hierarchical clustering has improved detection accuracy compared to other comparative algorithms.

Figure 2.7 shows the detection comparison results of a set of 5 perspectives (from left to right) on the Shelf database (Li 2020). In the matrix optimization-based result shown in Fig. 2.7a, the red bounding box in the first perspective and the yellow bounding box in the second perspective were originally supposed to correspond to the same person, but were mistakenly matched as two persons (with different box colors). This issue has been corrected in the results based on hierarchical clustering matching (all in red boxes).

Figure 2.8 further connects the detected key points in 3-D space to display human pose. The coordinate system of the 3-D results has been adjusted for visualization, representing only the interrelationships between human bodies and not their absolute positions. There are 4 persons in the scene, but 5 human bodies can be seen from Fig. 2.8a, where the yellow line represents the extra human body due to matching errors, indicating redundancy in the 3-D results. This issue does not appear in Fig. 2.8b, that is, the 3-D result is correct.

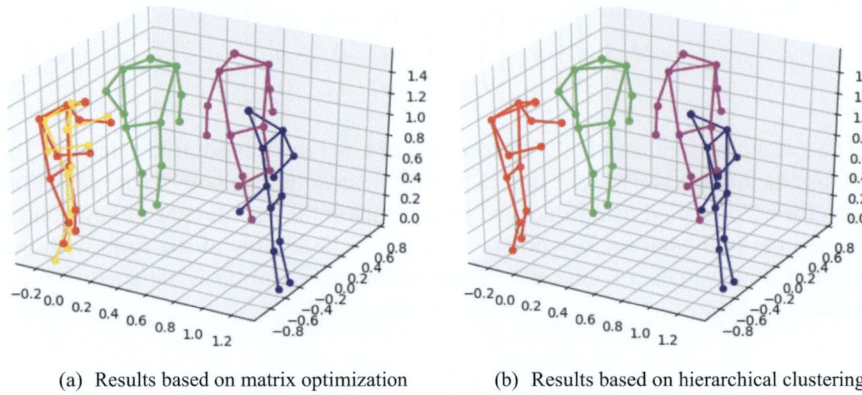

Fig. 2.8 Comparison results of detection on Shelf database (Li 2020)

References

Andriluka M, Pishchulin L, Gehler P, *et al.* 2-D human pose estimation: New benchmark and state of the art analysis. Proc. CVPR, 3686–3693, 2014.

Belagiannis V, Amin S, Andriluka M, *et al.* 3-D pictorial structures revisited: Multiple human pose estimation. IEEE-PAMI, 38(10): 1929–1942, 2016.

Bridgeman L, Volino M, Guillemaut J Y, *et al.* multi-person 3-D pose estimation and tracking in sports. Proc. CVPRW. 2487–2496, 2019.

Burenius M, Sullivan J, Carlsson S. 3-D pictorial structures for multiple view articulated pose estimation. Proc. CVPR, 3618–3625, 2013.

Cao Z, Simon T, Wei S E, *et al.* Real time multi-person 2-D pose estimation using part affinity fields. Proc. CVPR, 7291–7299, 2017.

Chen Y, Wang Z, Peng Y, *et al.* Cascaded pyramid network for multi person pose estimation. Proc. CVPR, 7103–7112, 2018.

Dindorf C, Dully J, Simon S, *et al.* Toward automated plantar pressure analysis: machine learning-based segmentation and key point detection across multicenter data. Frontiers in Bioengineering and Biotechnology, 13: #1579072. https://doi.org/10.3389/fbioe.2025.1579072, 2025.

Dong J, Jiang W, Huang Q, *et al.* Fast and robust multi-person 3-D pose estimation from multiple views. Proc. CVPR, 7792–7801, 2019.

Ershadi-Nasab S, Noury E, Kasaei S, *et al.* Multiple human 3-D pose estimation from multi-view images. Multimedia Tools and Applications, 77(12): 1557315601, 2018.

Girdhar R, Gkioxari G, Torresani L, *et al.* Detect and track: Efficient pose estimation in videos. Proc. CVPR, 350–359, 2018.

Hartley R, Zisserman A. Multiple View Geometry in Computer Vision. Cambridge university press, 2003, 2003

He K, Gkioxari G, Dollár P, *et al.* Mask RCNN. Proc. ICCV, 2980–2988, 2017.

Jhuang H, Gall J, Zuffi S, *et al.* Towards understanding action recognition. Proc. ICCV, 3192–3199, 2013.

Jiang J H, Xia N, Li C W, *et al.* Keypoint detection method for single person gymnastics actions based on multi-scale incremental learning. Acta Electronica Sinica, 52(5): 1730–1742, 2024a.

Jiang J H, Zhu X C, Ye X C. GAN-BodyPose: Real-time 3D human body pose data key point detection and quality assessment assisted by generative adversarial network. Image and Vision Computing, 149, 105144. https://doi.org/10.1016/j.imavis.2024.105144, 2024b.

Johnson S C. Hierarchical clustering schemes. Psychometrika, 32(3): 241–254, 1967.

Joo H, Liu H, Tan L, *et al.* Panoptic studio: A massively multi-view system for social motion capture. Proc. ICCV, 3334–3342, 2015.

Kavousinejad S, Vazirizadeh Y, Behnaz M, *et al.* Artificial intelligence framework for automated facial asymmetry detection using key-point analysis and neural networks. Journal of Imaging Informatics in Medicine. https://doi.org/10.1007/s10278-025-01558-8, 2025.

Laptev I. On space-time interest points. International Journal of Computer Vision, 64(2/3): 107–123, 2005.

Li W T, Xu X Y, Zhang Y-J. Temporal feature correlation for human pose estimation in videos. Proc. ICIP, 599–603, 2019, 2019.

Li W T. Human Pose Estimation with Feature Similarity between Images (Dissertation). Beijing, Tsinghua University, 2020.

Luo Y, Ren J, Wang Z, *et al.* LSTM pose machines. Proc. CVPR, 5207–5215, 2018.

Newell A, Yang K, Deng J. Stacked hourglass networks for human pose estimation. Proc. ECCV, 483–499, 2016.

Song J, Wang L, Van Gool L, *et al.* Thin-slicing network: A deep structured model for pose estimation in videos. Proc. CVPR, 4220–4229, 2017.

Zhang W F, Zhou Y M, Xu L, *et al.* A method of detecting phishing web pages based on Hungarian matching algorithm. Chinese Journal of Computers, 33(10): 1963–1975, 2010.

Zhang W, Zhu M, Derpanis K G. From actemes to action: A strongly supervised representation for detailed action understanding. Proc. ICCV, 2248–2255, 2013.

Zhang Y-J. A Selection of Image Understanding Techniques: From Fundamentals to Research Front. CRC Press, England, 2023.

Zhong Z, Zheng L, Zheng Z, *et al.* Camera style adaptation for person re-identification. Proc. CVPR, 5157–5166, 2018.

Zhu X C, Ye X C. GAN-BodyPose: Real-time 3D human body pose data key point detection and quality assessment assisted by generative adversarial network. Image and Vision Computing, 149, 105144. https://doi.org/10.1016/j.imavis.2024.105144, 2024.

Chapter 3
Spatiotemporal Trajectory

By tracking the motion of a point or a target along a straight line or curve, the (dynamic) trajectory of the point or target can be obtained (Yang 2024, Zhang 2024a, Zhao 2025). In the understanding of spatiotemporal behavior, learning and analyzing dynamic trajectories (Morris 2008) can characterize the behavior of various moving targets in a scene and provide a grasp of scene changes and motion states.

Trajectories and paths are closely related, but there are still some differences. The path mainly considers spatial location and is a collection of spatial points. Trajectory usually takes into account also the velocity, acceleration, etc., at various spatial positions. Someone calls it also active path, to emphasize the influence of motion. In general, paths mainly consider global connections, while trajectories also focus on some local features (if the concept of pixel connections is used, it can assume that paths basically correspond to passages, while trajectories also require connectivity).

The work of spatiotemporal trajectory analysis includes trajectory detection, tracking, modeling, learning, classification, recognition, etc.

The sections of this chapter are arranged as follows.

Section 3.1 introduces the basic principles and steps for trajectory analysis, emphasize modeling and learning. Some trajectory related activity analysis examples are also provided.

Section 3.2 introduces a method for classifying and recognizing trajectories of different target movements by using trajectory feature clustering trees.

3.1 Trajectory Learning and Analysis

Figure 3.1 shows a flowchart for dynamic trajectory learning and analysis of videos. With the help of input video, the first step is to detect the target. Here, either stationary cameras can be used to detect and track moving targets, or motion cameras can also be used to detect and track stationary or moving persons or organs, such as placing

Y.-J. Zhang, *Spatiotemporal Image Understanding*,
https://doi.org/10.1007/978-981-95-7130-7_3

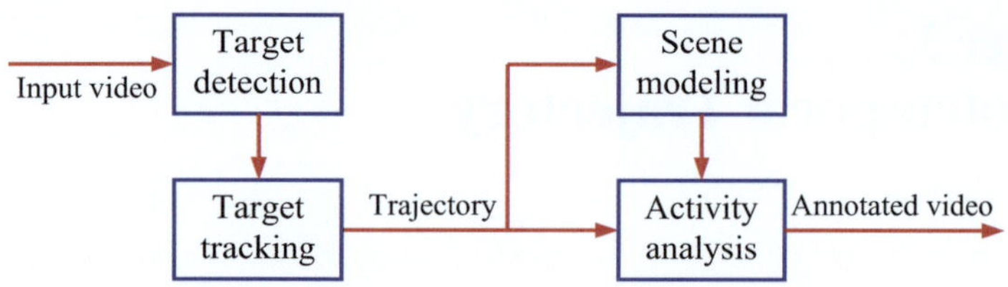

Fig. 3.1 Flowchart for dynamic trajectory learning and analysis of videos

the camera on a moving car to detect pedestrians on the roadside, as shown in (Jia 2007). In order to obtain the motion trajectories of different targets, various methods can be used, such as detecting vehicle trajectories as described in (Zhao 2024), and detecting pedestrian trajectories as described in (Wang 2024). In addition, it is also possible to consider combining trajectory segments, overcoming occlusion issues, and constructing complete trajectories, as shown in (Sun 2024). By blending the results of continuous detection and tracking, the motion trajectory of the target can be obtained. By utilizing such trajectories, a scene model can be automatically constructed. Finally, using such a model to analyze motion can also provide annotations for activities.

In scene modeling, the location of the image area where an event occurs can be defined as a **Point Of Interest** (POI) first, and then the **Activity Path** (AP) can be defined in the following learning steps. This path depicts how the target moves/travels between points of interest. The model constructed in this way is called the POI/AP model.

The main tasks learned in the POI/AP model are as follows.

(1) **Activity Learning**: Learning about activities can be achieved by comparing **trajectories**. The length of different trajectories may different, the key is to maintain a clear understanding of similarities.
(2) **Adaptation**: Study the techniques for managing POI/AP models. It enables technology to adapt online adding new activities, deleting activities that no longer continue, and validating models.
(3) **Feature Selection**: Determine the correct level of dynamic representation for a specific task. For example, the route of a car passed can be determined using only spatial location information, but its speed information is also required if an accident is to be detected.

3.1.1 Scene Modeling

The automatic modeling of scenes through dynamic trajectories includes the following three key steps (Makris 2005).

1. Tracking Target

Tracking the target requires maintaining the identity of each observable target in each frame. For example, a tracked target in a video of T frames will generate a series of inferred tracking states:

$$S_T = \{s_1,\ s_2,\ \cdots,\ s_t,\ \cdots,\ s_T\} \tag{3.1}$$

where each S_t can describe target's characteristics such as position, speed, appearance, shape, etc. The trajectory information based on these characteristics forms the cornerstone for further analysis. By carefully analyzing this information, one can identify and understand the activity.

2. Detecting Points of Interest

The primary task of scene modeling is to identify the regions of interest in the image. In the graph indicating the tracking target, these regions correspond to the nodes in the graph. The two types of nodes typically considered are entry/exit regions and stop regions. Taking a teacher teaching in a classroom as an example, the former corresponds to the classroom door, and the latter corresponds to the podium.

The entry/exit region refers to the position where a target enters or leaves the **Field Of View** (FOV), or where a tracked target appears or disappears. These regions are often modeled using a 2-D **Gaussian Mixture Model** (GMM), with $Z \sim \sum^{M}{}_{i=1} w_i N(\mu_i, \sigma_i)$, which includes M components. This model can be solved using the **Expectation–Maximization** (EM) algorithm. The incoming point data includes the position determined by the first tracking state, while the outgoing point data includes the position determined by the last tracking state. Consider using density criteria to distinguish states, where the mixed density in state i is defined as

$$d_i = \frac{w_i}{\pi\sqrt{|\sigma_i|}} > T_d \tag{3.2}$$

This is used to measure the compactness of Gaussian mixtures. Among them, the threshold

$$T_d = \frac{w}{\pi\sqrt{|\boldsymbol{C}|}} \tag{3.3}$$

indicates the average density of signal clustering. $0 < w < 1$ is a user-defined weight, and $\boldsymbol{C}$ is the covariance matrix of all points in the regional dataset. Compact mixing indicates the correct region, while loose mixing indicates tracking noise caused by tracking interruptions.

The stopping region originates from the landmark points in the scene, where the target tends to a fixed position over a period of time. The stopping region can be determined using two different methods: ① The speed of the tracked point in the region is below a predetermined lower threshold; ② All tracked points remain within a finite distance loop at least for a certain period of time. By defining the radius and time constants, the first method may still include slower moving targets, while adopting the second method can ensure that the target remains within a specific

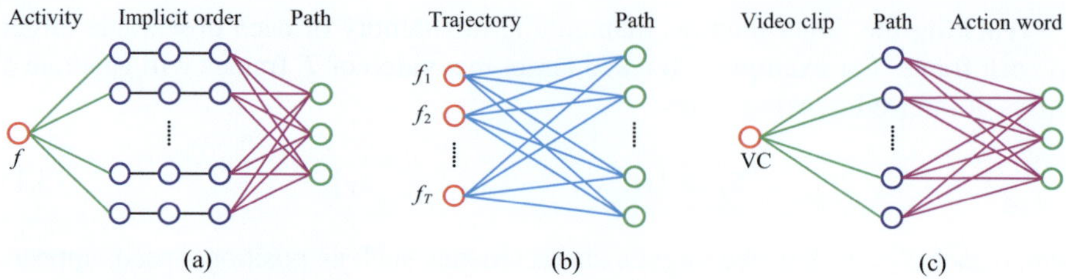

Fig. 3.2 Three basic structures of activity path learning algorithm

range. When analyzing activities, in addition to determining the location, it is also important to grasp the time spent in each stopping region.

3. Learning Activity Path

To understand behavior, it is necessary to determine the **Activity Path** (AP). POI can be used to filter out false alarms or tracking interruptions from the training set, retaining only trajectories that start after entering the activity region and end within the activity termination region. The tracking trajectory through the activity region is divided into two segments: entering and leaving the activity region. An activity should be defined between the two points of interest of the target's starting and ending actions.

In order to distinguish action targets that change over time (such as pedestrians walking or running along sidewalks), it is necessary to incorporate temporal dynamic information into path learning. Figure 3.2 shows three basic structures of the activity path learning algorithm. Their main differences include input types, motion vectors, trajectories (or the corresponding video clips), and the way motion is abstracted. In Fig. 3.2a, the input is a single trajectory started at time t, and the points in the path are implicitly sorted in time. In Fig. 3.2b, a complete trajectory is used as input for the learning algorithm to directly establish the output path. In Fig. 3.2c, the path is decomposed according to the video sequence, and the **video clip** (VC) is decomposed into a set of action words to describe the activity, or the video clip is labeled with a certain activity based on the appearance of the action words.

3.1.2 Trajectory Learning

To characterize the motion of the target, a sequence of dynamic measurements of the target's motion can be used. For example, a commonly used trajectory representation is a motion sequence:

$$G_T = \{\mathbf{g}_1, \mathbf{g}_2, \cdots, \mathbf{g}_T\} \tag{3.4}$$

where the motion vector

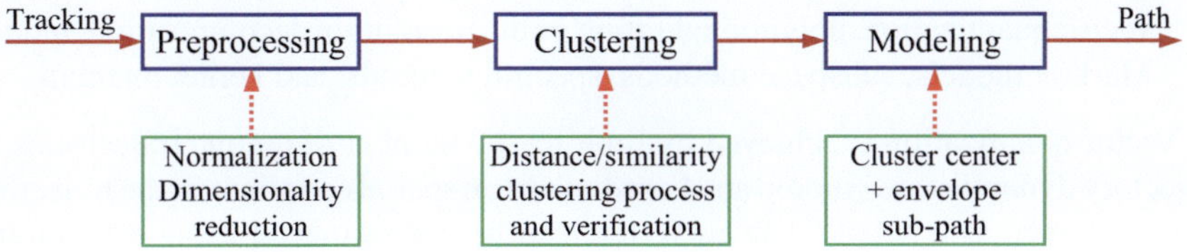

Fig. 3.3 Trajectory learning steps

$$\boldsymbol{g}_t = [x^t, y^t, v_x^t, v_y^t, a_x^t, a_y^t]^{\mathrm{T}} \tag{3.5}$$

represents the dynamic parameters of the target obtained from tracking at time t, including its position $[x, y]^{\mathrm{T}}$, velocity $[v_x, v_y]^{\mathrm{T}}$, and acceleration $[a_x, a_y]^{\mathrm{T}}$.

It is possible to learn AP in an unsupervised manner by using only trajectories, as shown in Fig. 3.3. The preprocessing step involves establishing trajectories for clustering, which mainly involves normalization and dimensionality reduction. The clustering step can provide a global and compact path model representation, with the main task of measuring distance or similarity during the clustering process. The modeling steps should provide a determined path, which mainly includes determining the cluster center and decomposing the sub paths. Although there are three separate sequential steps in Fig. 3.3, they are often combined together. Below are detailed explanations for each of the three steps.

1. Trajectory Preprocessing

Most of the work in path learning research requires obtaining trajectories suitable for clustering. When tracking, the main difficulty comes from the time-varying nature, which can lead to inconsistent trajectory lengths. At this point, some steps need to be taken to ensure meaningful comparisons can be made between inputs of different sizes. In addition, trajectory representation in clustering should be able to intuitively maintain the similarity of the original trajectory.

Trajectory preprocessing mainly includes two aspects:

(1) Normalization: The purpose is to ensure that all trajectories have the same length L_t. Two simple techniques are zero padding and extension. Filling in zeros is adding some zero terms after a shorter trajectory. Extension is the process of extending the last moment of the original trajectory to the desired length. Both have the potential to expand the trajectory space significantly. In addition to checking the training set to determine the length L_t of the trajectory, prior knowledge can also be used for resampling and smoothing. Resampling combined with interpolation can ensure that all trajectories have the same length L_t. Smoothing can be used to eliminate noise, and the smoothed trajectory can also be obtained by interpolation and sampling to obtain the desired length.

(2) Dimensionality Reduction: Dimensionality reduction maps trajectories to a new lower dimensional space, allowing for the use of more robust clustering methods. This can be achieved by assuming a trajectory model and determining the parameters that can most effectively describe the model. Common techniques include

vector quantization, polynomial fitting, multi-resolution decomposition, hidden Markov models, subspace methods, spectral methods, and kernel methods.

Vector quantization is achieved by limiting the number of unique trajectories. If trajectory dynamics are ignored and based solely on spatial coordinates, the trajectory can be viewed as a simple 2-D curve and can be approximated using a minimum mean square polynomial of order m (where w is the weight coefficient):

$$X(t) = \sum_{k=0}^{m} w_k t^k \tag{3.6}$$

In spectral methods, a similarity matrix $\boldsymbol{S}$ can be constructed for the training set, where element s_{ij} represents the similarity between trajectory i and trajectory j. It is also possible to construct the Laplacian matrix $\boldsymbol{L}$:

$$\boldsymbol{L} = \boldsymbol{D}^{-1/2}\boldsymbol{S}\boldsymbol{D}^{-1/2} \tag{3.7}$$

where $\boldsymbol{D}$ is a diagonal matrix, and its i-th diagonal element is the sum of the i-th row elements in $\boldsymbol{S}$.

By decomposing $\boldsymbol{L}$, its maximum K eigenvalues can be determined. Place the corresponding eigenvectors into a new matrix, with rows corresponding to the transformed trajectories in spectral space, which can be obtained using the K-means method.

Most researchers combine trajectory normalization and dimensionality reduction to process the original trajectory, ensuring that it can be processed using standard clustering techniques.

2. Trajectory Clustering

Clustering is a commonly used machine learning technique for determining structure in unlabeled data. It collects motion trajectories while observing the scene and categorizes them into similar categories. In order to generate meaningful clustering, the **trajectory clustering** process needs to consider three issues: ① Defining a distance (corresponding to similarity) measure; ② Determine the strategy for cluster updates; ③ Validate clustering. The following discussion is divided into two parts.

(1) Distance/Similarity Measurement: Clustering techniques rely on the definition of distance (similarity) measures. As mentioned earlier in the discussion of preprocessing, a major issue with trajectory clustering is that the length of trajectories generated by the same activity may vary. To solve this problem, either preprocessing methods can be used, or a size independent distance measure can be defined (if the lengths of the two trajectories G_i and G_j are the same):

$$d_{\mathrm{E}}(G_i, G_j) = \sqrt{(G_i - G_j)^{\mathrm{T}}(G_i - G_j)} \tag{3.8}$$

If the lengths of two trajectories G_i and G_j are different, the improvement of Euclidean distance not changing with size is to compare the trajectory vectors of two lengths m and n ($m > n$), and use the cumulative distortion of the last point $\boldsymbol{g}_{j,n}$:

$$d_{ij}^{(c)} = \frac{1}{m}\left\{\sum_{k=1}^{n} d_{\mathrm{E}}(\boldsymbol{g}_{i,k}, \boldsymbol{g}_{j,k}) + \sum_{k=1}^{m-n} d_{\mathrm{E}}(\boldsymbol{g}_{i,n+k}, \boldsymbol{g}_{j,n})\right\} \tag{3.9}$$

Euclidean distance is relatively simple, but its effect is not good in the presence of time offset, as only aligned sequences may match. For this purpose, the Hausdorff distance (Zhang 2024b) can be considered. Additionally, there is another distance measure that does not rely on the complete trajectory (without considering outliers). Assuming that the lengths of trajectories $G_i = \{\boldsymbol{g}_{i,k}\}$ and $G_j = \{\boldsymbol{g}_{j,l}\}$ are T_i and T_j, respectively, then

$$D_{\mathrm{o}}(G_i, G_j) = \frac{1}{T_i}\sum_{k=1}^{T_i} d_{\mathrm{o}}(\boldsymbol{g}_{i,k}, G_j) \tag{3.10}$$

where (δ is a positive number less than 1),

$$d_{\mathrm{o}}(\boldsymbol{g}_{i,k}, G_j) = \min_{l}\left[\frac{d_{\mathrm{E}}(\boldsymbol{g}_{i,k}, \boldsymbol{g}_{j,l})}{Z_l}\right] \qquad l \in \{\lfloor(1-\delta)k\rfloor, \cdots, \lceil(1+\delta)k\rceil\} \tag{3.11}$$

where Z_l is the normalization constant and also the variance at point l.

$D_{\mathrm{o}}(G_i, G_j)$ is used to compare trajectories with existing clusters. For comparing two trajectories, $Z_l = 1$ can be used. The distance measure defined in this way is the average normalized distance between any point and its best match point, where the best match point falls within a sliding time window centered at point l and the width of window is 2δ.

(2) Clustering Process and Validation: The preprocessed trajectories can be combined using unsupervised learning techniques, and the trajectory space can be decomposed into perceptually similar clusters (such as roads). There are various learning methods for clustering: ① Iterative optimization; ② Online adaptive; ③ Hierarchical method; ④ Neural network; ⑤ Symbiotic decomposition.

The paths learned through clustering algorithms need further validation as the actual number of categories is unknown. Most clustering algorithms require an initial value of the expected number of categories K, but this value is often incorrect. For this purpose, different K can be clustered separately, and the K corresponding to the best result can be selected as the true number of clusters. The criterion here can use the **Tightness and Separation Criterion** (TSC) to compare the distances between corresponding trajectories in different clusters. If the given training set is $D_T = \{G_1, G_2, \ldots, G_M\}$, then the criterion is

Fig. 3.4 Two types of trajectory modeling

$$\mathrm{TSC}(K) = \frac{1}{M} \frac{\sum_{j=1}^{K} \sum_{i=1}^{M} f_{ij}^2 d_{\mathrm{E}}^2(G_i, c_j)}{\min_{ij} d_{\mathrm{E}}^2(c_i, c_j)} \tag{3.12}$$

where f_{ij} is the fuzzy membership degree of trajectory G_i to cluster C_j (where the samples are represented by c_j).

3. Trajectory Modeling

After trajectory clustering, a graph model can be established based on the obtained paths for effective inference. The path model is a compact representation of clustering. There are two ways for **trajectory modeling**. The first approach considers a complete path, where the path from endpoint to endpoint has not only an average center of gravity/centerline, but also envelopes on both sides indicating the path range. There may also be some intermediate states along the path that provide measurement order, as shown in Fig. 3.4a. The second approach decomposes the path into several sub-paths, or represents the path as a tree containing sub-paths, and predicts the probability of the path from the current node to the leaf nodes, as shown in Fig. 3.4b.

3.1.3 Activity Analysis

Once the scene model is established, the activities and behaviors of the target can be analyzed. Using the surveillance video analysis to explain, one of its basic functions is to verify events of interest. Generally speaking, it is easy to define whether one is interested only in a specific environment. For example, the parking management system focuses on whether there are still available parking spaces, while the intelligent conference room system is concerned with communication between personnel. In addition to identifying specific behaviors, it is also necessary to examine all atypical events. By observing the scene for a long time, the system can conduct a series of activity analyses to learn which events are of interest.

Some typical activity analysis examples are as follows.

(1) **Virtual Fencing**: Any monitoring system has a certain monitoring range, and sentries can be set up at the boundary of this range to provide early warnings for events that occur within the range. This is equivalent to establishing a virtual fence at the boundary of the monitoring range, triggering analysis once there is

an intrusion. For example, controlling a high-resolution ***Pan-Tilt-Zoom*** (PTZ) camera to capture details of the intrusion site and starting to count the number of intrusions.

(2) **Speed Profiling**: Virtual fences only utilize location information, while with the help of target tracking technology, dynamic information can also be obtained to achieve speed-based warnings, such as vehicle speeding or road congestion.

(3) **Trajectory Classification**: Velocity analysis only utilizes the currently tracked data, and in practical applications, activity paths (APs) obtained from historical motion patterns can also be utilized. The behavior of newly emerging targets can be described using the **Maximum A Posteriori** (MAP) trajectory G:

$$L* = \arg\max_k p(l_k|G) = \arg\max_k p(G,\ l_k)p(l_k) \tag{3.13}$$

This helps determine which activity path can most fully explain the new data. Because the prior path distribution $p(l_k)$ can be estimated using the training set, the problem is simplified by using HMM for maximum likelihood estimation.

(4) **Anomaly Detection**: The detection of abnormal events is often an important task of monitoring systems. Because the activity path can indicate typical activities, if the new trajectory does not match the existing trajectory, anomalies can be detected. Abnormal patterns can be detected through intelligent thresholding:

$$p(l * |G) < L_l \tag{3.14}$$

where the value of the activity path l^* that is most similar to the new trajectory G and is still less than the threshold L_l; otherwise, an abnormal event occurred.

(5) **Online Activity Analysis**: Being able to analyze, identify, and evaluate activities online is more important than using the entire trajectory to describe motion. A real-time system should be able to quickly infer ongoing behavior based on incomplete data (often based on graph models). This can include two situations: ① Path prediction: Using existing tracking data to predict future behavior and refining the prediction when more data is collected. Non complete trajectories can be used to predict activities, which is represented as

$$\hat{L} = \arg\max_j p(l_j|W_t G_{t+k}) \tag{3.15}$$

where W_t represents the window function, G_{t+k} is the trajectory up to the current time t and k predicted future tracking states. ② Tracking anomalies: In addition to classifying the entire trajectory as anomalies, it is also necessary to be able to detect abnormal events when they occur. To achieve this, $W_t G_{t+k}$ can be used instead of G in Eq. (3.14). The window function W_t does not necessarily have to be the same as predicted, and the threshold may need to be adjusted according to the amount of data.

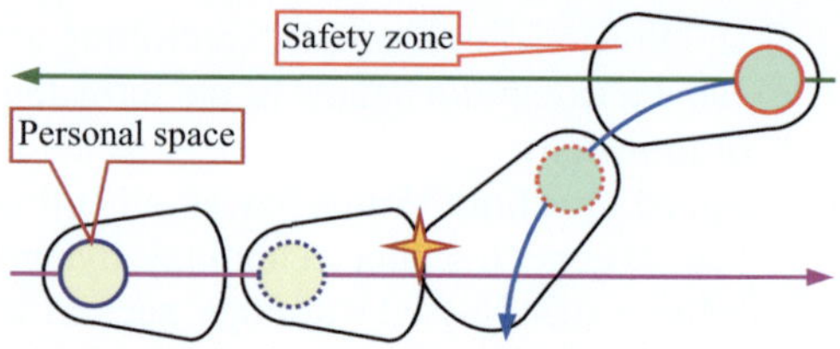

Fig. 3.5 Schematic diagram of using paths for vehicle collision assessment

(6) **Object Interaction Characterization**: Higher level analysis expects to further describe the interactions between targets. Similar to abnormal events, it is also difficult to strictly define target interactions. There are different types of interactions among different goals in different environments. Taking car collisions as an example, each car has its own spatial dimensions, which can be considered as personal space. When a car is in motion, a minimum safe distance (minimum safety zone) needs to be added to the personal space around the car. This space will change with the movement, and the faster the speed, the more the minimum safe distance increases (especially in the direction of travel). A schematic diagram is shown in Fig. 3.5, where personal space is represented by circles, while the safe region (around car) changes with speed (including size and direction). If the safety zones of two vehicles intersect, there is a possibility of collision, so it is necessary and possible to use this information for analysis to help plan the driving route. A hybrid deep learning model to predict vehicle trajectories with spatiotemporal interactions between several vehicles is proposed in (Zhang 2025).

Finally, it should be pointed out that for simple activities, analysis can be carried out solely based on the target position and velocity. However, for more complex activities, more measurements may be required, such as adding the curvature of the profile to distinguish peculiar motion trajectories. To provide more comprehensive coverage of activities and behaviors, it is often necessary to use a multi camera network. In addition, the activity trajectory may also originate from targets composed of interconnected components (such as the human body), in which case the activity needs to be defined relative to a set of trajectories.

3.2 Trajectory Feature Clustering Tree

Based on the motion trajectory, different methods can be used to classify and recognize various movements. The following introduces a method based on trajectory feature clustering tree (Chen 2016).

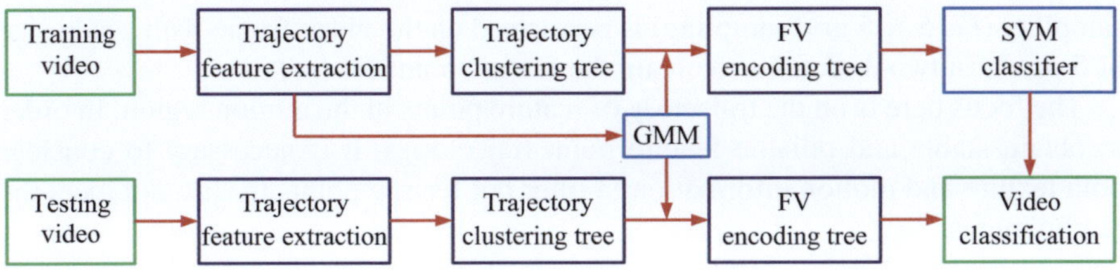

Fig. 3.6 Flow chart of trajectory feature clustering tree method

3.2.1 Flow Chart

The workflow diagram of this method is shown in Fig. 3.6, which is mainly divided into two stages: training and testing (see the upper and lower parts of the Fig. 3.6, respectively). During the training stage, trajectory features are first extracted from the training video. Then, based on the spatiotemporal position and shape information of the trajectory features, a clustering tree structure of trajectory is constructed, and a **Gaussian Mixture Model** (GMM) is trained using the trajectory features. Next, the GMM is used to encode the trajectory clusters contained in each node of the trajectory clustering tree using **Fischer Vector** (FV) encoding, resulting in the corresponding FV encoding tree structure. Finally, the **Support Vector Machine** (SVM) classifier is trained using tree structured vectors for classification.

In the testing stage, the similar process is conducted. Trajectory features are first extracted from the testing video, and a clustering tree structure of trajectory is constructed based on the spatiotemporal position and shape information of the trajectory features, with the help of the GMM trained using the trajectory features. Then, FV encoding is performed on the trajectory feature clusters contained in each node of the tree to obtain the corresponding FV encoding tree structure; Finally, the trained SVM classifier is used to perform video classification using the FV encoding tree obtained from the test video.

3.2.2 Trajectory Feature Extraction

Trajectory feature extraction includes two main steps: feature extraction and feature description.

1. Feature Extraction

The idea of extracting trajectory features from videos is to use optical flow fields to perform short-term motion tracking on densely sampled feature point sets, and to extract multiple descriptors within the spatiotemporal neighborhood of feature point trajectories (Wang 2013). Specifically, the Farnebäck algorithm (Farnebäck 2003) is used to calculate the dense optical flow field Ω_t of video frame I_t, and uniform dense sampling (*i.e.* 5×5 grid sampling) is performed on the video frame with a step size of 5 pixels in two directions to obtain the feature point set $\{p_t\}$.

The focus here is on the trajectory of feature points in the motion region. In order to obtain stable and reliable feature point trajectories, it is necessary to consider both texture and motion information to filter out feature points that do not meet the requirements.

(1) Texture Feature Points

In smooth regions of an image without texture, it is impossible to reliably track feature points. For this reason, it is necessary to remove the feature points of these smooth regions (Shi 1994). First, calculate the autocorrelation matrix $\boldsymbol{D}$ of the feature point p_t:

$$\boldsymbol{D} = \begin{bmatrix} d_x d_x & d_x d_y \\ d_y d_x & d_y d_y \end{bmatrix} \tag{3.16}$$

where d_x and d_y represent the gradients of feature point p_t in the x and y directions, respectively. Assuming that $(\lambda_1; \lambda_2)$ is the eigenvalue of matrix $\boldsymbol{D}$, then when $\min(\lambda_1; \lambda_2)$ is less than the pre-set threshold, the feature point will be removed from the feature point set.

(2) Motion Feature Points

For each sampled feature point $p_t = (x_t, y_t)$ in video frame I_t, the optical flow information after median filtering can be used to calculate its position p_{t+1} in the next video frame I_{t+1}:

$$p_{t+1} = (x_{t+1}, y_{t+1}) = (x_t, y_t) + (M \otimes \Omega_t)\big|_{(\bar{x}_t, \bar{y}_t)} \tag{3.17}$$

where M represents the median filtering function. The template size is 3×3. $(\bar{x}_t, \bar{y}_t)$ is the rounding position of the feature points (x_t, y_t). By continuously tracking the position of feature points in the next video frame, a feature point trajectory vector $\boldsymbol{P}$ can be obtained:

$$\boldsymbol{P} = [p_t, p_{t+1}, p_{t+2}, \cdots]^{\mathrm{T}} \tag{3.18}$$

Using optical flow fields to track feature points may result in deviations from their actual positions during the tracking process due to errors in optical flow calculations. To reduce the risk of tracking drift, the length of feature points in tracking can be limited, for example, to $L = 15$ frames. During the tracking process, some feature points may be lost or the tracking may end prematurely, resulting in some 5×5 regions having no feature points. At this point, it is necessary to add a sampling feature point in the region and perform the next step of tracking to ensure dense sampling. In addition, it is difficult to avoid some erroneous feature point trajectories in the process of feature point tracking (such as in static textured backgrounds or noisy regions), so it is necessary to make judgments based on the motion information of the trajectories. If the position of the trajectory changes very little or exceeds a specified threshold, it can be considered that these trajectories are incorrect, and the corresponding feature points will be removed from the feature point trajectory set.

Figure 3.7 shows a schematic diagram of tracking feature point trajectory for a weightlifting activity video (Chen 2016). The small (red) circles in the figure represents the position of the feature point at the current time, and the (green) vertical lines represents the motion trajectory of the feature point from the previous time to the current time.

2. Feature Description

After obtaining the trajectory of the feature points, it is necessary to extract descriptors that characterize the appearance and motion information from the spatiotemporal neighborhood of the trajectory. Firstly, consider the shape feature vector $\boldsymbol{T}$ of the trajectory

$$\boldsymbol{T} = [\Delta p_t,\ \Delta p_{t+1}\ , \cdots,\ \Delta p_{t+L-1}]^{\mathrm{T}} \tag{3.19}$$

where $\Delta p_t = p_{t+1} - p_t = (x_{t+1} - x_t,\ y_{t+1} - y_t)$ represents the displacement of the feature points at time t.

Normalizing the L_1 norm of the feature vector $\boldsymbol{T}$ can serve as a shape descriptor for trajectory features. Set the spatiotemporal neighborhood size of the trajectory to

Fig. 3.7 Schematic diagram of tracking feature point trajectory (Chen 2016)

$N \times N \times L$, where $N = 32$ pixels and $L = 15$ frames. Furthermore, the spatiotemporal neighborhood can be divided into sub blocks of $2 \times 2 \times 3$. Calculate the feature descriptors for each sub-block, such as **Histograms of Oriented Gradient** (HOG) (Dalal 2005), **Histogram of Optical Flow** (HOF) (Laptev 2008), and **Motion Boundary Histogram** (MBH) (Dalal 2006). Among them, HOG describes the appearance information in the spatial domain, HOF describes the motion information in the temporal domain, and MBH describes the relative motion information of feature point trajectories. Finally, concatenate the HOG, HOF, and MBH descriptors corresponding to each sub-block to form the final HOG, HOF, and MBH descriptors for the trajectory.

3.2.3 Feature Clustering Trees

On the basis of trajectory feature extraction, a feature clustering tree can be constructed. Here, the unsupervised hierarchical binary partitioning method (Gaidon 2014) is improved to obtain a data-driven tree decomposition structure that better reflects the spatiotemporal distribution of trajectory features. Firstly, calculate the similarity matrix $\boldsymbol{W} \in \mathrm{R}^{N \times N}$ between trajectory features, where N represents the number of trajectory features. In order to better reflect the spatiotemporal distribution of trajectories, the spatiotemporal position and shape information of trajectories are used to calculate the similarity between trajectories. These features include: spatiotemporal position $\boldsymbol{x} = (x_1, x_2, \ldots, x_L), \boldsymbol{y} = (y_1, y_2, \ldots, y_L), \boldsymbol{t} = (t, t+1, \ldots, t+L-1)$, and spatial variation information $\boldsymbol{v}_x = (\Delta x_1, \Delta x_2, \ldots, \Delta x_L)$, $\boldsymbol{v}_y = (\Delta y_1, \Delta y_2, \ldots, \Delta y_L)$. For each feature, a **Radial Basis Function** (RBF) kernel, that is, a Gaussian kernel function $k(f,f') = \exp[-\gamma d(f,f')^2]$, is used to calculate the similarity, where $d(f,f')$ calculates the Euclidean distance between two features, and where $\gamma = 1/(2\,\overline{d})$ is the normalization parameter, which represents the mean Euclidean distance between features. Finally, multiply the similarity matrices calculated from the five features to obtain the similarity matrix $\boldsymbol{W}$ for the trajectory features.

In the process of implementing binary partitioning, the original method revealed two problems that need to be solved: one is caused by isolated trajectory feature points, and the other is caused by the time difference between different video samples. They will be discussed separately below.

1. Isolated Trajectory Feature Points

In order to perform binary partitioning, it is necessary to establish a graph connection structure in the spatiotemporal space of trajectory features. The nodes in the graph represent trajectory features. If two trajectory features belong to K-nearest neighbors, there are connecting edges between the corresponding nodes. At this point, the K-D tree method can be used to quickly establish the K-nearest neighbor graph structure of the trajectory. Setting the number of neighbors to $K = 10$ can form a fully connected graph structure of trajectory features in the video. When dividing a node, the number of connected components in the trajectory features can be used to preferentially determine the division method with fewer connected components. However, in the process of continuous partitioning, the presence of many isolated trajectory feature points in the nodes can lead to an increase in the number of connected components, which affects the actual clustering effect. To solve this problem, it is possible to consider retaining only the maximum connected component within each node for the next layer partitioning, in order to avoid the impact of isolated trajectory feature points on clustering.

2. Video Sample Duration Difference

In reality, video samples vary greatly, and even videos of the same type of activity or behavior may have significantly different durations, resulting in a significant difference in the number of trajectory features extracted from them. To solve this problem, it is possible to consider using an adaptive node partitioning threshold. The dynamic threshold here can use multiple percentiles (such as 10%, 20%, …, 90%) to sequentially threshold the feature vectors and determine the minimum and maximum numbers of trajectory features contained in the nodes, avoiding the situation where the number of trajectory features of two nodes differs greatly during the partitioning process. This can also accelerate the clustering process.

3.2.4 *Fischer Vector Encoding Tree*

After obtaining the feature clustering tree, it is necessary to represent the trajectory features contained in each node of the clustering tree as vectors, using the **Fischer Vector** (FV) encoding method (Sánchez 2013). This encoding method utilizes first-order and second-order statistical information of features and cluster centers, which has stronger discriminative power than the K-means nearest neighbor encoding method and can achieve better classification performance. Specifically, 256,000 trajectory features are randomly selected from the training samples to train the **Gaussian Mixture Model** (GMM), with the number of GMMs set to $K = 256$. The encoding vector length corresponding to FV encoding is $2DK$, where D is the dimension of the feature. Finally, normalize the FV encoding vector, and connect features of the normalized FV encoding vectors, such as HOG, HOF, MBH, etc., together as the final FV encoding vector of the trajectory features contained in the node.

After obtaining the FV encoding tree of the video, it is necessary to define a kernel function that measures the similarity between different tree structures. The GraphHopper kernel function calculates the weighted average of node similarity by comparing the shortest paths between node pairs (Feragen 2013):

$$K(G_1, G_2) = \sum_{n_1 \in V_1} \sum_{n_2 \in V_2} w(n_1, n_2) k(n_1, n_2) \tag{3.20}$$

where, $w(n_1, n_2)$ counts the number of times nodes n_1 and n_2 appear at the same position in the shortest path.

In practice, due to the disorder between two sub-nodes in the clustering process of binary partitioning of trajectory features, the tree structure obtained by unsupervised clustering is not stable enough, so it is difficult to guarantee the effectiveness by directly using tree structure to measure similarity. Therefore, it can be considered to directly calculate the similarity between all node pairs as the kernel function:

$$K_{\mathrm{a}}(T_1, T_2) = w_r k(r_1, r_2) + \frac{1 - w_r}{|V_1||V_2|} \sum_{n_1 \in V_1} \sum_{n_2 \in V_2} k(n_1, n_2) \tag{3.21}$$

where r_1 and r_2 represent the root nodes of trees T_1 and T_2, respectively; n_1 and n_2 represent nodes in the non-root node sets V_1 and V_2, respectively; w_r represents the weighting coefficient, and when $w_r = 1$, it means directly using the bag of words model for behavior recognition. Equation (3.21) utilizes the similarity of all node pairs in the tree for calculation, which can be referred to as the kernel function of all tree node pairs.

The above kernel function only considers node similarity. It is possible to further consider edge similarity to fully utilize the structural information of the clustering tree. The encoding vectors of child nodes and parent nodes can be connected together as the vector representation of edges. This yields the kernel function for all tree edge pairs (where e indicates the edge):

$$K_{\mathrm{e}}(T_1, T_2) = w_r k(r_1, r_2) + \frac{1 - w_r}{|U_1||U_2|} \sum_{e_1 \in U_1} \sum_{e_2 \in U_2} k(e_1, e_2) \tag{3.22}$$

where e_1 and e_2 represent the edges formed by connecting non-root nodes with their parent nodes in trees T_1 and T_2, respectively; U_1 and U_2 respectively represent the sets of edges in two clustering trees.

In addition, the clustering effect of nodes with different similarities would not be the same. If all nodes are treated equally, it may affect the measurement performance of the final kernel function. For this reason, only the node pairs with the highest similarity can be considered when calculating the kernel function, so that all tree node pairs become (superscript (m) indicates the maximum)

$$K_{\mathrm{a}}^{(\mathrm{m})}(T_1, T_2) = w_r k(r_1, r_2) + (1 - w_r) \left[\frac{\sum\limits_{n_1 \in V_1} \max\limits_{n_2 \in V_2} \{k(n_1, n_2)\}}{|V_1|} + \frac{\sum\limits_{n_2 \in V_2} \max\limits_{n_1 \in V_1} \{k(n_1, n_2)\}}{|V_2|} \right] \tag{3.23}$$

Correspondingly, the kernel function of edge pairs in all trees becomes (superscript (m) indicates the maximum)

$$K_{\mathrm{e}}^{(\mathrm{m})}(T_1, T_2) = w_r k(r_1, r_2) + (1 - w_r)\left[\frac{\sum\limits_{e_1 \in U_1} \max\limits_{e_2 \in U_2} \{k(e_1, e_2)\}}{|U_1|} + \frac{\sum\limits_{e_2 \in U_2} \max\limits_{e_1 \in U_1} \{k(e_1, e_2)\}}{|U_2|}\right] \tag{3.24}$$

Finally, when calculating node similarity, weighted node kernel functions can be obtained based on the spatiotemporal distance between nodes:

$$K_{\mathrm{w}}(n_1, n_2) = \exp[-q \bullet d(n_1, n_2)^2]\langle \mathrm{FV}(n_1),\ \mathrm{FV}(n_2)\rangle \tag{3.25}$$

where q is a weighting coefficient.

The five kernel functions (corresponding to Eqs. (3.20)–(3.24), respectively) introduced earlier are all weighted sums of node kernel functions $K_{\mathrm{w}}(n_1, n_2)$. As long as the node kernel functions satisfy the positive definite condition, these five kernel functions satisfy the positive definite condition and can be directly combined with SVM classifiers.

3.2.5 Experimental Results and Analysis

The performance of the above algorithm was experimentally verified and compared with related algorithms using four databases (Chen 2016).

1. Experimental Algorithms and Databases

In the validation of the algorithm, on one hand, the original binary partition clustering method (Gaidon 2014) was considered, which is referred to as the original algorithm. On the other hand, the method of partitioning the features belonging to the maximum connected component within the node (referred to as Algorithm 1) and the method of using dynamic thresholds as the criteria for partitioning (referred to as Algorithm 2) were considered, separately. The algorithm introduced above that utilizes trajectory feature clustering trees can be referred to as Algorithm (1 + 2).

Four general video databases were used in the experiments: Hollywood2 database (Marszalek 2009), Olympic Sports database (Niebles 2010), HMDB51 database (Kuehne 2011), and UCF50 database (Reddy 2013). An overview of these four databases is shown in Table 3.1.

2. Comparison of Algorithm Effects

Table 3.1 Overview of four databases

Statistical item	Hollywood2	Olympic Sports	HMDB51	UCF50
Total number of behavior categories	12	16	51	50
Total number of video samples	1707	783	6766	6618
Number of test set samples	823	134	1530	250

The experimental results of the four algorithms mentioned above in the Olympic Sports database with significant differences in video duration are shown in Table 3.2 (bold numbers indicate the best). The evaluation indicator used is the **mean Average Precision** (mAP).

As shown in Table 3.2, both Algorithm 1 and Algorithm 2 have reduced the average number of nodes, which reduces the influence of isolated trajectory feature points, and can also accelerate the calculation of the clustering tree. The algorithm that combines them, Algorithm (1 + 2) performs even better.

3. Comparison of Kernel Functions

In Eq. (3.25), a node kernel function weighted by spatiotemporal distance is introduced. For the five kernel functions of Eqs. (3.20)–(3.24), another five kernel functions weighted by spatiotemporal distance can also be obtained with the help of Eq. (3.25). The experimental comparison results of these 10 kernel functions are shown in Table 3.3 (bold numbers indicate the best).

From the Table 3.3, it can be seen that:

(1) The kernel function $K(G_1, G_2)$ that considers the structural information of the clustering tree is not as effective as $K_a(T_1, T_2)$ and $K_e(T_1, T_2)$, indicating that

Table 3.2 Effects of four algorithms on Olympic sports database (Chen 2016)

Clustering algorithm	Average number of nodes	mAP(%)
Original algorithm	519	91.5
Algorithm 1	202	91.6
Algorithm 2	34	91.9
Algorithm (1 + 2)	**29**	**92.8**

Table 3.3 Comparison of different kernel functions and node kernel functions (Chen 2016)

Kernel function	Node kernel function	Hollywood2(%)	Olympic Sports(%)	HMDB51(%)	UCF50(%)
$K(G_1, G_2)$	K	62.3	90.5	55.5	88.5
	K_w	62.6	90.7	55.7	88.6
$K_e(T_1, T_2)$	K	64.1	92.4	59.1	91.4
	K_w	64.3	92.5	59.2	91.4
$K_e^{(m)}(T_1, T_2)$	K	64.3	92.5	59.2	91.4
	K_w	64.5	92.6	59.3	91.5
$K_a(T_1, T_2)$	K	64.0	91.9	58.9	91.3
	K_w	64.1	92.1	59.0	91.4
$K_a^{(m)}(T_1, T_2)$	K	64.4	92.8	59.2	91.5
	K_w	**64.6**	**92.9**	**59.3**	**91.7**

the structure of the clustering tree is not stable enough to measure the differences between different clustering trees.

(2) The kernel function $K_e^{(m)}(T_1, T_2)$, considering only with the maximum similarity node pair, performs better than $K_e(T_1, T_2)$. Similarly, the kernel function $K_a^{(m)}(T_1, T_2)$, considering only with the maximum similarity node pair, performs better than $K_a(T_1, T_2)$. Both indicate that all nodes should not be treated equally.

(3) The kernel functions $K_e^{(m)}(T_1, T_2)$ and $K_n^{(m)}(T_1, T_2)$ have similar effects, indicating that similarity measurement of edges in clustering trees is also effective.

(4) The effect obtained by weighting the spatiotemporal distance of node kernel functions has been improved, but not significantly. One possible factor is that the average spatiotemporal position of all features within the node is used here to represent the spatiotemporal position of the node. Due to the fact that a node may contain a large number of features, using the average value cannot well reflect the distribution of all features within the node. This still needs further investigation.

4. Comparison of Spatiotemporal Division

The division of time and space can be achieved using the **SpatioTemporal Pyramid** (STP). Figure 3.8 shows several ways to divide the spatiotemporal pyramid, namely: the undivided spatiotemporal method (denoted as O), the method of dividing time dimension into two parts (denoted as T2), the method of dividing space dimension into three parts (denoted as S3), and the method of simultaneously dividing time dimension into two parts and space dimension into three parts (denoted as T2 + S3).

The results obtained from experiments on the above-mentioned spatiotemporal partitioning methods are shown in Table 3.4. The results obtained using the undivided spatiotemporal approach (O) on the four databases are basically consistent with the original algorithm (Gaidon 2014). The use of the other three spatiotemporal partitioning methods (T2, H3, T2 + H3) resulted in varying degrees of performance degradation, particularly on the Hollywood2 database compiled from movie video clips. One explanation here is that the original algorithm used **Dense Trajectory Features** (DTF), while Algorithm 1, Algorithm 2, and Algorithm (1 + 2) all used **Improved Trajectory Features** (ITF). Although ITF features are more robust

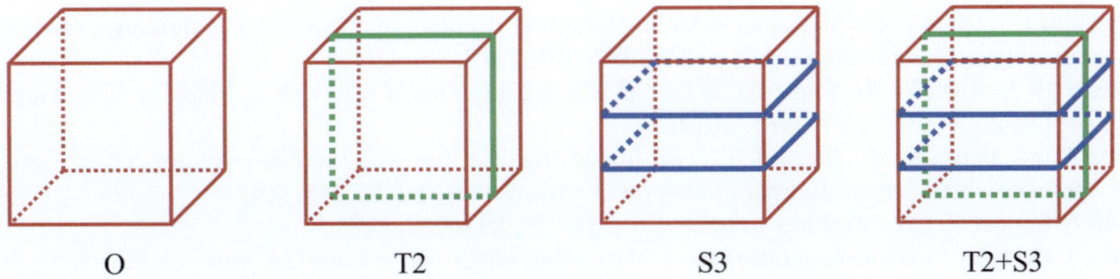

Fig. 3.8 Several spatiotemporal pyramid partitions

Table 3.4 Impact of spatiotemporal pyramid (Chen 2016)

Spatiotemporal pyramid	Hollywood2(%)	Olympic Sports(%)	HMDB51(%)	UCF50(%)
O	63.7	91.0	57.9	91.2
T2	38.9	59.8	56.8	83.0
S3	30.8	89.9	45.8	74.6
T2 + S3	34.1	69.6	44.3	69.8

than DTF features when there is camera motion, when combining ITF features with spatiotemporal partitioning, the number of features contained in each partitioned region varies greatly, and the resulting FV encoding vector cannot well describe the appearance and motion information of that region. This indicates that simple spatiotemporal partitioning methods are not effective for all features.

References

Chen Q Q, Zhang Y-J. Cluster trees of improved trajectories for action recognition. Neurocomputing, 173: 364–372, 2016.

Dalal N, Triggs B. Histograms of oriented gradients for human detection. Proc. CVPR, V1: 886–893, 2005.

Dalal N, Triggs B, Schmid C. Human detection using oriented histograms of flow and appearance. Proc. ECCV. 428–441, 2006.

Farnebäck G. Two-frame motion estimation based on polynomial expansion. Proc. Scandinavian Conference on Image Analysis, 363–370, 2003.

Feragen A, Kasenburg N, Petersen J, *et al.* Scalable kernels for graphs with continuous attributes. Proc. Advances in Neural Information Processing Systems, 216–224, 2013.

Gaidon A, Harchaoui Z, Schmid C. Activity representation with motion hierarchies. International Journal of Computer Vision, 107(3): 219–238, 2014.

Jia H X, Zhang Y-J. A survey of computer vision based pedestrian detection for driver assistance systems. Acta Automatica Sinica, 33(1): 84–90, 2007.

Kuehne H, Jhuang H, Garrote E, *et al.* HMDB: A large video database for human motion recognition. Proc. ICCV, 2556–2563, 2011.

Laptev I, Marszalek M, Schmid C, *et al.* Learning realistic human actions from movies. Proc. CVPR, 1–8, 2008.

Marszalek M, Laptev I, Schmid C. Actions in context. Proc. CVPR, 2929–2936, 2009.

Morris B T, Trivedi M. A survey of vision-based trajectory learning and analysis for surveillance. IEEE-CSVT, 18(8): 1114–1127, 2008.

Niebles J C, Chen C W, Fei-Fei L. Modeling temporal structure of decomposable motion segments for activity classification. Proc. ECCV, 392–405, 2010.

Reddy K K, Shah M. Recognizing 50 human action categories of web videos. Machine Vision and Applications, 24(5): 971–981, 2013.

Sánchez J, Perronnin F, Mensink T, *et al.* Image classification with the Fisher vector: Theory and practice. International Journal of Computer Vision, 105(3): 222–245, 2013.

Shi J, Tomasi C. Good features to track. Proc. CVPR, 593–600, 1994.

Sun J, Du G M. Tracklet generation method by submodular optimization for multi-object tracking. Journal of Electronics & Information Technology, 46(3): 995–1004, 2024.

Wang H, Schmid C. Action recognition with improved trajectories. Proc. ICCV, 3551–3558, 2013.

Wang R Y, Zhou Y D, Wu D P, *et al.* Pedestrian trajectory prediction method based on group perception. Journal on Communications, 45(12): 44–56, 2024.

Yang C Q, Xu M D, Liang X W, *et al.* RFS-Filters-based resolvable group target tracking technology: A review. Signal Processing, 40(10): 1763–1772, 2024.

Zhang P, Lei W M, Zhao X L, *et al.* A survey on multi-target multi-camera tracking methods. Chinese Journal of Computers, 47(2): 287–309, 2024a.

Zhang Z S, Xu T, Zhou J H, *et al.* An improved hybrid model for vehicle trajectory prediction considering spatiotemporal interactions. Transportmetrica B-Transport Dynamics, 13(1): 2440589. https://doi.org/10.1080/21680566.2024.2440589, 2025

Zhang Y-J. Image Engineering (V.3): Image Understanding (5th Edition). Beijing: Tsinghua University Press, 2024b.

Zhao W H, Wang W, Wan Z L. Vehicle trajectory prediction based on spatiotemporal Transformer feature fusion. Journal on Communications, 45(11): 267–276, 2024.

Zhao Y H, Wang C H, Wang H Y, *et al.* Toward high-quality spatiotemporal recommendation: Trajectory recovery based on spatial and temporal dependencies. IEEE Trans-BD, 11(4): 1628–1639, 2025.

Chapter 4
Action Classification and Recognition

The understanding of behavior needs to be based on the judgment of actions, that is, the classification and recognition of various actions that occur in the scene. Different actions and combinations of actions reflect different behaviors. Visual based human action classification and recognition is the process of labeling images (also videos, image sequences) with action (class) labels. On the basis of detecting and representing the motion trajectory observed in images or videos, human action and motion recognition can be transformed into a classification problem.

Various techniques for action classification and recognition have been proposed, but work in this area is still ongoing. For example, to enhance the accuracy of action classification, multisensory data is used in (Abro et al. 2025). In addition to utilizing information from static images, it also mainly relies on the unique temporal dynamic information in videos. In videos, the information content within different frame images varies, and attention mechanisms can be used to focus more on those frame images with more important content.

The sections of this chapter are arranged as follows.

Section 4.1 introduces basic action classification techniques, including direct classification, time state models, and direct detection techniques.

Section 4.2 discusses action recognition methods for various activities as well as various networks used for action recognition.

Section 4.3 introduces an action classification method that combines pose and contextual information, and discusses specifically classifiers based on pose and context.

Section 4.4 analyzes two methods using attention mechanisms for classifying and recognizing actions in videos. One method utilizes attention mechanism to generate candidate actions, while the other embeds attention mechanism into the temporal action detection process.

Y.-J. Zhang, *Spatiotemporal Image Understanding*,
https://doi.org/10.1007/978-981-95-7130-7_4

4.1 Action Classification

Various forms of techniques can be used for classifying actions (Poppe 2010), three types of commonly used techniques are: ① Direct classification; ② Time state models; ③ Action detection.

1. **Direct Classification**

In direct classification methods, there is no specific focus on the time domain. Here, the information of all frames in the observation sequence can be combined into a single representation, or actions can be recognized and classified separately for each frame image.

In many cases, the representation of images is high-dimensional, resulting in a significant amount of matching computation for classification and recognition. In addition, the representation may also include interference factors such as noise. This requires obtaining compact and robust feature representations in low dimensional space to achieve action classification. The dimensionality reduction techniques from high to low dimensions can be achieved using both linear and nonlinear methods. For example, **Principal Component Analysis** (PCA) is a typical linear method, while **Local Linear Embedding** (LLE) is a typical nonlinear method.

The classifiers used for direct classification can be different. For example, discriminative classifiers focus on how to distinguish different categories (such as SVM), rather than modeling each category. Different classifiers can be used in combination. For example, in the boost framework, a strong classifier can be constructed using a series of weak classifiers (each maybe expressed using only 1-D representation). Bootstrap methods, in addition to AdaBoost (Zhang 2024a), also include LPBoost, which can obtain sparse coefficients and converge quickly.

2. **Time State Models**

The time state model includes the generative model and the discriminative model.

The **generative model** models each action category by learning the joint distribution between all observed actions (considering all variations). The discriminative model learns the probability of action categories under observation conditions. It does not model categories separately, but focuses on the differences between different categories.

The most typical generative model is the **Hidden Markov Model** (HMM), where the hidden states correspond to various steps in the action process. Hidden states model the transition probability and observation probability. This is based on two independent assumptions: one is that the state transition depends only on the previous state, and the other is that the observation depends only on the current state. The variants of HMM include **Maximum Entropy Markov Model** (MEMM), **Factored-State Hierarchical Hidden Markov Model** (FS-HHMM), **Hierarchical Transition Variable Hidden Markov Model** (HVT-HMM), etc.

The **discrimination model** models the conditional distribution of a given observation and combines multiple observations to distinguish different action categories.

This model is advantageous for distinguishing related actions. **Conditional Random Field** (CRF) is a typical discriminative model, whose improvements include **Factorial Conditional Random Field** (FCRF) and **Generation of Conditional Random Field** (GCRF).

3. **Action Detection**

Traditional methods based on action detection do not explicitly model the representation of objects in images, nor do they model actions. It associates observation sequences with numbered video sequences to directly detect (defined) actions. For example, video clips can be described as bags of words encoded at different time scales, where each word corresponds to a gradient orientation of a local patch. Local patches with slow temporal changes can be ignored, allowing representation to mainly focus on significant motion region. Neural network-based methods can learn long-term temporal dependencies and spatial contextual information, and use spatiotemporal cross perception networks to extract spatiotemporal features (Ke et al. 2024).

When the moving action has periodicity, the action is cyclical, that is, a **cyclic action** (such as walking or running). At this point, time-domain segmentation can be achieved by analyzing the self-similarity matrix. Further markers can be added to the human body by tracking the markers and constructing a self-similarity matrix using an affine distance function. The self-similarity matrix can be transformed to frequency domain, then, the peaks in the spectrum correspond to the frequency of motion (such as distinguishing between walking or running people, and calculating the period of gait). By analyzing the matrix structure, the types of actions can be determined.

The main methods for representing and describing human body movements can be divided into two categories: ① Appearance based methods: Directly using descriptions of the foreground, background, contour, optical flow, and changes in the image; ② Method based on human body model: Using the human body model to represent the structural characteristics of the behavior person, such as using a sequence of human joint points to describe actions. Regardless of the method used, the detection of the human body and the detection and tracking of important parts of the human body such as the head, hands, feet, etc. play an important role.

Figure 4.1 shows some action example images from the Weizmann action recognition database (Blank et al. 2005). From top to bottom, the left column shows in turn the High five on the head (jack), Lateral movement (side), Bend down (bend), Walking (walk), and Running (run), while the right column shows in turn the Wave one hand (wave1), Wave two hands (wave2), Single foot forward jump (skip), Jump forward with both feet (jump), and Jump in place with both feet (pjump).

Fig. 4.1 Example images of 10 actions in Weizmann action recognition database (Blank et al. 2005)

4.2 Action Recognition

The representation and recognition of actions and activities is a field that has developed to some extent but is still deepening. The methods used usually depend on the researcher's purpose. In scene interpretation, representations can be independent of the objects generated by the activity (such as people or cars). In monitoring applications, the focus is generally on human activities and interactions. In holistic methods, global information is superior to component information, such as when determining a person's gender. For simple actions such as walking or running, local methods can also be considered, which focus more on detailed actions or action primitives. There are still many recent works in action recognition, such as (Chamusca et al. 2025), (Chung et al. 2025), (Ding et al. 2025), (Han et al. 2024), (Hu et al. 2024), (Kumain et al. 2005), (Liu et al. 2024), (Liu et al. 2025), (Meurie 2025).

4.2.1 Action Recognition in Various Activities

Because action recognition has different requirements in different activity scenarios, it also needs to be analyzed differently.

1. **Holistic Recognition**

Holistic recognition emphasizes the recognition of the entire human body or the complete organs of a single human body. For example, human walking and gait can be recognized based on the entire body structure and the dynamic information of entire body. The vast majority of methods are based on the silhouette or contour of the human body, without distinguishing between different parts of the body. For example, a human based identity recognition technology uses human silhouettes and uniformly samples their contours, and then performs PCA processing on the decomposed contours. To calculate the spatiotemporal correlation, various trajectories can be compared in the eigen-space. On the other hand, using dynamic information can identify the identity of a person and determine what work this person is doing. Based on body part recognition, actions are recognized through the position and dynamic information of each body part.

2. **Pose Modeling**

The recognition of human actions is closely related to the estimation of human (body) pose. The human pose can be divided into action pose and (body) position pose. The former corresponds to the human body's action behavior at a certain moment, while the latter corresponds to the orientation state of the human body in 3-D space.

There are three main methods for representing and calculating human pose.

(1) Method based on appearance: It does not directly model the physical structure of a person, but analyzes human pose using information such as color, texture, and contour. Because only the appearance information in 2-D images is utilized, it is difficult to determine the 3-D pose of the human body.
(2) Method based on human body model: First, line graph model, 2-D or 3-D model is used to model the human body, and then the human body pose is estimated by analyzing the parameterized human body model. This type of method usually requires high image resolution and object detection accuracy.
(3) Method based on 3-D reconstruction: First, multiple cameras are used to obtain multiple images of 2-D moving targets at different positions (with different perspectives), and corresponding point matching is then used to reconstruct them into 3-D moving targets. Finally, camera parameters and imaging formulas are manipulated to estimate the human pose in 3-D space.

Modeling pose can be based on spatiotemporal interest points (see Sect. 2.1). If only the spatiotemporal **Harris interest point detector** is used, the obtained spatiotemporal interest points are mostly located in regions of sudden motion changes. This type of point count is relatively small and belongs to the sparse type, which may result in the loss of important motion information in the video, and leading to detection failure. To overcome this problem, dense spatiotemporal interest points can also be extracted using the intensity of motion, fully capturing the changes generated by motion. For example, the motion intensity can be calculated by convolving the image with a spatial Gaussian filter and a temporal Gabor filter (Zhang 2024a). After extracting spatiotemporal interest points, first establish descriptors for each point, and then model each pose. One specific method is to first extract the spatiotemporal feature points of posts from the training sample library as the underlying features, so that each pose corresponds to a set of spatiotemporal feature points. Then, unsupervised classification methods are used to classify the pose samples, in order to obtain clustering results for typical poses. Finally, a Gaussian mixture model based on the **Expectation–Maximization** (EM) strategy is used to model each typical pose category.

A recent trend in pose estimation in natural scenes is to overcome the problem of tracking with a single view in unstructured scenes, and pose detection is often performed in a single frame image. For example, based on robust component detection and probabilistic combination of components, it has been possible to obtain good estimates of 2-D poses in complex movie videos.

3. **Activity Reconstruction**

Actions cause changes in body pose. If each stationary pose of the human body is defined as a state, then using the state space method (also known as the probability network method), multiple states can be switched through transition probabilities to construct an activity sequence by traversing between the states of the corresponding pose.

Based on the estimation of pose, significant progress has been made in automatically reconstructing human activities from videos. The original model-based analysis-synthesis scheme utilizes multi view video capture to effectively search the pose space. Many recent methods focus more on obtaining the overall movement of the body rather than emphasizing the precise construction of details.

Significant progress has been made in single view human activity reconstruction using **stochastic sampling techniques**. The current focus is on using learned models to constrain activity-based reconstruction. Research has shown that using strong prior models can aid in tracking specific activities in a single view.

4. **Interactive Activities**

Interactive activities are relatively complex and can be divided into two categories: ① Interaction between people and the environment, such as riding a bicycle or picking up a book; ② Interpersonal interaction often refers to the communication activities or contact behaviors of two or more persons, which are to some extent the combination of individual activities (considered as basic units). Single person activities can be described using probability graph models. The probability graph model is a powerful tool for modeling continuous dynamic feature sequences, with a mature theoretical foundation. The disadvantage of probability graph models is that the topology of the model depends on the structural information of the activity itself, and for complex interactive activities, a large amount of training data is generally required to learn the topology of the graph model. To combine individual activities, **Statistical Relationship Learning** (SRL) methods can also be used. SRL is a machine learning method that integrates relational/logical representation, probabilistic inference, machine learning, and data mining to obtain likelihood models of relational data.

5. **Group Activities**

Quantitative changes lead to qualitative changes, resulting in a significant increase in the number of targets participating in activities, which can bring about new problems and new research. For example, group target motion analysis mainly focuses on human flow, traffic flow, and dense biological populations in nature. It studies the representation and description methods of group target motion, analyzes the motion characteristics of group targets, and investigates the influence of boundary constraints on group target motion. At this point, the grasp of the unique behavior of special individuals will be placed in a relatively secondary position, and more attention will be paid to abstracting individuals and describing the entire collective activity. For example, some studies draw on macroscopic kinematics theory to explore the motion laws of particle flow and establish a theory of particle flow motion. On this basis, semantic analysis is conducted on the dynamic evolution phenomena such as aggregation, dissipation, differentiation, and merging in group target activities to explain the overall trend and situation of the scene.

In group activity analysis, the number of individuals participating in the activity is often a fundamental data. For example, many public places (such as squares, sports stadium entrances and exits, etc.) require the statistics on pedestrian flow. Figure 4.2 shows a scene of counting the number of persons get in or get out in a monitoring scene (Jiang et al. 2009). Although there are many different types of persons in the scene and their movements (speed, directions, etc.) are varied, at this time the only focus is on the number of persons (marked by two circles) within a specific range (the region enclosed by a box).

6. **Scene Interpretation**

Unlike the recognition of specific targets in a scene, **scene interpretation** mainly considers the entire image rather than focusing on verifying specific targets or persons. Many methods used in practice only consider the results captured by the camera, observing the general movement of the target (without necessarily determining its identity), in order to learn and recognize activities. This strategy is more effective when the target is small enough to be represented as a point in 2-D space.

Fig. 4.2 Screen of counting the number of persons in the monitoring scene (Jiang et al. 2009)

For example, a system for detecting abnormal situations includes the following steps. Firstly, the 2-D position, velocity, size, and binary silhouette of the target in the image are extracted, and an example codebook using vector quantization is generated. To consider the temporal relationship among different targets, symbiotic (co-occurrence) statistics can be used here. Then the probability functions between the examples in the two codebooks are iteratively defined and the binary tree structure is determined, where leaf nodes correspond to the probability distribution in the co-occurrence statistical matrix, and higher-level nodes correspond to simple scene activities (such as pedestrian or vehicle movements). Finally, by further combining and analyzing the information of various nodes, an interpretation of the scene can be provided.

4.2.2 Various Networks for Action Recognition

In recent years, deep learning and neural networks have been widely applied in action recognition work (Guo et al. 2024). Table 4.1 summarizes some deep learning-based action recognition networks from the perspective of network structure.

4.3 Action Classification Combining Pose and Context

Generally, the recognition of actions requires the use of videos or sequence images. This is because different actions may have common or similar poses, and it is not necessarily possible to distinguish actions based solely on a single pose. The following introduces an action classification method that combines pose and context information (environmental information) in still images (Zheng et al. 2012).

The workflow of this method is shown in Fig. 4.3. Firstly, the **Poselet Activation Vector** (PAV) is used as a feature to learn an action classifier based on the pose model, which contains pose information for various types of actions. Using sparse coding to construct visual dictionaries for both foreground and background separately, and to concatenate the **Bag of Feature** (BoF) representations of the two dictionaries to obtain contextual information. Next, the contextual information is used to obtain a context-based action classifier. Given a test image, the probability outputs of two classifiers corresponding to each test action can be combined to determine the credibility of the image in this action category, and the image with the highest credibility can be used as the predicted action model.

Table 4.1 Comparison of various action recognition networks (Guo et al. 2024)

Network	Principle	Advantage	Disadvantage	Improvement examples
3-D CNN	Stack consecutive frames of the video to form cube data, and use 3-D convolution kernels for feature extraction	It can effectively extract spatiotemporal information, has fast training speed, and can be combined with other networks to improve recognition performance, making it more suitable for use with sufficient training data	It has a large number of parameters and high requirements for equipment. When the training data volume is too small, overfitting may occur	P3D ResNet (Qiu et al. 2017) uses $1 \times 3 \times 3$ convolutional layers and $3 \times 1 \times 1$ convolutional layers in a parallel or cascaded manner to replace the original $3 \times 3 \times 3$ convolutional layers, forming the P3D module. Then, drawing on the residual network structure, the P3D module is combined to alleviate the problem of large parameter count
TS-CNN	Using two convolutional neural networks with the same structure to separately process the spatial and temporal information of the video	Convolutional neural networks can be used to separately extract temporal and spatial features	Real time recognition still needs improvement	The SlowFast network framework (Feichtenhofer et al. 2019) uses a low frame rate approach to collect spatial information, a high frame rate approach to collect temporal information, and finally fuses spatiotemporal information through lateral connections
LSTM and RNN	LSTM is a commonly used structural model with the ability to process time-domain data. When combined with CNN, it can effectively enhance the network's ability to obtain long-term information	LSTM filters useful information through input gates, forget gates, and output gates, forgets useless information, and has a certain effect on dealing with gradient vanishing problems	The combination of LSTM and CNN has many parameters, which increases the difficulty of training and makes it difficult to accurately and effectively model CNN when it is complex	Video LSTM (Li et al. 2018) introduces attention mechanism in LSTM to better capture action information, obtains spatial correlation between video frames through CNN, and completes spatiotemporal localization of actions with attention mapping and video level action labels CLA net (Wu et al. 2023) incorporates attention mechanism on the basis of CNN-LSTM to further optimize features

(continued)

Table 4.1 (continued)

Network	Principle	Advantage	Disadvantage	Improvement examples
Trans-former	A deep learning model with self-attention mechanism that can effectively obtain global information and perform long-term dependency modeling	It can effectively obtain global information, thereby better capturing long-term features, and it also has parallel computing capability	The converter has high computational complexity, weak generalization ability, and is prone to overfitting when there are insufficient training samples	VTN (Neimark 2021) uses 2-D CNN and Transformer to respectively obtain feature information and focus on long-term information to balance speed and accuracy IA-RED2 (Pan 2021) learns to find and discard irrelevant patches to reduce computational complexity
GCN	Graph Convolutional Networks extend convolution operations from images to graph data	The processing effect of skeleton information is better than that of CNN and RNN	High computational cost, insufficient spatiotemporal feature extraction	Shift GCN (Cheng et al. 2020) uses displacement graph operation and lightweight point convolution to reduce computational costs Integrating attention concentration mechanism into LSTM and GCN to fully extract spatiotemporal features (Gao et al. 2022), improving the accuracy of recognizing similar actions

4.3.1 Action Classifier Based on Pose

The action classifier based on pose model mainly focuses on the foreground and can solve the problems of scale and viewpoint changes. Below, a specific action pose model is first introduced, and then an action classifier based on the activation vector of the pose model is described.

1. **Specific Action Pose Model**

A **pose model** is a type of part/component model that reflects the basic structural elements of the human body in a certain pose. To train a pose model, it is necessary to first annotate the training set and define distance measures to collect primitives (structural elements) in the structural space. Then, it is required to extract gradient histogram features from the collected positive samples (poselets) and random negative samples. Finally, these features are taken as input to SVM classifiers for training pose models, and a greedy method is used to select a set of pose models based on their convergence ability. Each pose model describes a prominent part of the human body.

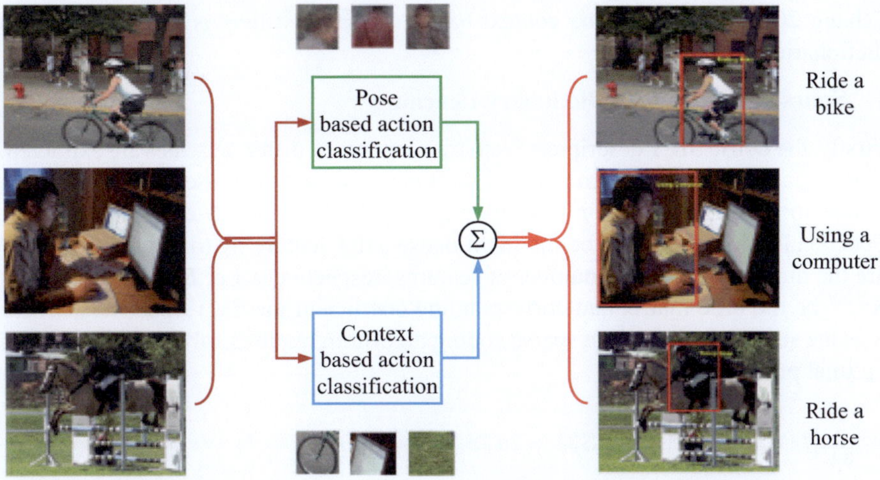

Fig. 4.3 Process of action classification method combining pose and context in still images (Zheng et al. 2012)

The detection of pose models should not only consider the similarity of structural space, but also the similarity of appearance. Although pose models can be used for human detection, their discriminative power is not strong enough when recognizing image actions, so particular **Action Specific Poselets** (ASPs) model are still needed. These ASPs can be obtained by limiting positive training samples belonging to the same action category.

2. **Action Features and SVM Classifier**

The **Poselet Activation Vector** (PAV) reflects the response distribution of the foreground pose model. For each specific action's pose model p_i, a sliding window can be used to detect the corresponding sample unit, and only the detection results that intersect with the true value by more than 20% can be collected. The detection results belonging to the same pose model are added up as the value of the i-th component of PAV. Finally, the SVM classifier can be used for pose based action classification by using PAV as a feature.

4.3.2 Action Classifier Based on Context

In action recognition, contextual information is defined as the symbiosis between the action and the environment. The context provides useful information for identifying actions in an image. For example, when a person uses a computer, the environment is usually indoors (unlike riding a bike), and there are usually display devices and/or tables in the image. In the following, how to build a context-based action classifier will be discussed. Firstly, the sparse coding for dictionary learning is introduced

(Zhang 2024b), and then the context-based action classifiers is learned based on dictionaries.

1. **Sparse Encoding for Dictionary Learning**

Firstly, the dense SIFT descriptors from training sets of different scales are extracted. Then, sparse coding to learn a visual dictionary is used. The use of sparse coding is due to its effectiveness in constructing raw features and determining patterns. Specifically, let $\boldsymbol{X} \in \mathrm{R}^{D\times N}$ be the input dense SIFT feature matrix, where D and N are the dimensionality and number of features, respectively. Let $\boldsymbol{B} \in \mathrm{R}^{D\times K}$ and $\boldsymbol{S} \in \mathrm{R}^{K\times N}$ be the base matrix and corresponding coefficient matrix, respectively, where K is the size of the base. The sparse coding algorithm requires solving the following optimal problem:

$$\min_{\mathbf{B},\mathbf{S}}\big[f(\mathbf{B},\mathbf{S})\big] = \|\mathbf{X}-\mathbf{BS}\|_{\mathrm{F}}^2 + 2\alpha\|\mathbf{S}\|_1 \quad \text{s.t. } \|B_{\cdot i}\|^2 = 1, \quad \forall i = 1, 2, \cdots, K \tag{4.1}$$

where $\boldsymbol{B}_{\cdot n}$ and $\boldsymbol{B}_{k\cdot}$ represent the n-th column and k-th row of matrix $\boldsymbol{B}$, respectively; α is the regularization coefficient that controls the fitting effect and balances sparsity. The use of L_1-norm regularization term here is to enhance the sparsity of $\boldsymbol{S}$.

Although the Eq. (4.1) needs to be optimized is not convex (monotonic) for both $\boldsymbol{B}$ and $\boldsymbol{S}$, it is convex for $\boldsymbol{B}$ (when $\boldsymbol{S}$ is fixed) or $\boldsymbol{S}$ (when $\boldsymbol{B}$ is fixed), respectively. Therefore, the problem can be decomposed into two sub optimization problems and solved using alternating minimization techniques. The first regularized least squares problem is

$$\min_{\mathbf{S}}\big[f(\mathbf{S})\big] = \|\mathbf{X}-\mathbf{BS}\|_{\mathrm{F}}^2 + 2\alpha\|\mathbf{S}\|_1 \tag{4.2}$$

The second regularized least squares problem is

$$\min_{\mathbf{B}}\big[f(\mathbf{B})\big] = \|\mathbf{X}-\mathbf{BS}\|_{\mathrm{F}}^2 \quad \text{s.t. } \|B_{\cdot i}\|^2 = 1, \quad \forall i = 1, 2, \cdots, K \tag{4.3}$$

There is a closed form solution for minimizing Eq. (4.2) relative to a single row (first subscript):

$$\begin{aligned}\mathbf{S}_{k\cdot} &= \arg\min_{\mathbf{S}_{k\cdot}} \big\{\|\mathbf{X}-\mathbf{BS}\|_{\mathrm{F}}^2 + 2\alpha\|\mathbf{S}\|_1\big\} \\ &= \max\big\{[\mathbf{B}_{\cdot k}]^{\mathrm{T}}\mathbf{X} - [\mathbf{B}_{\cdot k}]^{\mathrm{T}}\mathbf{BS}^k,\ \alpha\big\} + \min\big\{[\mathbf{B}_{\cdot k}]^{\mathrm{T}}\mathbf{X} - [\mathbf{B}_{\cdot k}]^{\mathrm{T}}\mathbf{BS}^k,\ -\alpha\big\}\end{aligned} \tag{4.4}$$

where

$$\mathbf{S}_{p\cdot}^k = \begin{cases}\mathbf{S}_{p\cdot} & p \neq k \\ 0 & p = k\end{cases} \tag{4.5}$$

There is a closed form solution for minimizing Eq. (4.3) relative to a single column (second subscript):

$$\mathbf{S}_{k\cdot} = \arg\min_{\mathbf{S}_{k\cdot}} \|\mathbf{X} - \mathbf{BS}\|_F^2 = \frac{\mathbf{X}[\mathbf{S}_{k\cdot}]^T - \mathbf{B}^k\mathbf{S}[\mathbf{S}_{k\cdot}]^T}{\|\mathbf{X}[\mathbf{S}_{k\cdot}]^T - \mathbf{B}^k\mathbf{S}[\mathbf{S}_{k\cdot}]^T\|_2} \tag{4.6}$$

where

$$\mathbf{B}^k_{\cdot p} = \begin{cases} \mathbf{B}_{\cdot p} & p \neq k \\ 0 & p = k \end{cases} \tag{4.7}$$

2. **Context Representation and Classifier**

Assuming that $\boldsymbol{Y}_{fg} \in \mathrm{R}^{D\times M1}$ and $\boldsymbol{Y}_{bg} \in \mathrm{R}^{D\times M2}$ are two dense SIFT descriptors extracted from an image, $\boldsymbol{B}_{fg} \in \mathrm{R}^{D\times K1}$ and $\boldsymbol{B}_{bg} \in \mathrm{R}^{D\times K2}$ are dictionaries learned from the training set using sparse coding, where D is the dimensionality of the features, M_1 and M_2 are the number of slices in the foreground and background, respectively, and K_1 and K_2 are the number of bases in the foreground and background dictionaries, respectively. If f_B is the encoding operator for dictionary $\boldsymbol{B}$, then the representations $\boldsymbol{S}_{fg} \in \mathrm{R}^{K1\times M1}$ and $\boldsymbol{S}_{bg} \in \mathrm{R}^{K2\times M2}$ for $\boldsymbol{Y}_{fg}$ and $\boldsymbol{Y}_{bg}$ on $\boldsymbol{B}_{fg}$ and $\boldsymbol{B}_{bg}$ can be obtained as follows:

$$\begin{aligned} \mathbf{S}_{fg} &= f_{B_{fg}}(\mathbf{Y}_{fg}) \\ \mathbf{S}_{bg} &= f_{B_{bg}}(\mathbf{Y}_{bg}) \end{aligned} \tag{4.8}$$

where the columns of $\boldsymbol{S}_{fg}$ and $\boldsymbol{S}_{bg}$ are the reconstruction coefficients of the dictionary.

If p: $\mathrm{R}^{K\times N} \rightarrow \mathrm{R}^K$ is the summary operator, then

$$\begin{aligned} \mathbf{Z}_{fg} &= p(\mathbf{S}_{fg}) \\ \mathbf{Z}_{bg} &= p(\mathbf{S}_{bg}) \end{aligned} \tag{4.9}$$

where $\mathbf{Z}_{fg} \in \mathrm{R}^{K1}$ and $\mathbf{Z}_{bg} \in \mathrm{R}^{K2}$ are the representation of the foreground and background of the image, respectively.

Next, concatenate $\mathbf{Z}_{fg}$ and $\mathbf{Z}_{bg}$ together to obtain the contextual representation $\mathbf{Z} \in \mathrm{R}^{K1+K2}$ of the image:

$$\mathbf{Z} = \left[\mathbf{Z}_{fg}^{\mathrm{T}},\ \mathbf{Z}_{bg}^{\mathrm{T}}\right]^{\mathrm{T}} \tag{4.10}$$

Finally, the context-based action classifier can be obtained by learning the contextual representation of the training set.

After constructing the pose-based action classifier and the context-based action classifier, the actions can be classified and judged according to the process shown in Fig. 4.3. Figure 4.3 also presents several classification results.

4.4 Action Detection Based on Attention Mechanism

Detecting actions is usually done through video. For example, Video Action Detection (VAD) aims to detect actors and classify their actions in a video, in which VAD suffers more from classification rather than localization of actors (Lee et al. 2025). The information contained in multiple frames of a video could be different, such as some frames where an action is taking place, while others are mainly background or even without an action person. Different computational weights should be assigned to different frames in order to more effectively utilize video information. With the help of attention mechanism, the importance of different frames can be determined, and information within different frames can be utilized differently.

Below two methods for classifying and recognizing actions in videos using **visual attention mechanisms** will be introduced. One approach is to combine attention mechanisms with video candidate action generation tasks, using a two-level attention module to weight and fuse different time segments in the video (Liu et al. 2018). Another approach is to combine attention mechanisms with temporal action detection tasks, using attention pooling modules that incorporate attention mechanisms instead of traditional regional pooling modules to weight video features at different locations (Liu 2019).

4.4.1 Candidate Action Generation

Candidate action generation is to determine the candidate positions of actions that need to be classified and recognized from the video. The flowchart of candidate action generation based on attention mechanism is shown in Fig. 4.4 (Liu et al. 2018), which mainly includes three threads: ① Constructing the segment pyramid; ② Utilizing temporal attention fusion features; ③ Classification and regression.

1. **Constructing the Segment Pyramid**

Divide the video into segments and organize them into a pyramid structure. Each segment in the pyramid is composed of three parts pieced together:

$$S_k^n = \{f_i\}_{k-n}^{k} \cup \{f_i\}_{k}^{k+n} \cup \{f_i\}_{k+n}^{k+2n} \tag{4.11}$$

where n represents the layer of the pyramid, and the total number of layers is N, that is, $n = 1, 2,.., N$. Each segment $S_k{}^n$ is composed of three frame groups spliced together (subscript indicates the start frame, superscript indicates the end frame), $\{f_i\}_{k-n}^{k}$ representing the preceding frame group, $\{f_i\}_{k}^{k+n}$ representing the middle frame group, and $\{f_i\}_{k+n}^{k+2n}$ representing the following frame group. The length of segments at different levels varies, but the length of the preceding frame group, middle frame group, and following frame group in the segment can be the same.

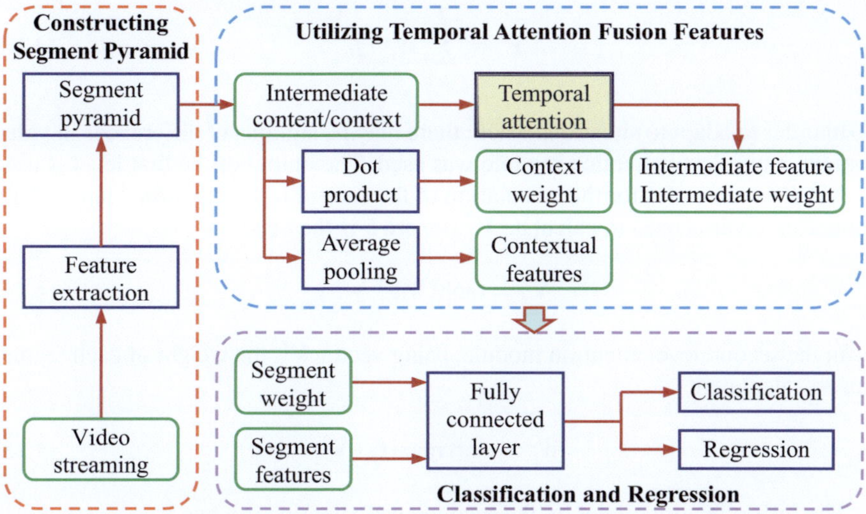

Fig. 4.4 Flow chart of candidate action generation based on attention mechanism

To improve efficiency, features can be extracted from the entire video first, and then utilized on each segment with the help of the extracted features. If the total length of the video is T, it can be evenly divided into T/m small segments, each containing m frames. For each small segment, a pre-trained neural network is used to extract features, and when computing the features of different segments in the pyramid, the features of these small segments can be reused for fusion.

2. **Utilizing Temporal Attention Fusion Features**

Expand the temporal attention module in Fig. 4.4, as shown in Fig. 4.5. It contains two (hierarchical) attention modules with a fully connected layer in between.

Firstly, input the continuous video segment features $\{f_i\}_1^T$ into the attention module of the first level, which has a trainable vector $\boldsymbol{V}^1$ with the same length as the feature vector. By using vector $\boldsymbol{V}^1$, the weight of each feature can be calculated:

$$W_i^1 = \text{soft}\max(\mathbf{f}_i \cdot \mathbf{V}^1) \tag{4.12}$$

The fusion feature output by the first level attention module is

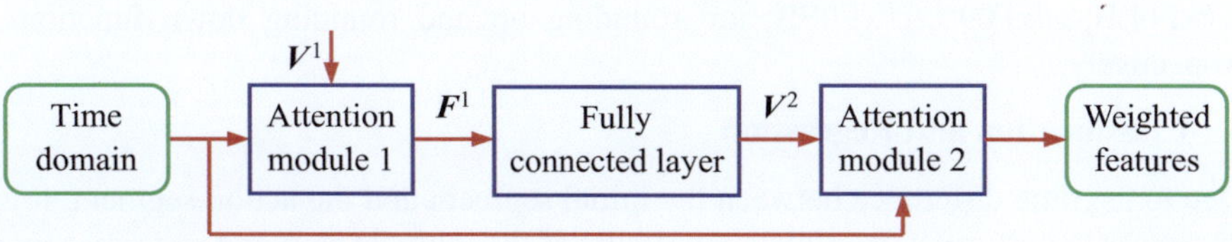

Fig. 4.5 Temporal attention module

$$\mathbf{F}^1 = \sum_{i=1}^{T} W_i^1 \cdot f_i \tag{4.13}$$

In order to adapt to situations where there may be significant differences in video content, a two-level attention module was used. The output of the first level is used to calculate vector $\boldsymbol{V}^2$ for the calculation of the second level attention. Here, a fully connected layer is used to calculate $\boldsymbol{V}^2$ (where b is the bias):

$$\mathbf{V}^2 = \tanh(W\mathbf{F}^1 + b) \tag{4.14}$$

In the second level attention module, using vector $\boldsymbol{V}^2$, the weight of each feature can be calculated:

$$W_i^2 = \text{soft}\max(\mathbf{f}_i \cdot \mathbf{V}^2) \tag{4.15}$$

The fusion feature output by the second level attention module is

$$\mathbf{F}^2 = \sum_{i=1}^{T} W_i^2 f_i \tag{4.16}$$

When fusing features, for each video pyramid segment, only the features of the intermediate content (mainly containing actions) are subjected to attention weighting operations, while the contextual features (mainly corresponding to the background) are subjected to average pooling operations.

To improve algorithm performance, the weights of the attention model can also be included in subsequent computational processing. For $\boldsymbol{V}^2$ obtained from a video segment, calculate the dot product $W_i = \boldsymbol{f}_i \cdot \boldsymbol{V}^2$ in both the middle content and context sections. Due to the different scales of different segments, the lengths of the weight sequence obtained may also be different. In order to facilitate the subsequent calculation of the neural network, linear interpolation operation can be used to interpolate the weights to the maximum length:

$$\hat{W}_i = (\lceil i/L \rceil - i/L) W_{\lfloor i/L \rfloor} + (i/L - \lfloor i/L \rfloor) W_{\lceil i/L \rceil} \tag{4.17}$$

where W is the original weight, $\hat{W}$ is the interpolation weight, L represents the maximum segment length;  and  are rounding up and rounding down functions, respectively.

3. **Classification and Regression**

Due to the time difference between the initial segment and the action segment, it is necessary to perform a coordinate regression of the segment start and end times first in order to align different segments.

Let S represent the start time, E represent the end time, C represent the center position of the segment, L represent the length of the segment, subscript b represents the segment before regression, and a represent the segment after regression. By using a fully connected layer to calculate two parameters: D_C (the coordinate difference between the centers of the target segment and the starting segment) and D_L (the length difference between the target segment and the starting segment), and using them for regression, the coordinates of the regressed segment can be represented as

$$C_a = \frac{S_b + E_b}{2} + g_C D_C (E_b - S_b) \tag{4.18}$$

$$S_a = C_a - \frac{E_b - S_b}{2} \exp(g_L D_L) \tag{4.19}$$

$$E_a = C_a + \frac{E_b - S_b}{2} \exp(g_L D_L) \tag{4.10}$$

$$L_b = E_b - S_b \tag{4.11}$$

$$L_a = E_a - S_a \tag{4.12}$$

$$D_L = L_b - L_a \tag{4.13}$$

where g_C and g_L are fixed coefficients, and in practice, $g_C = g_L = 0.1$ can be taken.

4. **Experiments Results and Analysis**

Some algorithm experiments were conducted using the THUMOS14 database (Jiang et al. 2014), (Liu et al. 2018). The evaluation indicator used is the **Average Recall Average Number** (AR-AN) curve, with the horizontal axis representing the average number of candidate segments (retrieved) contained in each video and the vertical axis representing the **Temporal Intersection of Union** (T-IoU) when the threshold is between [0.5, 1]. T-IoU measures the degree of overlap between two time segments. For two time segments A and B, their temporal intersection of union will be ($| \cdot |$ represents the length of the time segment)

$$\text{T - IoU} = \frac{|A \cap B|}{|A| + |B| + |A \cap B|} \tag{4.14}$$

If the T-IoU value is larger, it represents a greater degree of overlap between two time segments.

Below two experiments and their results are given.

(1) **Comparison of Temporal Attention**

The experiment considered four methods for calculating temporal attention: ① Single-layer, combining contextual information and weighted weight information; ②

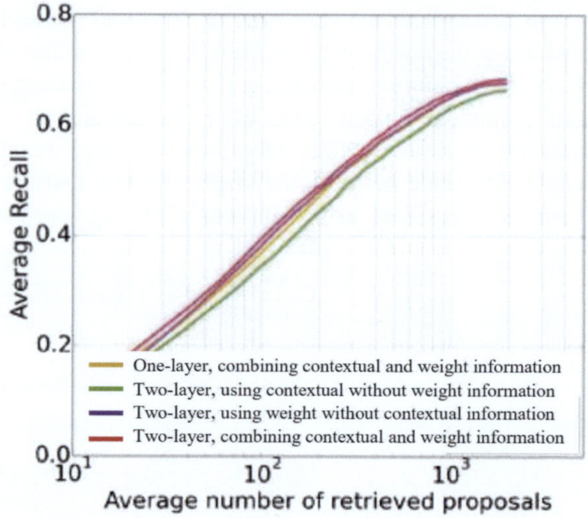

Fig. 4.6 AR-AN curves obtained from different temporal attention modules (Liu et al. 2018)

Two-layer cascading, using contextual information without weighted weight information; ③ Two-layer cascading, using weighted weight information, without using contextual information; ④ Two-layer cascading, combining contextual information and weighted weight information.

The calculated AR-AN curve is shown in Fig. 4.6. As can be seen from Fig. 4.6, the performance of cascading two layers and combining contextual information and weighted weighting information is the best.

(2) **Algorithm Comparison**

The above algorithm, which combines the **Temporal Attention Network** (TAN), was compared with some other candidate action generation algorithms, including DAPs (Escorcia et al. 2016), SCNN-prop (Shou et al. 2016), Sparse-prop (Caba et al. 2016), SST (Buch et al. 2017), and TURN (Gao et al. 2017). Figure 4.7 shows the AR-AN curves of the performance of each algorithm. As can be seen from Fig. 4.7, the introduction of temporal attention significantly improves the performance.

4.4.2 *Temporal Action Detection*

Temporal action detection is to detect actions that need to be classified and recognized from videos. The flowchart of temporal action detection based on attention mechanism is shown in Fig. 4.8 (Liu 2019), which mainly includes three threads: ① Extracting convolutional features; ② Determining candidate actions; ③ Detecting actions.

Fig. 4.7 Comparison of AR-AN curves for candidate action generation algorithms (Liu et al. 2018)

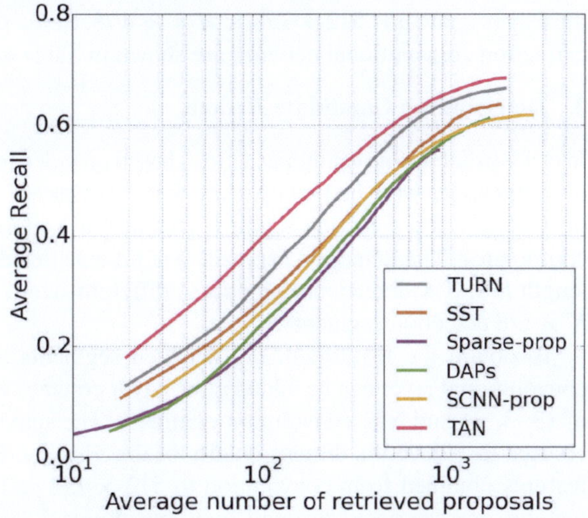

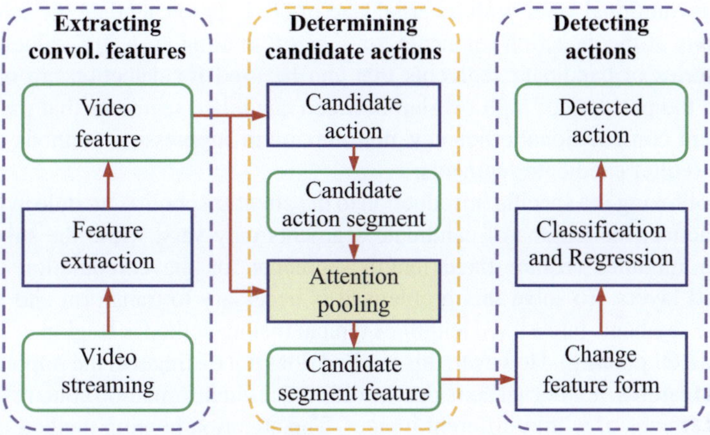

Fig. 4.8 Temporal action detection flowchart

1. **Extracting convolutional features**

The input video includes a series of color image frames with dimensions of $3L \times H \times W$, where 3 is for color channels, L is the frame rate (which can be determined by the video memory), H and W are the height and width of the image, respectively (both taken as 112).

To extract video features, a 3-D convolutional network is used. Compared to dual stream networks, 3-D convolutional networks can extract both spatial and temporal features using a single network. Specifically, the 3-D convolutional network C3D (Tran 2015) was used from the Layer conv1a to the Layer conv5b, where the Layer conv5b has 512 feature channels, and the final feature dimension extracted from the Layer conv5b is $512 \times L/8 \times H/8 \times W/8$. Some parameters of the 3-D feature extraction convolutional network are shown in Table 4.2.

2. **Determining Candidate Actions**

In order to determine candidate actions based on video features, detection segments of different scales were first set up. Here, it is necessary to calculate the confidence value of whether each detection segment contains an action, and to regress the segment coordinates. The detection segment is a time segment cut from a video feature of length $L/8$. If K detection segments of different sizes are set, there will be a total of $K \times L/8$ detection segments.

To obtain the features of the detected segments at each time position, a 3-D convolutional layer can be added after Layer conv5b, with a convolution kernel size of (3, 3, 3) and 512 convolution channels. The maximum pooling operation can be used to reduce the dimensionality of the $512 \times L/8 \times H/8 \times W/8$ dimensional features obtained from convolution to $512 \times L/8 \times 1 \times 1$ dimension. Firstly, the features are processed through two convolutional layers with kernel sizes of (1, 1, 1) and 512 feature channels to weight their representative power. Next, input it into a convolutional layer with a kernel size of (1, 1, 1) to calculate the scores and regressions of the detection segments for K sizes, totaling $(1 + 2)K$ values. In this way, a series of candidate segments that can be used for detection are obtained. To avoid the problem of high overlap between candidate segments that may affect subsequent computational efficiency, non-maximum suppression methods can also be used to filter candidate segments.

The following is a specific introduction to the attention pooling module in Fig. 4.8.

In practice, the lengths of candidate segments may vary, while the subsequent detection modules require fixed length segments for the computation of fully connected layers. To solve this problem, it is necessary to transform and fuse the candidate segments into a fixed length. A typical fusion method is **Region of Interest pooling** (ROI pooling). However, this method does not distinguish the importance of different features, nor does it consider the differences in information content between different frames or within different images. The attention pooling method attempts to achieve better results by weighting features at different (temporal) frames and different (spatial) positions differently.

Table 4.2 Some parameters of 3-D feature extraction convolutional network (Liu 2019)

Layer	Number of feature channels	Kernel size	Layer	Number of feature channels	Kernel size
conv1a	64	(3, 3, 3)	pool3	–	(2, 2, 2)
pool1	–	(1, 2, 2)	conv4a	512	(3, 3, 3)
conv2a	128	(3, 3, 3)	conv4b	512	(3, 3, 3)
pool2	–	(2, 2, 2)	pool4	–	(2, 2, 2)
conv3a	256	(3, 3, 3)	conv5a	512	(3, 3, 3)
conv3b	256	(3, 3, 3)	conv5b	512	(3, 3, 3)

The approach taken here has some similarities with that in Sub-Sect. 4.4.1, but having two main differences: one is that the spatiotemporal features considered here are three-dimensional, and the other is that the features of the candidate segments are divided into $4 \times 2 \times 2$ blocks.

Firstly, input the 512-D features $\{f_{i,j,k}\}$ of the entire video segment into the attention module of the first level. This module has a trainable vector $\boldsymbol{V}^1$, which has the same length as the feature vector. By using vector $\boldsymbol{V}^1$, the weight of each feature can be calculated:

$$W_{i,j,k}^1 = \operatorname{soft\,max}(\mathbf{f}_{i,j,k} \cdot \mathbf{V}^1) \tag{4.15}$$

The fusion feature output by the first level attention module is

$$\mathbf{F}^1 = \sum_{i=1}^{T} W_{i,j,k}^1 \cdot f_{i,j,k} \tag{4.16}$$

In order to adapt to the situations where the contents of different videos do not change significantly within segments, but there may be significant changes between segments, a two-level attention module is also used. Still using the fused features output from the entire segment of the first level to calculate vector $\boldsymbol{V}^2$ for the computation of the second level attention. Here, a fully connected layer is also used to calculate $\boldsymbol{V}^2$ (where b is the bias):

$$\mathbf{V}^2 = \tanh(W\mathbf{F}^1 + b) \tag{4.17}$$

In the second level attention module, vector $\boldsymbol{V}^2$ and the Sigmoid function are used to partition and calculate the weight of each feature:

$$W_{i,j,k}^2 = \frac{4 \times 2 \times 2}{\sum_{i,j,k} \operatorname{Sigmoid}(\mathbf{f}_{i,j,k} \cdot \mathbf{V}^2)} \operatorname{Sigmoid}(\mathbf{f}_{i,j,k} \cdot \mathbf{V}^2) \tag{4.18}$$

where the fraction on the right side of the equal sign is the normalization coefficient to ensure that the fused feature scale is consistent with the feature scale of the regional pooling operation. In the following, take the weighted features

$$\hat{\boldsymbol{f}}_{i,j,k} = W_{i,j,k}^2 \cdot \boldsymbol{f}_{i,j,k} \tag{4.19}$$

and divide them into blocks of $4 \times 2 \times 2$. Finally, calculate the average value on each block to obtain the fused features. In this way, the features of candidate segments with varying lengths are fused into fixed length features at the output of the attention pooling module.

3. **Detecting Actions**

To detect actions, the features of $512 \times 4 \times 2 \times 2$ are first transformed into 8192-D vector features. After processing through two fully connected layers of 4096-D, the category score and coordinate regression coefficient of each candidate segment can be obtained. For each candidate segment, calculate coefficients D_C (the coordinate difference between the centers of the target segment and the starting segment) and D_L (the length difference between the target segment and the starting segment) for coordinate regression:

$$D_C = \frac{C^* - C}{L} \tag{4.20}$$

$$D_L = \log\left[\frac{L^*}{L}\right] \tag{4.21}$$

where C represents the center position of the segment, L represents the length of the segment; The asterisk (*) indicates the value of the actual action segment.

4. **Experiments Results and Analysis**

The algorithm was tested on the THUMOS14 database (Jiang et al. 2014) using the **mean Average Precision** (mAP) as the evaluation indicator. When doing classification, the calculation of mAP involves three steps: ① Obtaining the **precision-recall** (P-R) curve for each category; ② Calculate the area under the P-R curve for each category to obtain the **Average Precision** (AR); ③ Calculate the average AR value for each category.

Below are the results of two comparative experiments.

(1) **Regional Pooling and Attention Pooling**

The results obtained by using regional pooling and attention pooling separately are shown in Table 4.3 (bold numbers indicate the best), which presents the mAP values with different T-IoU (as shown in Eq. (4.14)) thresholds.

As shown in Table 4.3, under high T-IoU thresholds, the mAP performance of attention pooling is better than that of regional pooling. But at low T-IoU thresholds, the mAP performance of regional pooling is better than that of attention pooling. One explanation for this phenomenon is that for lower quality video segments with low T-IoU values, when calculating attention weights, the frame images of candidate segments contain both action and background parts. At this time, the calculation of attention weights is affected by two different types of features, making it difficult for the feature vectors in the attention module to calculate effective semantic features,

Table 4.3 Comparison of regional pooling and attention pooling (Liu 2019)

Pooling method	T-IoU threshold						
	0.1	0.2	0.3	0.4	0.5	0.6	0.7
Regional pooling	**54.3**	**53.0**	**49.6**	42.0	31.3	24.4	15.2
Attention pooling	53.5	52.7	48.5	**42.5**	**32.2**	**26.1**	**16.5**

Table 4.4 Comparison between attention pooling method and other methods (Liu 2019)

Comparison method	T-IoU Threshold				
	0.1	0.2	0.3	0.4	0.5
SCNN	47.7	43.5	36.3	28.7	19.0
R-C3D	54.5	51.5	44.8	35.6	28.9
SSN	**66.0**	**59.4**	**51.9**	41.0	29.8
Attention pooling	53.5	52.7	48.5	**42.5**	**32.2**

thereby affecting their performance. In segments with high T-IoU values, the frame images of candidate segments mainly contain action information, and the calculated feature vectors have clear semantic features, which can improve the detection effect.

(2) **Method Based on Attention Pooling and Other Methods**

The attention pooling-based method was experimentally compared with several other methods, including SCNN (Shou 2016), R-C3D (Zhao et al. 2017), and SSN (Xu et al. 2017), and the results are shown in Table 4.4 (bold numbers indicate the best). As shown in Table 4.4, the performance of the attention pooling-based method is comparable to these comparison methods, and its performance is even better at high T-IoU thresholds.

References

Abro I A, Alhasson H F, Alharbi S S, *et al.* Advanced biosignal-RGB fusion with adaptive neuro fuzzy classification for high-precision action recognition. IEEE Access, 13, 57287-57310. https://doi.org/10.1109/ACCESS.2025.3553196 (2025).

Blank B, Gorelick L, Shechtman E, *et al.* Actions as space-time shapes. ICCV, 2: 1395-1402 (2005).

Buch S, Escorcia V, Shen C, *et al.* SST: Single-stream temporal action proposals. Proc. CVPR, 2911–2920 (2017).

Caba H F, Carlos N J, Ghanem B. Fast temporal activity proposals for efficient detection of human actions in untrimmed videos. Proc. CVPR, 1914–1923 (2016).

Chamusca I L, Pagano T P, Loureiro R B, *et al.* Enhancing context awareness in augmented reality environments: a review of opportunities and challenges in object and action recognition through machine learning. Discover Applied Science, 7(7): 750. https://doi.org/10.1007/s42452-025-07033-x (2025).

Cheng K, Zhang Y, He X, *et al.* Skeleton-based action recognition with shift graph convolutional network. Proc. CVPR, 183–192 (2020).

Chung J L, Ong L Y, Leow M C. A systematic literature review of optimization methods in skeleton-based human action recognition. IEEE Access, 13(2): 116713-116728 (2025).

Ding H, Guo C, Sun J, *et al.* Motion-driven adaptive frame selection strategy for video action recognition. Eurasip Journal on Image and Video Processing, 2025(1): 12. https://doi.org/10.1186/s13640-025-00675-2 (2025).

EscorciaV, Heilbron F C, Niebles J C, *et al.* DAPs: Deep action proposals for action understanding. Proc. ECCV, 768–784 (2016).

Feichtenhofer C, Fan H, Malik J, *et al.* Slowfast networks for video recognition. Proc. ICCV, 6202–6211 (2019).

Gao Z J, Gu Q Y, Han Z H. Human action recognition based on LSTM-GCN network fusing with attention mechanism. Modern Electronics Technique, 45(19): 93-98 (2022).

Gao J, Yang Z, Chen K, *et al.* Turn tap: Temporal unit regression network for temporal action proposals. Proc. ICCV, 3628–3636 (2017).

Guo J J, Ye J W, Kong Y Y, *et al.* Research progress in human behavior recognition based on deep learning. Journal of Zhongkai University of Agriculture and Engineering, 37(4): 55-64 (2024).

Han Z W, Yang H, Wu S Q, *et al.* Action recognition network combining spatiotemporal adaptive graph convolution and transformer. Journal of Electronics & Information Technology, 46(6): 2587-2595 (2024).

Hu Z P, Wang X Y, Chen D P, *et al.* Skeleton fine-grained action recognition model with spatiotemporal feature calibration and correlation decoupling. Signal Processing, 40(12): 2178-2192 (2024).

Jiang Y G, Liu J, Zamir A R, *et al.* Thumos challenge: Action recognition with a large number of classes. https://www.crcv.ucf.edu/THUMOS14/ (2014).

16. Jiang H X, Zhang Y J. Automatic people counting based on machine learning in intelligent video surveillance. Video Engineering, (4): 78-81 (2009).

Ke X, Miao X, Guo W Z. Real-time action detection based on spatiotemporal interaction perception. Acta Electronica Sinica, 52(2): 574-588 (2024).

Kumain S C, Singh M, Awasthi L K, *et al.* AI and ML techniques in image processing and object detection. Springer Nature Singapore, 2025 (2005)

Lee J, Kim T, Lee I, *et al.* Classification matters: Improving video action detection with class-specific attention. Lecture Notes in Computer Science, 15078, 450–467. https://doi.org/10.1007/978-3-031-72661-3_26 (2025)

Li Z Y, Gavrilyuk K, Gavves E, *et al.* VideoLSTM convolves, attends and flows for action recognition. Computer Vision & Image Understanding, 166: 41-50 (2018).

Liu C Y. Attention Based Video Temporal Action Proposal and Localization (Dissertation). Beijing, Tsinghua University (2019).

Liu L Z, Yang Y, Xia Y J, *et al.* Study on video action recognition based on augment negative example multi-granularity discrimination model. Journal on Communications, 45(12): 28-43 (2024).

Liu C Y, Huang H, Gao Z K, *et al.* A survey on action and event recognition with detectors for video data. Web Intelligence, 23(2): 275-291 (2025).

Liu C Y, Xu X Y, Zhang Y-J. Temporal attention network for action proposal. Proc. ICIP, 2281–2285 (2018).

Meurie C, Lézoray O. A comprehensive review of on-board action recognition models in public transportation systems. Expert Systems with Applications, 29: 128311. https://doi.org/10.1016/j.eswa.2025.128311 (2025).

Neimark D, Bar O, Zohar M, *et al.* Video transformer network. Proc. ICCV, 3163–3172 (2021).

Pan B, Jiang Y, Panda R, *et al.* A-RED: Interpretability-aware redundancy reduction for vision transformers. Advances in Neural Information Processing Systems, 34: 24898-24911 (2021).

Poppe R. A survey on vision-based human action recognition. Image and Vision Computing, 28: 976-990 (2010).

Qiu Z, Yao T, Mei T. Learning spatiotemporal representation with pseudo-3D residual networks. Proc. ICCV, 5534–5542 (2017).

Shou Z, Wang D, Chang S F. Temporal action localization in untrimmed videos via multi-stage CNNs. Proc. CVPR, 1049–1058 (2016).

Tran D, Bourdev L, Fergus R, *et al.* Learning spatiotemporal features with 3D convolutional networks. Proc. ICCV, 4489–4497 (2015).

Wu D H, Xu J, Chen J B, *et al.* Human activity recognition algorithm based on CNN-LSTM with attention mechanism. Science Technology and Engineering, 23(2): 681-689 (2023).

Xu H, Das A, Saenko K. R-C3D: Region convolutional 3D network for temporal activity detection. Proc. ICCV, 5783–5792 (2017).

Zhang Y-J. Image Engineering (V.2): Image Analysis (5th Edition). Beijing: Tsinghua University Press (2024a).

Zhang Y-J. Image Engineering (V.3): Image Understanding (5th Edition). Beijing: Tsinghua University Press (2024b).

Zhao Y, Xiong Y, Wang L, *et al.* Temporal action detection with structured segment networks. Proc. ICCV, 2914–2923 (2017).

Zheng Y, Zhang Y-J, Li X, *et al.* Action recognition in still images using a combination of human pose and context information. Proc. ICIP, 785–788 (2012).

Chapter 5
Activity Modeling and Recognition

Activities are generally larger in scale, longer in duration, and involve multiple actions. It depends on both the actors (action initiators) and the environment. Activities often represent complex actions performed by multiple persons in a sequence (and possibly interacting) (Yan et al. 2024). In order to better identify activities, it is usually necessary to establish corresponding models and conduct comprehensive analysis. Many of the tasks here involve cognitive computation of visual information (Luo 2010), (Maley 2024).

According to the model established for the activity, different methods and means can be used to identify the activity. On the one hand, the mutual relationship between actors and actions can be jointly considered, and on the other hand, the application of various deep learning techniques can also be considered. (Forsyth and Ponce 2012) provides some websites related to activity recognition research. A review of some related technologies can be found in (Abu-Bakar 2019), (Gayathri and Mamatha 2025), (Host and Ivasic-Kos 2022), (Kumar et al. 2024), (Miranda et al. 2022), (Saha et al. 2024).

The sections of this chapter are arranged as follows.

Section 5.1 introduces the basic methods and classifications of action modeling and activity modeling.

Section 5.2 discusses several techniques for joint modeling of actors and actions.

Section 5.3 introduces the human skeleton representation and provides an analysis on various networks using skeleton data for activity modeling and recognition.

Y.-J. Zhang, *Spatiotemporal Image Understanding*,
https://doi.org/10.1007/978-981-95-7130-7_5

5.1 Action and Activity Modeling

Activities consist of a combination of actions, and the recognition of activities requires several steps from image sequences to high-level interpretation (Turaga et al. 2008).

(1) Obtain input video or sequence images.
(2) Extract refined low-level image features.
(3) Obtain mid-level action descriptions based on low-level features.
(4) Starting from basic actions for high-level semantic interpretation.

The activity recognition system commonly used in practical applications is hierarchical. The bottom layer includes foreground–background segmentation module, tracking module, and object detection module. The middle layer mainly consists of the action recognition module (for action prediction methods related to action recognition, please refer to (Zhang et al. 2023)). The most important thing at higher levels is the inference engine, which encodes the semantics of activities based on low-level action primitives and actions, and provides an overall understanding based on the learned model.

As pointed out in Sect. 1.2, in terms of abstraction, the level of activity is higher than that of action. From a technical perspective, modeling and recognition of actions and activities often use different techniques and have characteristics ranging from simple to complex. Many commonly used modeling techniques for actions and activities can be classified according to Fig. 5.1 (Turaga et al. 2008).

5.1.1 Action Modeling

The methods for modeling actions are mainly divided into three categories (Fig. 5.1): **Non-parametric modeling**, **Volumetric modeling**, and **Parametric time-series modeling**. Non-parametric methods extract a set of features from each frame of the video and match the features with previously stored templates. Volumetric methods (often using stereo techniques) does not extract features frame by frame, but rather treats the video as a 3-D volume of voxel intensity and extends standard 2-D image features (such as scale space extremum, spatial filter response, etc.) to 3-D. Parametric

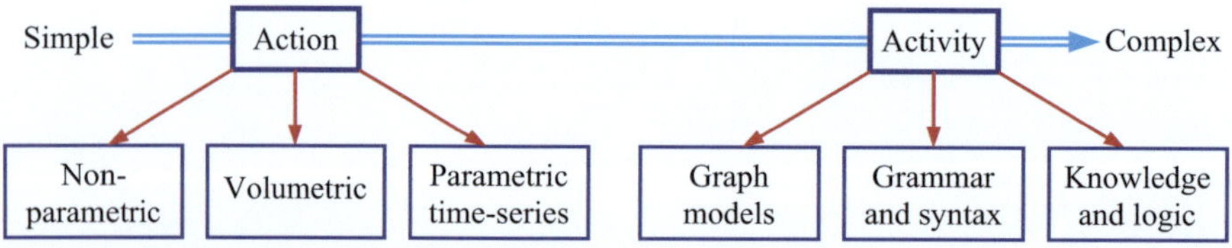

Fig. 5.1 Classification of action and activity modeling techniques

time-series methods dynamically models the time of motion and estimates specific parameters of a set of actions from the training set.

1. **Non-parametric Modeling**

Common methods of non-parametric modeling include the following.

(1) Based on 2-D Template

The method of using 2-D templates includes the following steps: ① Performing motion detection; ② Tracking the target in the scene; ③ Establishing a cropping sequence containing the target. The change in scale can be compensated for by normalizing the target size. It then calculates the periodicity index for a given action, and if the periodicity is strong, performing action recognition. To identify action, the periodic sequence is segmented into independent periods using the estimation of period. The average period is decomposed into several time segments and the flow-based features for each spatial point in each segment is calculated. The flow features from each segment are averaged into a single frame. The average flow frame during the activity cycle constitutes the template for each action group.

A typical method is to construct a **temporal template** as a model for actions. Specifically, the background is extracted first, and then the background blocks extracted from a sequence are combined into a still image. There are two ways to combine them here: One is to assign the same weight to all frames in the sequence, and the resulting representation can be called a **Motion Energy Image** (MEI); Another approach is to assign different weights to different frames in the sequence. Generally, new frames are given larger weights, while existing frames are given smaller weights. The resulting representation can be called a **Motion History Image** (MHI). For a given action, the combined images could be used to form a template. Calculate the invariant moment of the template's region (Zhang 2024a) and identify it.

(2) Based on 3-D Target Model

The 3-D target model is a model established for spatiotemporal targets, typical examples include the generalized cylindrical model (Zhang 2024b), 2-D contour stacking model, etc. The 2-D contour stacking model contains the shape and motion information of the target, from which geometric features of the target surface, such as peaks, pits, valleys, ridges, etc., can be extracted (Zhang 2024b). If the 2-D contour is replaced with a blob in the background, a **binary space–time volume** is obtained.

(3) Based on Manifold Learning Method

Many action recognition techniques involve data in high-dimensional space. Because the feature space becomes exponentially sparse with increasing dimensionality, constructing an effective model requires a large number of samples. To this end, the manifold where the learning data is located can be used to determine the intrinsic dimension of the data, which has fewer degrees of freedom and is beneficial for designing effective models in low dimensional spaces. The simplest method to reduce dimensionality is **Principal Component Analysis** (PCA), which assumes that the data is in a linear subspace. In practical applications, except for very special cases, the data would not be located in the linear subspace, and in this case, it is necessary to learn manifold eigen-geometry methods from a large number of samples. Nonlinear dimensionality reduction techniques allow data points to be represented based on their proximity to each other in nonlinear manifolds. Typical methods include **Local Linear Embedding** (LLE), **Laplacian eigenmaps**, etc.

2. **Volumetric Modeling**

Common methods of volumetric modeling include the following.

(1) Based on Spatiotemporal Filtering

Spatiotemporal filtering is an extension of spatial filtering, which refers to using a bank of spatiotemporal filters to treat the data of the **video volume**. Specific features can be further obtained based on the response of the filter bank. It is hypothesized that the spatiotemporal properties of cells in the visual cortex can be described by spatiotemporal filter structures, such as **oriented Gaussian kernels and their derivatives**, and **oriented Gabor filter banks**. For example, video clips can be considered as spatiotemporal volumes defined in *XYT*, and for each voxel (x, y, t), Gabor filter banks (Zhang 2024a) can be used to calculate local epigenetic models with different orientations, spatial scales, and individual temporal scales. The result can be used to identify actions using the average spatial probability of each voxel in a frame image. Because the analysis of actions is conducted on a single time scale, this method cannot be applied to situations where the frame rate varies. To achieve this, locally normalized spatiotemporal gradient histograms can be extracted at several time scales, and then the χ^2 statistics between the histograms can be used to match the input video with the stored samples. Gaussian kernel can also be used for filtering in the spatial domain, and Gaussian differentiation can be used for filtering in the temporal domain. After thresholding the response, it can be combined into a histogram. This method can provide simple and effective features for far-field (non-close range) videos.

The filtering method can be easily and quickly implemented through effective convolution. But in most applications, the bandwidth of the filter is unknown in advance, requiring the use of multiple large filter banks at both temporal and spatial scales to effectively capture actions. Due to the fact that the output response of each filter should have the same dimensionality as the input data, the use of large filter banks with multiple temporal and spatial scales is subject to certain limitations.

(2) Based on Components

A video can be seen as a collection of many local components, each with its own unique motion pattern. A typical method is to use the spatiotemporal point of interest representation in Sect. 2.1. In addition to using **Harris interest point detectors**, clustering can also be performed on spatiotemporal gradients extracted from the training set. In addition, the bag of words model (Zhang 2024b) can also be used to represent actions, where the bag of words model can be obtained by extracting spatiotemporal interest points and clustering features.

Because **points of interest** are essentially local, long-term correlations are ignored. To solve this problem, **correlogram** can be used. Consider a video as consisting of a series of collections, each containing content from a sliding window within a small time period. This method does not directly perform global geometric modeling on local components, but rather treats them as a feature package. Different actions can contain similar spatiotemporal components, but can have different geometric relationships. If global geometric information is combined into component-based video representation, it can form a **constellation** of components. When there are many components, the model becomes more complex. It is also possible to combine the constellation model and bag of words model (including feature packets) into a hierarchical structure, where the high-level constellation model has only a small number of components, and each component is included in the low-level feature packet. This technique combines the advantages of both models.

In most component-based methods, the detection of components is usually based on various linear operations such as filtering, spatiotemporal gradients, etc. Such descriptors are sensitive to apparent changes, noise, occlusion, etc. However, due to their inherent locality, these methods are more robust to non-stationary backgrounds.

(3) Based on Sub-volume Matching

Sub-volume matching refers to the matching between sub-volumes in a video and a template. For example, actions can be matched with templates from the perspective of spatiotemporal motion. The main difference between this method and the component-based method is that it does not require extracting action descriptors from extreme points in the scale space, but rather checks the similarity between two local spatiotemporal blocks (patches) by comparing the motion between two blocks. However, performing relevant calculations on the entire video is time-consuming. One way to solve this problem is to extend the successful fast Haar features (box features) in object detection to 3-D. The Haar features in 3-D are the output of the 3-D filter bank, with filter coefficients of 1 and -1. By combining the outputs of these filters with boosting methods (Zhang 2024a), robust performance can be obtained. Another method is to treat the video volume as a collection of arbitrarily shaped sub-volumes, each of which is a spatially consistent stereoscopic volume that can be obtained by clustering voxels that are visually and spatially close. Next, the given video will be segmented into multiple sub-volumes or **super-voxels**. The final action template is matched by searching for the minimum volume set that maximizes the overlap rate between the sub-volume set and the templates.

The advantage of sub-volume matching is that it is more robust to noise and occlusion, and if combined with optical flow features, it is also more robust to apparent changes. The disadvantage of sub-volume matching is that it is susceptible to background changes.

(4) Based on Tensor

Tensor is an extension of 2-D matrices in multidimensional space. A 3-D space–time volume can naturally be viewed as a tensor with three independent dimensions. For example, a person's actions, identity, and joint trajectories can be viewed as three independent dimensions of a tensor. Decomposing the total data tensor into dominant patterns (similar to the extension of PCA) can extract the corresponding actions and **signature** of the person performing the action. Of course, the 3-D of the tensor can also be directly taken as the 3-D of the spatiotemporal domain, *i.e.* (x, y, t).

The tensor-based method provides a direct way to match videos as a whole, without considering the mid-level representations used in the previous methods. In addition, other types of features (such as optical flow, spatiotemporal filter response, etc.) can also be easily combined by increasing the tensor dimension.

3. **Parameter Time Series Modeling**

The above two modeling methods are suitable for relatively simple actions, while the modeling methods introduced below are suitable for complex actions that span time domains, such as complex dance steps in ballet videos and special gestures of instrumentalists.

(1) Hidden Markov Model

Hidden Markov Model (HMM) is a typical model of state space, which is effective in modeling time series data and has good generalization and discriminative properties. It is suitable for tasks that require recursive probability estimation. In the process of constructing a discrete HMM, the state space can be viewed as a finite set of discrete points. Their evolution over time can be modeled as a series of probabilistic steps from one state to another. The three key issues of HMM are **inference**, **decoding**, and **learning**. The earliest use of HMM for recognizing actions was tennis shot actions, such as forehand stroke, forehand intercept, backhand stroke, backhand intercept, spike, etc. Among them, it is necessary to model a series of background subtracted images into HMM corresponding to specific categories. HMM can also be used to model actions that change over time, such as gait.

Single person actions can be modeled using a single Hidden Markov Model. For multi person interaction actions, a pair of HMMs can be used to represent alternating actions. In addition, domain knowledge can be integrated into the construction process of HMMs, or HMMs can be combined with object detection to leverage the connections between actions and (acted) objects. For example, prior knowledge of state duration can be combined into the framework of HMM, and the resulting model is called a **semi-Hidden Markov Model** (semi-HMM). If a discrete label is added to the state space for modeling high-level activity, a mixed state HMM can be constructed, which can be used to model non-stationary activity.

(2) Linear Dynamic System

Linear Dynamic Systems (LDS) are more generalized than Hidden Markov models (HMM), as they do not limit the state space to a finite set of symbols but can be continuous values in the R^k space, where k is the dimension of the state space. The simplest linear dynamic system is a first-order time invariant Gaussian Markov process, which can be represented as

$$\mathbf{x}(t) = A\mathbf{x}(t-1) + \mathbf{w}(t) \quad \mathbf{w} \sim N(0, \mathbf{P}) \tag{5.1}$$

$$\mathbf{y}(t) = C\mathbf{x}(t) + \mathbf{v}(t) \quad \mathbf{v} \sim N(0, \mathbf{Q}) \tag{5.2}$$

where $\boldsymbol{x} \in \mathrm{R}^d$ is the d-D state space; $\boldsymbol{y} \in \mathrm{R}^n$ is the n-D observation vector; $d < < n$; $\boldsymbol{w}$ and $\boldsymbol{v}$ are the process and observation noise, respectively, both of which are Gaussian distributions with zero mean and covariance matrices $\boldsymbol{P}$ and $\boldsymbol{Q}$. Linear dynamic systems can be seen as an extension of the continuous state space of Hidden Markov models (with Gaussian observation models), which are more suitable for processing high-dimensional time series data, but still not very suitable for non-stationary actions.

(3) Non-linear Dynamic System

Consider the following sequence of actions: A person first bends down to pick up an item, then walks towards to a table and places the item on it, and finally sits on a chair aside. This includes a series of short steps, each of which can be modeled using LDS. The entire process can be seen as a transition between different LDSs. The most common form of time-varying LDS is

$$\mathbf{x}(t) = A(t)\mathbf{x}(t-1) + \mathbf{w}(t) \quad \mathbf{w} \sim N(0, \mathbf{P}) \tag{5.3}$$

$$\mathbf{y}(t) = C(t)\mathbf{x}(t) + \mathbf{v}(t) \quad \mathbf{v} \sim N(0, \mathbf{Q}) \tag{5.4}$$

Compared with the previous Eqs. (5.1) and (5.2), both A and C in the above two equations can vary over time. To solve such complex dynamic problems, commonly used methods are **Switching Linear Dynamic Systems** (SLDS) or **Jumping Linear Systems** (JLS). Switching linear dynamic systems includes a set of linear dynamic systems and a switching function that changes model parameters by switching between models. To identify complex motion, a multi-layer approach containing multiple levels of abstraction can be used. The lowest layer is a series of input images, and the upper layer includes regions with consistent motion states, called blob. The next high layer is a combination of time-based blob trajectories, and the highest layer includes a Hidden Markov model (HMM) that represents complex activity.

Although the switching linear dynamic system has stronger modeling and description capabilities than Hidden Markov models (HMM) and linear dynamic systems (LDS), learning and reasoning in switching linear dynamic systems are more complex and generally require the use of approximation methods. In practical applications, it is difficult to determine the appropriate number of switching states, often requiring a large amount of training data or complex manual adjustments.

5.1.2 Activity Modeling

Compared to actions, activities not only last longer, but most of the activity applications that people pay attention to, such as monitoring and content-based indexing, include multiple action persons. Their activities not only interact with each other, but also influence each other with **contextual entities**. For modeling complex scenes, it is necessary to represent and infer the intrinsic structure and semantics of complex activities at a high level. The methods for modeling activities are mainly divided into three categories (see Fig. 5.1): Graph models, Synthesis methods, as well as Knowledge-based and logic-based methods. The specific discussion is as follows.

1. **Graph Models**

Common graph models include the following.

(1) Belief network

Belief Network (BN), also known as **Bayesian Network** (BN), is a directed graph that simulates causal relationships in human reasoning processes. First, encode a set of random variables into **Local Conditional Probability Density** (LCPD), and then encode the complex conditional dependencies within it. **Dynamic Belief Network** (DBN, also known as **Dynamic Bayesian Network**) is a generalization of simple belief networks obtained by combining the temporal dependencies between random variables.

Compared to traditional HMMs that can only encode one latent variable, DBN can encode complex conditional dependencies between several random variables. For example, the interactions between two persons (such as pointing, squeezing, pushing, hugging, etc.) require a two-step process to be used for modeling. First, performing the pose estimation by using Bayesian networks, and then modeling the temporal evolution of the posture by using DBN. The contextual information derived from other targets in the scene can be used to recognize actions, while Bayesian networks can be used to explain interactions between persons or objects.

If considering the dependencies between multiple random variables, DBN is more versatile than HMM. But in DBN, the time model is also a Markov model just like in HMM, and the basic DBN model can only handle the activity of sequences. The development of graph models for learning and reasoning enables them to model structured activity. However, learning local conditional probability density for large networks often requires a large amount of training data or complex manual adjustments by experts, which limits the use of DBN in large-scale environments.

By the way, there are many estimation methods for human posture, which can be found in reviews (Li et al. 2024) and (Xu et al. 2024).

(2) Petri net

Petri net is a mathematical tool used to describe the relationship between conditions and events. It is especially suitable for modeling and visualizing various activities such as **sequencing**, **concurrency**, **synchronization**, and **resource sharing**. Petri

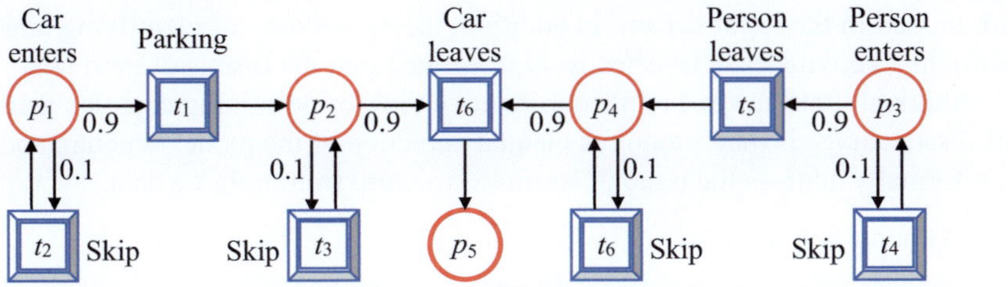

Fig. 5.2 An example of a probability Petri net representing a car retrieval activity from a garage

net is a bipartite graph that contains two types of nodes: position and transition, where position refers to the state of the entity and transition refers to the change in the entity's state.

An example of using a probabilistic Petri net to represent a car pickup activity from a garage is shown in Fig. 5.2. The positions in the figure are marked as p_1, p_2, p_3, p_4, p_5, and the transition in the figure are marked as t_1, t_2, t_3, t_4, t_5, t_6. In this Petri net, p_1 and p_3 are the starting nodes, and p_5 is the ending node. A car enters the scene and places a token at position p_1. Transition t_1 can be activated at this time, but it still needs to wait for the relevant conditions (the car needs to be parked in a nearby parking space) to be met before it can officially start. At this point, remove the token at p_1 and place it at p_2. Similarly, when a person enters a parking space, place the token at p_3, and transition t_5 starts after the person leaves the parked car. Next, the token will be removed from p_3 and placed at p_4.

Now, a token has been placed at each allowed position during transition t_6, and when the relevant conditions (the car leaving the parking space) are met, it can be started/ignited (fire). Once the car leaves, t_6 ignites, all tokens are removed, and a token is placed at the final position p_5. In this example, sorting, concurrency, and synchronization are all occurred.

Petri net was once used to develop a system for high-level interpretation of image sequences. Among them, the structure of the Petri net needs to be determined in advance, which is a complex task for large networks that represent complex activities. The above work can be semi-automated by automatically mapping a small set of logical, spatial, and temporal operations to the graph structure. With this approach, an interactive tool for querying video surveillance can be developed that maps user query requirements to Petri net. However, this method is based on deterministic Petri nets and generally cannot handle the uncertainty in low-level modules such as trackers and object detectors.

In practice, real human activities are not completely consistent with strict models, which allow for differences from the expected sequence and impose penalties for significant differences. The concept of **Probabilistic Petri Net** (PPN) was proposed for this purpose. In PPN, transitions are associated with weights, which record the probability of transition initiation. By utilizing skip transitions and allowing for low probabilities as penalties, it is possible to achieve robustness when observations are missed in the input stream. In addition, the uncertainty of identifying targets or unfolding activities can be effectively integrated into the tokens of Petri net.

Although Petri net is a relatively intuitive tool for describing complex activities, its disadvantage is that it requires manual depiction of the model structure and does not formally address the issue of learning structure from training data.

(3) Other graph models

In response to the shortcomings of DBN, especially the limitations on sequence activity description, some other graph models have also been proposed. Under the DBN framework, some graph models have been constructed for modeling complex temporal relationships such as sequences, time periods, parallelism, synchronization, etc. A typical **Past-Now-Future** (PNF) structure can be used to model complex time sorting situations. Additionally, a propagation network can be used to represent activities that use partial sorting time intervals. These activities will be constrained by time, logical order, and activity interval length. The method based on the propagation network regards a time scalable activity as a series of event labels. With the help of context and specific constraints related to the activity, it may be discovered that sequence labels have some inherent partial sorting properties. For example, you need first to open your mailbox before you can view emails. By utilizing these constraints, the activity model can be viewed as a set of subsequences that represent partial sorting constraints of different lengths.

2. **Synthesis Method**

The synthesis method is mainly implemented through grammar concepts and rules.

(1) Grammar

Grammar uses a set of production rules to describe the structure of processing. Similar to grammar in language models, production rules specify how to construct sentences (activities) from words (activity primitives) and how to recognize sentences (videos) that meet the rules of a given grammar (activity model). The early grammar for recognizing visual activities was used for target disassembly work, and at that time, there was no probability model in the grammar. The subsequent application is **Context Free Grammar** (CFG), which is used for modeling and recognizing human motion and multi-person interaction. A hierarchical process is used here, where the lower layer is a combination of HMM and BN, and the interaction between the higher layers is modeled using CFG. The method of context free grammar has a strong theoretical foundation and can model structured processes. In the synthesis method, it is only necessary to enumerate the **primitive events** that need to be detected and to define the production rules for high-level activities. Once the rules for CFG are constructed, existing parsing algorithms can be utilized.

Because the deterministic syntax expects high accuracy at lower levels, it is not suitable for situations where errors are caused by tracking errors and missed observations at lower levels. In complex scenarios that require the participation of multiple time connections (such as parallelism, overlay, synchronization, etc.), it is often difficult to improve the effectiveness of manually constructing syntax rules. Learning grammar rules from training data is a promising alternative method, but it has been proven to be very difficult in general situations.

(2) Stochastic grammar

The algorithms used to detect low-level primitives are often essentially probabilistic algorithms. **Stochastic Context Free Grammar** (SCFG) has probabilistically extended the context free grammar, making it more suitable for practical visual models. SCFG can be used to model the semantics of activities (whose structure is assumed to be known). Among them, HMM is used in the detection of low-level primitives. The production rules of grammar are supplemented by probabilities and introduce a skip transition. It can improve the robustness of insertion errors in the input stream and also enhance the robustness of low-level modules. SCFG can also be used to model multi-tasking activities (including multiple independent execution threads, intermittent related interactions, etc.).

In many cases, it is often necessary to associate additional attributes or features with event primitives. For example, the exact location of the event primitive occurrence may be important for describing the event, but it may not have been pre-recorded in the set of event primitives. In this case, attribute grammar has stronger descriptive power than traditional grammar. Probabilistic attribute grammar has been used to handle multi-agent activities in monitoring.

An example of attribute grammar for airplane passenger boarding attributes is presented as follows. As shown in Fig. 5.3, production rules and event primitives such as "appearance", "departure", "move around", and "move away" are used to describe activities. The event primitive is further associated with attributes such as the location where the event appears and disappears, the classification of a group of targets (class), and the identification of related entities (idr).

Although SCFG is more robust to errors and missed detections in the input stream than CFG, it is still limited in modeling temporal relationships, like CFG.

3. **Knowledge and Logic**

Knowledge and logic are closely related.

(1) Logic based approach

The logic-based approach relies on strict logical rules to describe domain knowledge in a general sense to describe activities. Logical rules can be used to describe domain knowledge input by users or to represent high-level reasoning results in an intuitive

$S \rightarrow$ BOARDING$_N$

BOARDING $\rightarrow$ appear$_0$ CHECK$_1$ disappear$_1$

(isPerson (appear, class) $\wedge$ isInside (appear.location, Gate) $\wedge$ isInside (disappear.location, Plane))

CHECK $\rightarrow$ moveclose$_0$ CHECK$_1$

CHECK $\rightarrow$ moveaway$_0$ CHECK$_1$

CHECK $\rightarrow$ moveclose$_0$ moveaway$_1$ CHECK$_1$

(isPerson (moveclose, class) $\wedge$ moveclose.idr = moveaway.idr

Fig. 5.3 Example of grammar for airplane passenger boarding attributes and user readable form. **Declarative models** use scene structures, events, etc., to describe all expected activities. The activity model includes the interaction between targets in the scene. A hierarchical structure can be used to identify a series of actions performed by an agent. The symbol descriptors of actions can be extracted from low-level features through intermediate levels. Next, a rule-based approach is used to approximate the probability of a particular activity occurring by matching the properties of the agent with the expected distribution (represented by mean and variance). This method considers an activity consisting of several action threads, each of which can be modeled as a finite random state automaton. The constraints between different threads propagate in a temporal logical network.

When representing and identifying high-level activities in a system based on logical programming, low-level modules are first used to detect event primitives, and then high-level inference engines based on Prolog are used to identify activities represented by logical rules between event primitives. These methods do not directly address uncertainty issues in the observed input stream. To address these issues, a combination of logical and probabilistic models can be used, where logical rules are represented by using first-order logical predicates. Each rule is also associated with a weight indicating the accuracy of the rule. Further reasoning can be carried out using Markov logic networks.

Although logic-based methods provide a natural approach that combines domain knowledge, they often involve time-consuming reviews of whether constraints are met. Additionally, it is not yet clear how much domain knowledge needs to be integrated. It can be expected that combining more knowledge will make the model more rigorous, but it is not easy to generalize to other situations. Finally, logical rules require domain experts to perform time-consuming traversal for each configuration.

(2) Ontological approach

In most practical configurations using the aforementioned methods, the definition of symbol activity is constructed empirically. Rules such as grammar rules or a set of logical rules are manually specified. Although experience-based design is fast and often effective, its generalizability is poor and limited to specific design situations. Therefore, there is also a need for a centralized representation of activity definitions or an algorithm independent to activity ontology. Ontology can standardize the definition of activities, allow porting of specific configurations, enhance interoperability between different systems, and facilitate replication and comparison of system performance. Typical practical examples include classifying conference videos, analyzing social interactions in nursing rooms, and setting up interactive actions in banks.

Since 2003, **video event challenge workshop** has been held internationally to integrate various abilities, and a domain ontology based on general knowledge has been constructed. The conference has defined six areas of video surveillance: ① Perimeter and internal security; ② Monitoring of railway intersections; ③ Visual banking monitoring; ④ Visual subway monitoring; ⑤ Warehouse security;  Airport apron safety. The conference also guided the development of two formal languages, one is **Video Event Representation Language** (VERL), which is used to achieve ontology representation of complex events based on simple sub-events;

Fig. 5.4 Example of describing a car parade activity using ontology concepts

```
PROCESS (cruise-parking-lot (vehicle v, parking-lot lot),
Sequence (enter (v, lot),
    Set-to-zero (i),
    Repeat-Until (
        AND (inside (v, lot), move-in-circuit (v), increment (i)),
        Equal (i, n)),
    Exit (v, lot)))
```

another is **Video Event Markup Language** (VEML), which is used to annotate events in videos.

Here is an example of an ontology. Figure 5.4 is an example of using ontology concepts to describe car cruising activities. This ontology records the number of times a car turns on the road without stopping in the parking lot. If this number exceeds a threshold, it can be considered as detecting a parade activity.

Although ontologies provide concise high-level activity definitions, they do not guarantee the provision of the correct "hardware" to "parse" ontologies used for identifying tasks.

5.2 Actor-Action Joint Modeling

As research deepens, the categories of actors and actions that need to be considered in **spatiotemporal activity understanding** are constantly increasing. In many cases, there will be multiple entities of different categories performing actions of different categories. For this purpose, it can be considered to model the actor-action joint model (Xu et al. 2015). In fact, jointly detecting a set of several targets in an image is more robust than separately detecting a single target. Through joint modeling, it is possible to effectively achieve spatiotemporal activity understanding in complex situations. The research on the relationship between actor and action is also the foundation of video based visual question answering (such as (Shih et al. 2016) and (Wu et al. 2017)) and autonomous driving of automobiles.

For this purpose, the video can be viewed as a 3-D image $f(x, y, t)$ and represented using the graph structure $G = (N, A)$. Among them, the node set $N = (n_1, n_2, \ldots, n_M)$ represents M voxels (or M hyper-voxels), and the arc set $A(n)$ represents the voxel set in the neighborhood of a certain node n in N. Assuming that the actor tag set is represented by X and the action tag set is represented by Y.

Consider a set of random variables $\{x\}$ representing the actors and a set of random variables $\{y\}$ representing the actions. The actor-action understanding problem can be regarded as a maximum a posteriori problem:

$$(x^*, y^*) = \arg\max_{x,y} P(x, y|M) \tag{5.5}$$

The general actor-action understanding problem includes three situations: ① Single label actor-action recognition; ② Multi label actor-action recognition; ③

Actor-action semantic segmentation, which correspond to three stages of granularity refinement.

5.2.1 *Single Label Actor-Action Recognition*

Single-label actor-action recognition is the coarsest granularity scenario, corresponding to general action recognition problems. Firstly, consider the case where both x and y are scalars. In this case, Eq. (5.5) represents the scenario where a single actor x initiates a single action y in a given video. There are three models that can be used in this scenario (more discussion in Sect. 5.2.3).

(1) Naïve Bayes model

Assuming that the actor-action is independent of each other, that is, any actor can initiate any action. At this point, a set of classifiers needs to be trained in the action space to classify different actions. This is the simplest method, but it does not emphasize the existence of various combinations of actor-action (tuples), that is, some actors may not be able to initiate all actions, or some actors can only initiate certain actions. Therefore, when there are many different actors and actions, using Naïve Bayes models may result in some unreasonable combinations (such as human flying, bird swimming, etc.).

(2) Joint product space model

Considering that the actor space X and action space Y can generate a new label space Z, such as using the product relationship $Z = X \times Y$. In the joint product space, a classifier can be directly learned for each actor-action tuple. Obviously, this method emphasizes the existence of actor-action tuples and can eliminate unreasonable combinations. In addition, it is possible to use more cross actor-action features to learn more discriminative classifiers. However, this method may not be able to effectively utilize the commonalities across different actors or different actions, such as the need for both adults and children to take steps and swing their arms when walking.

(3) Tri-layer model

The tri-level model unifies the Naïve Bayes model and the joint product space model, simultaneously learning classifiers in the actor space X, action space Y, and joint actor-action space Z. When reasoning, infer Bayesian elements and joint product space elements separately, and then linearly combine them to obtain the final result. It not only models the interaction between actors and actions, but also models the initiation of different actions by the same actor and the initiation of the same action by different actors.

5.2.2 Multi Label Actor-Action Recognition

In practical applications, many videos have multiple actors and/or initiate multiple actions, known as multi label situations. At this point, both x and y are binary vectors with dimensions $|X|$ and $|Y|$. If there is an i-th type of actor in the video, the value of x_i is 1, otherwise x_i is 0. Similarly, if there is a j-th type of action in the video, the value of y_j is 1, otherwise y_j is 0. This generalized definition does not confine specific elements in x to specific elements in y. This will help to independently compare the multi label performance of actor-action combinations with the multi label performance of actor-action tuples.

For example, in order to study the situation where multiple actors initiate multiple actions, a corresponding video database called **Actor-Action Database** (A2D) was constructed (Xu et al. 2015). Among them, a total of 7 actor categories were considered: adults, infants, cats, dogs, birds, cars, and balls; as well as 9 action categories were considered: walking, running, jumping, rolling, climbing, crawling, flying, eating, and no action (not in the first 8 categories). The main actors include articulated structures such as adults, infants, cats, dogs, and birds; but they also include rigid bodies such as cars and balls. Many actors can initiate the same action, but no actor can initiate all actions. Therefore, although there are theoretically 63 possible combinations, some of them are unreasonable (or almost never occur), resulting in a total of 43 reasonable actor-action tuples. For these 43 tuples, 3782 video clips from YouTube are collected by using 43 actor-action tuples of text, with lengths ranging from 24 to 332 frames (an average of 136 frames per video clip). The numbers of video clips corresponding to each actor-action tuple are shown in Table 5.1. The blank spaces in the table correspond to unreasonable actor-action tuples, and no video clips were collected. As shown in Table 5.1, the numbers of video clips corresponding to various actor-action tuples are most around one hundred.

In the 3782 video clips, the number of video clips containing different numbers (1 ~ 5) of actors, the number of video clips containing different numbers (1 ~ 5) of actions, and the number of video clips containing different numbers (1 ~ 5) of

Table 5.1 Numbers of video clips corresponding to various actor-action tuples in the database (Xu et al. 2015)

	Walking	Running	Jumping	Rolling	Climbing	Crawling	Flying	Eating	No action
Adults	282	175	174	105	101	105		105	761
Infants	113			107	104	106			36
Cats	113	99	105	103	106			110	53
Dogs	176	110	104	104		109		107	46
Birds	112		107	107	99		106	105	26
Cars		120	107	104			102		99
Balls			105	117			109		87

Table 5.2 Number of video clips corresponding to actor, action, and actor-action labels in the database (Xu et al. 2015)

	1	2	3	4	5
Actor	2794	936	49	3	0
Action	2639	1037	99	6	1
Actor-Action	2503	1051	194	31	3

actor-actions are shown in Table 5.2. As shown in Table 5.2, in more than one-third of the video clips, the number of actors or actions is greater than 1 (in the last 4 columns of the bottom row of the table, including one actor initiating two or more actions or two or more actors initiating one action).

For the case of **multi label actor-action recognition**, three classifiers can be considered similar to the case of single label actor-action recognition. That is, the multi label actor-action classifier using Naïve Bayes model, the multi label actor-action classifier in the joint product space, and the actor-action classifier based on a tri-level model that combines the first two classifiers.

Multi label actor-action recognition can be seen as a retrieval problem. The experiment conducted on this database (using 3036 segments as the training set and 746 segments as the test set, with similar proportions of various combinations) showed that the performance of the multi label actor-action classifier based on the joint product space was better than that of the multi label actor-action classifier based on Naïve Bayes model, and the actor-action classifier based on the tri-level model could still improve the performance (Xu et al. 2015).

5.2.3 Actor-Action Semantic Segmentation

Actor-action semantic segmentation is the most fine-grained case in actor-action activity understanding, and can also embrace other coarser grained problems such as detection and localization. The main task is to find labels for the actor-action of each voxel throughout the entire video. Still define two sets of random variables $\{x\}$ and $\{y\}$, whose dimensions are determined by the number of voxels or hyper-voxels, and $x_i \in X$ and $y_j \in Y$. The objective function of Eq. (5.5) remains unchanged, but implementing the $P(x, y|M)$ graph model requires completely different assumptions about the various relationships between the actor variable and the action variable.

Below these relationships is discussed in detail. Firstly, the method based on Naïve Bayes model is introduced, which can handle the labels of two classes separately. Further, the method based on the joint product space model is introduced, which utilizes the combination $[x, y]$ to jointly consider the actor and action. Next, a two-level model that considers the relationship between actor variables and action variables is introduced. Finally, a tri-level model that considers both the connections within categories and between categories is introduced.

1. **Naïve Bayes Model**

Similar to the situation in single label actor-action recognition, the Naïve Bayes model can be represented as

$$\begin{aligned} P(x, y|M) = P(x|M)P(y|M) &= \prod_{i \in M} P(x_i)P(y_i) \prod_{i \in M} \prod_{j \in A(i)} P(x_i, x_j)P(y_i, y_j) \\ &\propto \prod_{i \in M} q_i(x_i)r_i(y_i) \prod_{i \in M} \prod_{j \in A(i)} q_{ij}(x_i, x_j)r_{ij}(y_i, y_j) \end{aligned} \tag{5.6}$$

where q_i and r_i encode the potential function defined in the actor-action model, respectively; q_{ij} and r_{ij} encode the potential functions in the set of actor nodes and the set of action nodes, respectively.

Now the classifier $\{f_c|c \in X\}$ is trained on the actor set and the classifier $\{g_c|c \in Y\}$ is trained on the action set using features. The potential function of paired edges has the form of a contrast sensitive Potts model as follows:

$$q_{ij} = \begin{cases} 1 & x_i = x_j \\ \exp[-k/(1 + \chi_{ij}^2)] & \text{otherwise} \end{cases} \tag{5.7}$$

$$r_{ij} = \begin{cases} 1 & y_i = y_j \\ \exp[-k/(1 + \chi_{ij}^2)] & \text{otherwise} \end{cases} \tag{5.8}$$

where ${\chi^2}_{ij}$ is the χ^2 distance between the feature histograms of nodes i and j, k is the parameter to be learned from the training data. Actor-action semantic segmentation can be obtained by independently solving these two flat condition random fields.

2. **Joint Product Space**

Consider a new set of random variables $z = \{z_1, z_2, \ldots, z_M\}$, also defined on above all voxels or hyper-voxels in a video, and select labels from the actor-action product space $Z = X \times Y$. This method jointly obtains actor-action tuples as unique elements, but cannot model the common factors of actor-action in different tuples (the models introduced later can solve this problem). This yields a single-layer graph model:

$$\begin{aligned} P(x, y|M) &= P(z|M) = \prod_{i \in M} P(z_i) \prod_{i \in M} \prod_{j \in A(i)} P(z_i, z_j) \\ &\propto \prod_{i \in M} s_i(z_i) \prod_{i \in M} \prod_{j \in A(i)} s_{ij}(z_i, z_j) = \prod_{i \in M} s_i([x_i, y_i]) \prod_{i \in M} \prod_{j \in A(i)} s_{ij}([x_i, y_i], [x_j, y_j]) \end{aligned} \tag{5.9}$$

where s_i is the potential function of the product space label of the joint actor-action, s_{ij} is the nodal potential function between two nodes corresponding to the combination $[x, y]$. Specifically, s_i includes the classification score obtained by the trained actor-action classifier $\{h_c|c \in Z\}$ for node i, and the form of s_{ij} is the same as Eqs. (5.7) or (5.8). As an intuitive diagram, please refer to Fig. 5.5a and b.

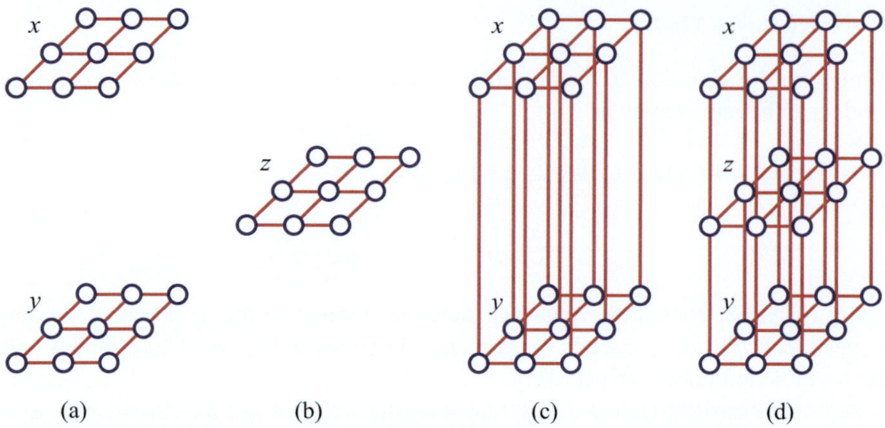

Fig. 5.5 Schematic diagram of different graph models

3. **Bi-Layer Model**

Given the actor node x and the action node y, the **bi-layer model** uses edges encoding the combined potential function to connect each random variable pair $\{(x_i, y_i)^M{}_{i=1}\}$, directly obtaining the covariance across the actor-action labels.

$$\begin{aligned} P(x, y|M) &= \prod_{i\in M} P(x_i, y_i) \prod_{i\in M} \prod_{j\in A(i)} P(x_i, x_j)P(y_i, y_j) \\ &\propto \prod_{i\in M} q_i(x_i)r_i(y_i)t_i(x_i, y_i) \prod_{i\in M} \prod_{j\in A(i)} q_{ij}(x_i, x_j)r_{ij}(y_i, y_j) \end{aligned} \tag{5.10}$$

where $t_i(x_i, y_i)$ is the potential function obtained by learning the labels of the entire product space, which can be obtained like s_i in Fig. 5.5a and b, as shown in Fig. 5.5c, with the addition of cross level connecting edges.

4. **Tri-Layer Model**

The Naïve Bayes model shown in Eq. (5.6) does not consider the relationship between the actor variable x and the action variable y. The joint product space model of Eq. (5.9) combines the characteristics of cross actor-action and the interaction features within neighboring nodes of the actor-action node. The bi-layer model of Eq. (5.10) adds actor-action interactions between separated actor nodes and action nodes, but does not consider the spatiotemporal variations of the interactions.

The following is a **tri-layer model** that can explicitly model the spatiotemporal changes in Fig. 5.5d, combining all nodes of the joint product space with the actor node and action node:

$$
\begin{aligned}
P(x, y, z|M) &= P(x|M)P(y|M)P(z|M) \prod_{i \in M} P(x_i, z_i)P(y_i, z_i) \\
&\propto \prod_{i \in M} q_i(x_i)r_i(y_i)s_i(z_i)u_i(x_i, z_i)v_i(y_i, z_i) \\
&\prod_{i \in M} \prod_{j \in A(i)} q_{ij}(x_i, x_j)r_{ij}(y_i, y_j)s_{ij}(z_i, z_j)
\end{aligned}
\tag{5.11}
$$

where

$$
u_i(x_i, z_i) = \begin{cases} w(y_i'|x_i) & \text{for } z_i = [x_i', y_i'] \text{ there is } x_i = x_i' \\ 0 & \text{otherwise} \end{cases} \tag{5.12}
$$

$$
v_i(y_i, z_i) = \begin{cases} w(x_i'|y_i) & \text{for } z_i = [x_i', y_i'] \text{ there is } y_i = y_i' \\ 0 & \text{otherwise} \end{cases} \tag{5.13}
$$

where $w(y_i{'}|x_i)$ and $w(x_i{'}|y_i)$ are the classification scores of the conditional classifier specifically trained for the tri-layer model.

These conditional classifiers are the main reasons for performance improvement. The action specific, separable classifiers based on actor type conditions can utilize the unique characteristics of actor-action tuples. For example, when an actor "adult" is given and a conditional classifier is trained on the action "eat", all other actions of the actor "adult" can be considered as negative training samples. In this way, the tri-layer model considers all connections in the actor space, action space, and joint product space. In other words, the previous three basic models were all special cases of the tri-layer model. It can be proven that maximizing (x^*, y^*, z^*) of Eq. (5.11) can also maximize Eq. (5.5) (Xu et al. 2016).

5.3 Networks Using Skeleton Representation

The human body can be viewed as a joint system, consisting of rigid segments (limbs) connected by joint points (usually represented as a skeleton sequence or skeleton diagram). When recognizing human activities and behaviors, taking into account the position changes of these joints and the motion of these line segments, it is possible to recognize their activities and infer their behavior (Karthika et al. 2025).

The use of skeleton data for action recognition has several advantages. Firstly, skeleton data is a 3-D coordinate sequence of multiple skeleton joints, so its topological structure can be modeled using prior knowledge. In addition, compared with RGB data, it has better robustness not only to external noise such as lighting and occlusion, but also to changes in human scale or viewing angle. Finally, due to the fact that the number of human joints in the skeleton data is generally much smaller than the number of pixels in the image, it can improve the computational efficiency of the model.

5.3.1 Skeleton Representation

The human **skeleton** can be represented as a graph with skeleton joints as nodes and bones as edges. This graph can be denoted as $G = (V, E, X)$, where $V = \{v_1, v_2, \ldots, v_N\}$ is a set of N nodes; E is the set of all edges, which can be formulated as the adjacency matrix $\boldsymbol{A} \in \mathrm{R}^{N \times N}$, and its element a_{ij} reflects the strength of the correlation between nodes v_i and v_j. The neighborhood of v_i can be represented as $N(v_i) = \{v_j | a_{ij} \neq 0\}$. X is a feature set of N nodes, which can be formulated as a matrix $\boldsymbol{X} \in \mathrm{R}^{N \times C}$, where C represents the number of channels. The feature of node v_i can be represented as $\boldsymbol{x}_i \in \mathrm{R}^C$.

Many activity recognitions are based on the human skeleton, and the definition and representation of the skeleton are often related to the application purpose. In some applications, not only the joints of the skeleton need to be considered, but also the connections between these joints. Therefore, some skeleton representations not only consider the joints themselves, but also their connections, and different skeletal models use different numbers of joints and/or connection. The following will provide some examples of skeleton representations (for the convenience of seeing the total number of nodes, the head nodes are labeled with the maximum value).

(1) A skeleton representation with 11 joint points (Liu et al. 2020b), as shown in Fig. 5.6.
(2) A skeleton representation with 16 joint points (Ke et al. 2017), as shown in Fig. 5.7.
(3) A skeleton representation with 18 joint points (Yan et al. 2018), as shown in Fig. 5.8.
(4) A skeleton representation with 25 joint points (Caetano et al. 2019a), as shown in Fig. 5.9.
(5) A skeleton representation with 20 joint points (Shi et al. 2023), as shown in Fig. 5.10. In Fig. 5.10, the names of the human body parts or regions corresponding to each joint point are also indicated.

In addition, in order to evaluate the posture of gymnastics actions, (Jiang et al. 2024) adopted a skeleton representation with the same topology as Fig. 5.10. The only

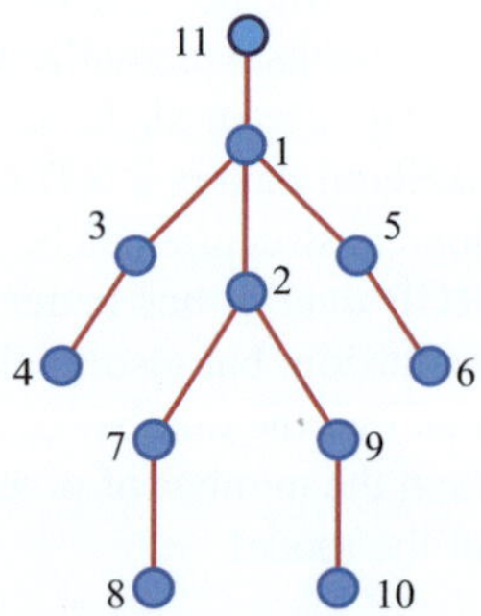

Fig. 5.6 A skeleton representation with 11 joint points (Liu et al. 2020b)

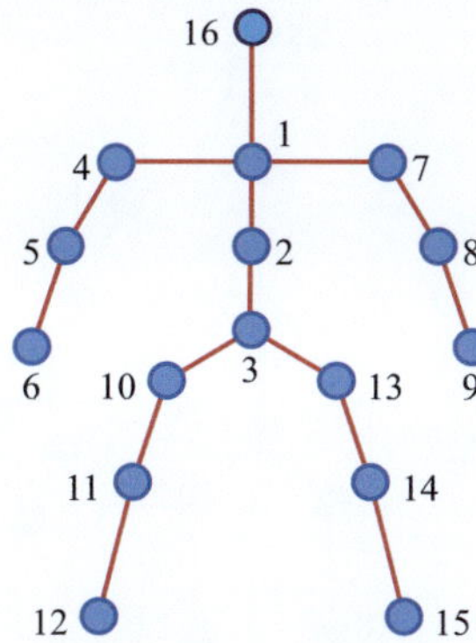

Fig. 5.7 A Skeleton representation with 16 joint points (Ke et al. 2017)

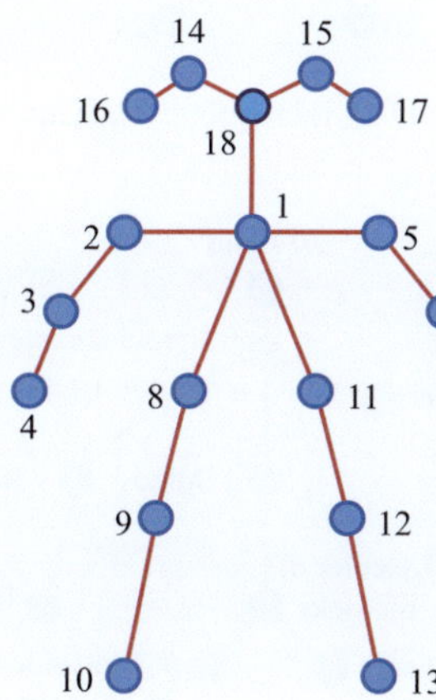

Fig. 5.8 A skeleton representation with 18 joint points (Yan et al. 2018)

differences include, due to the characteristics of gymnastics movements, changing joint point 12 in Fig. 5.10 to the left fingertip; change joint point 13 in Fig. 5.10 to the right fingertip, change joint point 18 in Fig. 5.10 to the tip of the left foot, change joint 19 in Fig. 5.10 to the tip of the right foot.

(6) A skeleton representation with 16 joint points (Du et al. 2024), as shown in Fig. 5.11 (where the names of the corresponding human body parts for each joint point are marked). In Fig. 5.11, these joint points have also been divided into five groups: ① Joints 1, 2, 3; ② Joints 4, 5, 6; ③ Joints 7, 8, 9; ④ Joints 10, 11, 12; ⑤ Joints 13, 14, 15, 16. With this grouping, the motion characteristics of joints in each local group can also be extracted to help determining the human pose and movement.

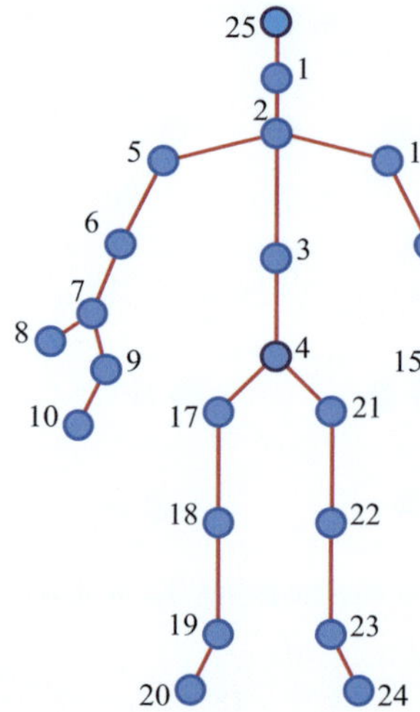

Fig. 5.9 A skeleton representation with 25 joint points (Caetano et al. 2019a)

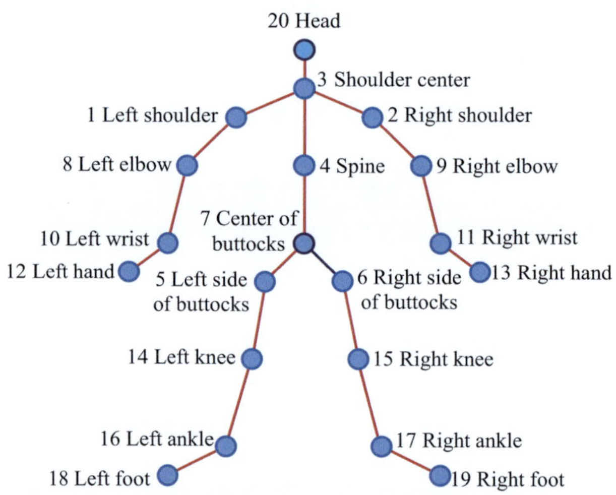

Fig. 5.10 A skeleton representation with 20 joint points (Shi et al. 2023)

(6) A skeleton representation with 14 joint points and 8 motion chains (Du and Ikenaga 2025), as shown in Fig. 5.12 (where the names of the corresponding human body parts for each joint point are marked). In Fig. 5.12, the complex structure of the human body is modeled using highly interconnected joints and motion chains, which can further help understand the structure and motion of the human body. A joint point is the position where two or more joints intersect, and different types of joints allow for different, flexible ranges of motion. The

Fig. 5.11 A skeleton representation with 16 joint points and joint grouping (Du et al. 2024)

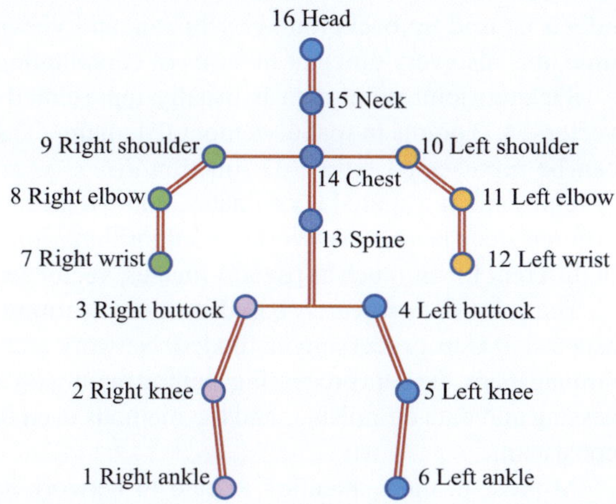

Fig. 5.12 A skeleton representation with 14 joint points and 8 motion chains (Du and Ikenaga 2025)

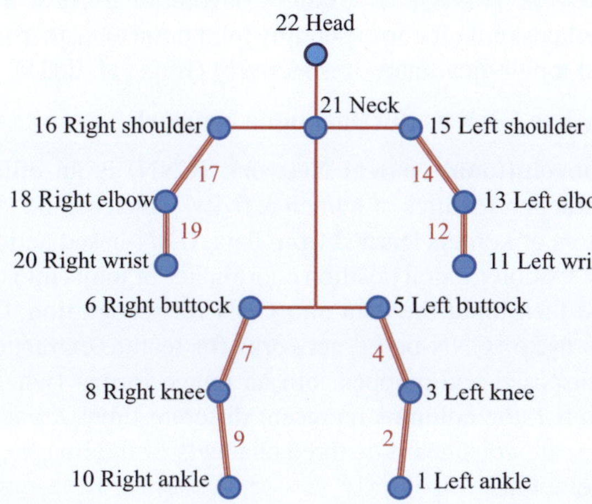

motion chain represents the limbs or body parts between joints, which can be layered, meaning that the movement of higher-level joints affects the position of downstream joints.

5.3.2 Backbone Network Architecture

Activity recognition with the help of action recognition is considered as a high-level recognition. Compared with RGB data and/or depth data, skeleton joint point data corresponds to higher-level features of the human body and is not easily affected by the appearance of the scene. In addition, it can better avoid lighting changes, noise effects caused by background occlusion, and viewing angle changes. At the same time, it is also very efficient in terms of computation and storage.

Skeleton joint point data is usually represented as a series of point coordinate vectors (4-D points in spatial–temporal domain). That is, **joints** (**articulation point**) can be represented by a 5-D function $J(l, x, y, z, t)$, where l is the label, (x, y, z) represents the spatial coordinates, and t represents the temporal coordinates. In different deep learning networks and algorithms, joint point data are often represented in different forms (such as pseudo-images, vector sequences, and topological maps).

The joint data research based on deep learning method mainly involves three aspects: ① Data processing method; ② Network architecture; ③ Data fusion method. Among them, the data processing method mainly involves whether to perform preprocessing and data de-noising, and the methods used for data fusion are also relatively consistent.

At present, more attention is paid to network architecture, and there are three commonly used ones: ① Convolutional Neural Network (CNN); ② Recurrent Neural Network (RNN); ③ Graph Convolutional Network (GCN). The representation methods of their corresponding joint point data are pseudo images, vector sequences, and topological maps, respectively (Liu et al. 2021).

1. **Use CNN as the Backbone Network**

Convolutional Neural Network (CNN) is an efficient network architecture for extracting features of human activity, which can be identified by local convolutional filters or kernels learned from data. CNN-based action recognition methods encode the spatiotemporal position coordinates of joints into rows and columns, respectively, and then input the data into CNN for recognition. Generally, in order to facilitate the use of CNN-based networks for feature extraction, the joint point data will be transposed and mapped into an image format (where the rows represent different joints l, the columns represent different times t, and the 3-D space coordinates (x, y, z) are considered as three channels of the image), and then perform convolution operation.

Table 5.3 briefly summarizes some recent techniques using CNN for activity recognition, they are suitable for improving the detection and recognition accuracy for the complex interactions.

1. **Use RNN as the Backbone Network**

Recurrent neural networks (RNNs) can process sequence data of varying lengths. The activity recognition method based on RNN first represents the joint point data as a vector sequence, which contains the position information of all relevant nodes in a time (state) sequence; then the vector sequence is sent to the activity recognition network with RNN as the backbone. The **Long Short-Term Memory** (LSTM) model is a variant of RNN because its unit states can decide which temporal states should be left behind and which should be forgotten. It has greater advantages in processing time-series data such as joint video.

Table 5.4 briefly summarizes some recent techniques for activity recognition using LSTMs as network structures for activity recognition.

Table 5.3 Some recent technologies using CNN

S/N	Characteristic and description	Advantage and disadvantage	Reference
1	Dual stream fusion of RGB information and joint point information is designed to improve accuracy. Extract key frames before sending RGB video information to CNN to reduce training time	Short training time	(Ji et al. 2019)
2	Use a pose-based approach for activity recognition. The CNN framework includes three semantic modules: ① Spatial posture CNN; ② Temporal posture CNN; ③ Action CNN. It can be used as a supplementary semantic flow of RGB flow and optical flow	The network structure is simple, but the accuracy is not prominent	(Yan et al. 2019)
3	3-D activity recognition based on tree structure and reference joint using skeleton image	Low training efficiency	(Caetano et al. 2019a)
4	The time dynamics are encoded by calculating the motion amplitude and direction of the skeleton joints. Use different time scales to calculate the motion value of the joint to filter the noise	It can effectively filter the motion noise in the data	(Caetano et al. 2019b)
5	Recoding skeleton joint information with geometric algebra	High speed but low accuracy	(Li et al. 2019c)

Table 5.4 Some recent technologies using LSTM

S/N	Characteristic and description	Advantage and disadvantage	Reference
1	Adding multi-mode feature fusion strategy to the trust gate of spatiotemporal LSTM	The recognition accuracy is improved, but the training efficiency is reduced	(Liu et al. 2017a)
2	The **Global Context-aware Attention LSTM** (GCA-LSTM) network, which is mainly composed of two layers of LSTM, is used. The first layer generates global background information, and the second layer adds an attention mechanism to better focus on the key joint points of each frame	It can better focus on the key joint points of each frame	(Liu et al. 2017b)
3	Expand GCA-LSTM and add coarse-grained and fine-grained attention mechanisms	The recognition accuracy is improved, but the training efficiency is reduced	(Liu et al. 2018)
4	A dual stream attention loop LSTM network is proposed. The cyclic relation network learns the spatial features in a single skeleton, and the multilayer LSTM learns the temporal features in the skeleton sequence	Make full use of joint information to improve recognition accuracy	(Zheng et al. 2019)

3. **Use GCN as the Backbone Network**

The collection of human skeleton joints can be viewed as a topology graph. Topological graph is a kind of non-Euclidean structure data, in which the number of adjacent vertices of each node may be different, so it is difficult to calculate convolution with a fixed-size convolution kernel, so it cannot be directly processed by CNN. **Graph convolutional networks** (GCNs) can directly deal with topological graphs. Here, it is only necessary to represent the joint point data as a topology graph, in which the vertices in the space domain are connected by space arcs, the corresponding joint points between adjacent frames in the time domain are connected by time arcs, and the space coordinate vector is used as the attribute feature of each joint point.

Table 5.5 briefly summarizes some recent techniques for using GCNs as network structures for activity recognition.

4. **Use Hybrid Network as the Backbone Network**

Table 5.5 Some recent technologies using GCN

S/N	Characteristic and description	Advantage and disadvantage	Reference
1	Using the higher-order polynomial of adjacency matrix, an encoder-decoder method is designed to capture the implicit joint correlation and obtain the physical structure link between the joints	High model complexity	(Li et al. 2019a)
2	Neural architecture search is used to construct graph convolution network, in which cross entropy evolution strategy is combined with importance hybrid method to improve sampling efficiency and storage efficiency	High sampling and storage efficiency	(Peng et al. 2019)
3	In order to improve the efficiency of spatiotemporal information processing, spatial residual layer and dense connection enhancement block are introduced into spatiotemporal graph convolution network	It is easy to combine with the mainstream spatiotemporal convolution method	(Wu et al. 2019)
4	Based on the motion dependence between human joints and bones, the dual flow adaptive graph convolution network is improved by representing the skeleton data as a directed acyclic graph	High recognition accuracy	(Shi et al. 2019)
5	A novel symbiotic graph convolution network is proposed, which includes not only the activity recognition function module, but also the action prediction module	The two modules promote each other in improving the accuracy of activity recognition and motion prediction	(Li et al. 2019b)
6	Using pseudo graph convolution network with time and channel attention mechanism, not only key frames can be extracted, but also input frames with more features can be filtered out	Key frames can be extracted, but some key information may be ignored	(Yang et al. 2020)

Joint point-based activity recognition research can also use hybrid networks, making full use of the feature extraction capabilities of CNN and GCN in the spatial domain and the advantages of RNN in time series classification. In this case, the original joint node data should be represented by the corresponding data format according to the needs of different hybrid networks.

Table 5.6 briefly summarizes some recent techniques using hybrid networks for activity recognition.

5.3.3 Network Construction Methods

On the basis of skeleton representation, various networks and techniques can be used for recognizing actions and activities. Many networks take the advantages of fusion of different features, information, models, structures, etc. (Dahou et al. 2025), (Hassan and Feizi-Derakhshi 2025). The following gives a brief introduction to some methods for constructing different networks (Ming 2022).

1. **Graph Convolutional Network Combining Spatiotemporal Modeling Features**

This method (Cheng et al. 2021) is based on skeleton representation, which inputs spatiotemporal modeling features into a graph convolutional network for feature learning. The high-order fast Chebyshev polynomial of spectral convolution is used for approximation to detect activities related to the limbs of two persons in multi person interaction actions. In order to increase the accuracy of action recognition, on the one hand, the connections between skeleton joint points were divided into three categories for respective design, and on the other hand, a **Slice Recurrent Neural Network** (SRNN) was used to capture the dependency information of the entire action sequence.

The entire working flowchart is shown in Fig. 5.13. First, OpenPose (Cao et al. 2017) is used to estimate the coordinates of all joint points in the video. Divide the connections of these joint points into three categories: ① Intra frame single person connections; ② Two-person interactive connections; ③ Inter frame connections (the first two are intra frame connections).

In addition to considering the internal connections between joint points, namely physical connections (corresponding to the lines in the skeleton diagram), single person connections also take into account the potential associations representing non-physical connections between joint points (multiple joint points will move simultaneously when performing actions, such as the left and right hands moving towards each other when clapping). In addition to considering the corresponding connections of joints that are prone to similar changes (such as when two persons embrace, their actions are basically the same), interactive connections also consider the potential connections between other joints. In addition to considering the connections between joint points within the original frame, inter frame connections also need

Table 5.6 Some recent technologies using hybrid networks

S/N	Network	Characteristic and description	Advantage and disadvantage	Reference
1	CNN + LSTM	A view adaptive scheme including two view adaptive neural networks is designed. The view adaptive loop network is composed of the main LSTM and the view adaptive sub network, which sends the joint point representation under the new viewpoint to the main LSTM network to determine the activity recognition. The view adaptive convolution network is composed of the main CNN and the view adaptive sub network, which sends the joint point representation under the new observation viewpoint to the main CNN to determine the activity category. Finally, the classification scores of the two parts of the network are fused	It combines the advantages of CNN to extract activity features in the spatial domain and RNN to extract activity features in the time domain. Changes in different perspectives have little effect on the recognition results	(Zhang et al. 2019)
2	CNN + GCN	Combining CNN and GCN, it does not only consider the extraction of activity characteristics in space–time domain, but also learning frequency patterns with the help of residual frequency attention method	Added learning of frequency	(Hu et al. 2019)

(continued)

Table 5.6 (continued)

S/N	Network	Characteristic and description	Advantage and disadvantage	Reference
3	GCN + LSTM	Using the **Attention-enhancement Graph Convolution** LSTM (AGC-LSTM) network, it can not only extract the activity features in the spatial and temporal domains, but also increase the time duration at the top AGC-LSTM layer by adding the time perception field, so as to enhance the ability to learn the high-level features, and to reduce the computational cost	Enhanced ability to learn high-level features and reduced computational cost	(Si et al. 2019)
4	GCN + LSTM	Learning spatiotemporal context information from human joint point data with focusing and diffusion mechanism by using bidirectional attention graph convolution network	High recognition accuracy	(Gao et al. 2019)
5	GCN + CNN	The semantics of the joint points (frame index and joint type) are fed to the semantic perception graph convolution layer and the semantic perception convolution layer together with the position and speed of the joint points as part of the network input	Reduced model complexity and improved recognition accuracy	(Zhang et al. 2020)

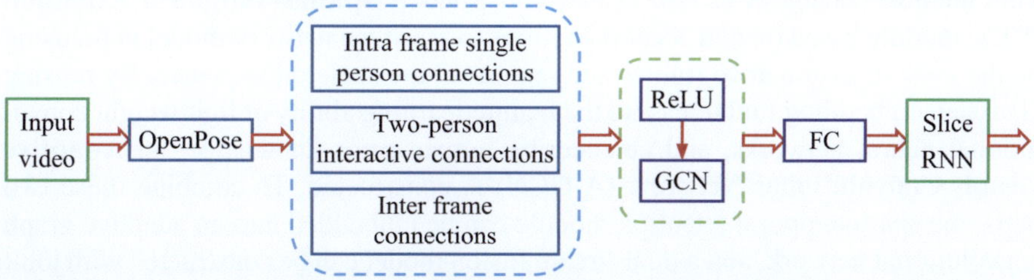

Fig. 5.13 Graph convolutional network combining spatiotemporal modeling features

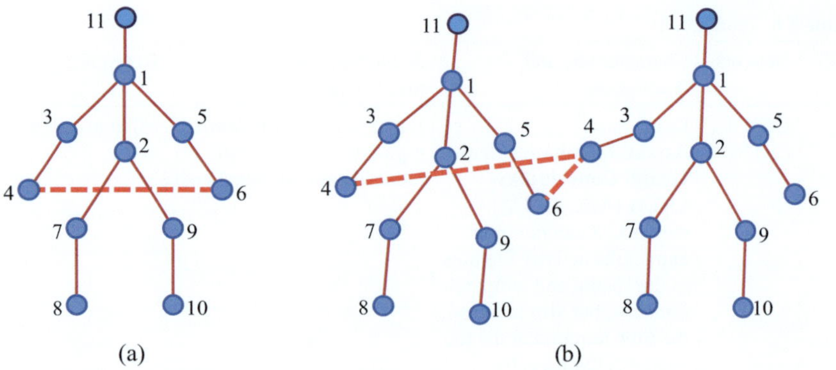

Fig. 5.14 Two examples of intra frame connections each

to consider the connections between a joint point in the current frame and its corresponding neighborhoods in the previous and next frames (due to temporal variations). Figure 5.14 shows examples of the first two types of intra frame connections. The thick dashed line in Fig. 5.14a indicates a correlation between the movements of the left and right hands during clapping. The thick dashed line in Fig. 5.14b indicates a person shaking hands with another person using both hands.

In order to obtain dependency information of action sequences, **Recurrent Neural Networks** (RNNs) can be used for processing time series. However, in traditional RNNs, the current node information is only related to the previous node, which can only model short-term dynamic information. Therefore, a sliced RNN network model is needed to solve this problem. In the sliced RNN model, the input sequence is divided into multiple sequence segments, and an independent RNN network is used for computation on each segment. If RNN feature extraction is performed on each relatively short sequence segment, the information transfer between layers can preserve long-term dependency information to a greater extent.

2. **Combining Spatiotemporal Attention Mechanism and Adaptive Graph Convolutional Network**

This method (Zhang et al. 2021) first constructs a **Spatial–Temporal Attention** (STA) module based on non-local operations to assist the network model in focusing on the most discriminative frames and regions in the skeleton sequence. By reusing Gaussian embedding functions and the feature learning ability of lightweight convolutional neural networks, and considering human prior knowledge, an **Adaptive Graph Convolutional Network** (A-GCN) is constructed. To combine these two parts, the spatiotemporal attention module can be embedded into an adaptive graph convolutional network, and a dual stream fusion model can be constructed with joint information, skeleton information, and their respective motion information to achieve activity recognition.

The spatiotemporal attention module includes a spatial attention module and a temporal attention module. These two modules can respectively capture the correlation information between intra frame joints and inter frame joints. The input feature dimension of the spatiotemporal attention module is the same as the output feature dimension and can be embedded between various convolutional layers. The feature dimension here is the product of the number of channels, frames, and joints.

In adaptive graph convolutional networks, both prior knowledge constructed by the human body (representing the topological structure of the graph's adjacency matrix) and global contextual information (generated by data-driven adjacency matrix) are considered.

In dual stream fusion, the joint information related to the joint position, skeleton information related to the direction of the joint connection, and their respective motion information (joint motion information can be represented by the vector pointing from the source joint point to the target joint point, and skeleton motion information can be represented by the change vector between the joint point source connection and the joint point target connection) are first fused into two network branches. Then, the individual models are trained from each network branch. Finally, by fusing the two models, the final prediction result can be obtained.

3. **Graph Convolutional Network with Spatial–Temporal Feature Enhancement**

This method (Cao et al. 2023) proposes using **Spatial–Temporal Feature Enhanced Graph Convolutional Network** (STFE-GCN) for multi-steam activity recognition. The network includes an L-layer (in reality, $L = 10$) spatial–temporal feature enhancement graph convolution module, which mainly incorporated spatial feature enhancement, temporal feature enhancement, and channel attention modules, as shown in Fig. 5.15.

In the spatial feature enhancement module, the **Graph Attention Mechanism** (GAT) in the spatial domain is used (Veličković 2018) to mine the structural features of the human body spatial domain. Specifically, different weight coefficients are assigned based on the importance of the connection between joint points and adjacent joint points, and an attention coefficient matrix is generated to replace the original adjacency matrix that represents the topological structure of the human body.

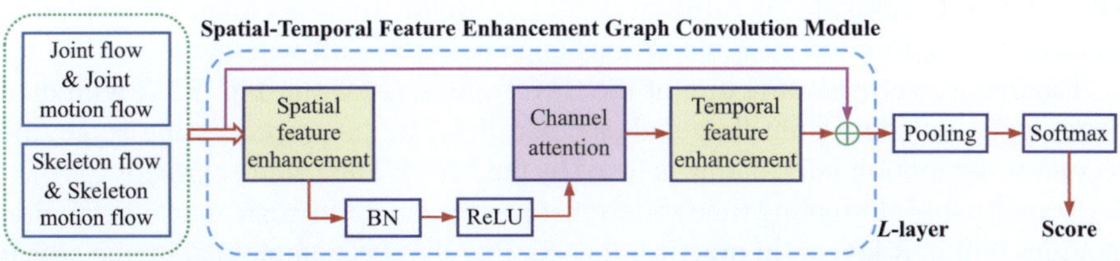

Fig. 5.15 Graph convolutional network with spatiotemporal feature enhancement

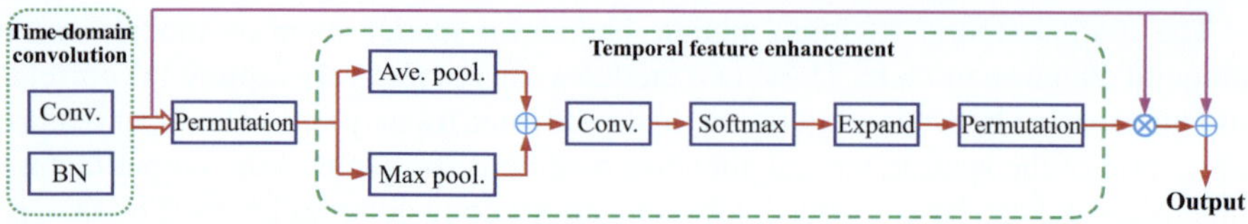

Fig. 5.16 Time domain feature enhancement module

The channel attention module utilizes the **Efficient Channel Attention Network** (ECA-Net) (Wang et al. 2019) to enhance channel attention, which is beneficial for the model to extract spatiotemporal features of samples.

The temporal feature enhancement module adopts a hybrid pooling method to enhance time-domain feature extraction, and its framework and process can be seen in Fig. 5.16. For the input features, activity features are first extracted through convolution, and then Batch Normalization (BN) is performed (their combination is called time-domain convolution). Next, the channel and time domains are dimension swapped, and feature extraction and fusion are performed in parallel using average pooling (extracting global contextual features in the time domain) and max pooling (extracting key action features in the time domain). In the following, the fused features are extracted through convolution, normalized using the Softmax function, and expanded to the feature size before mixing pooling using the "Expand" function. The channel and temporal dimensions are then permuted and multiplied with the residuals. Finally, the permutation result obtained by multiplication in this way is added to the residual to obtain the final feature output. The temporal feature enhancement module not only extracts time-domain key action features and global contextual features, but also combines the features extracted by time-domain convolution, thus being able to extract comprehensive time-domain features from activity information.

4. Space–Time Correlated Transformer

This method (Lu and Yang 2024) constructs a **Spatial–Temporal Correlated Transformer** (STCTrans), which mainly includes designing a **Motion Fusion Module** (MFM) to fuse motion flow information into the basic flow branch to reduce training costs, designing a local spatiotemporal module that integrates time shift transformer to construct short-term spatiotemporal joint dependencies, and designing a **Multi-Scale Temporal Convolution** (MSTC) module to extract long-term temporal features and to promote information exchange between shift windows.

The overall network structure of the STCTrans is shown in Fig. 5.17, with dual flow inputs including joint flow and skeleton flow. In the preprocessing stage, the second-order motion information is fused by the MFM. The feature extraction is then performed using alternating time shift transformers and multi-scale time convolution modules within R layers (in practice, $R = 8$). Finally, it is compressed by the global average pooling layer and sent to the Softmax classifier to obtain the final prediction score.

A comparative experiment was conducted between this method and some related methods using two databases, NTU RGB + D and NTU RGB + D 120 (see

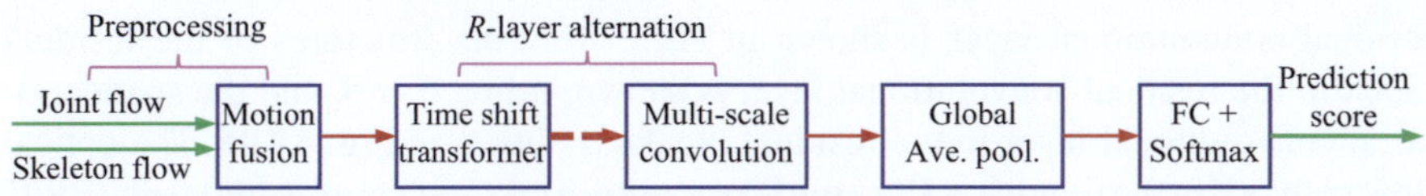

Fig. 5.17 Overall network structure of the space–time correlated transformer

Sect. 5.3.3) (Liu et al. 2020a). Table 5.7 presents some experimental results on the NTU RGB + D 120 database (Lu and Yang 2024, with bold numbers indicate the best. This database contains 114,480 skeleton sequence samples obtained from 155 different camera angles and from 106 individuals (113,945 were used in the experiment). Among them, each skeleton sequence sample contains 3-D coordinate data of 25 joint points (Fig. 5.19). This database contains 120 action categories, and the evaluation of effectiveness can be divided into two situations: ①**Cross Sub** (X-Sub): Divided into training set (63,026) and testing set (50,919) based on the person's ID; ② **Cross Setup** (X-Set): Divided into training set (54,468) and testing set (59,477) based on sample ID.

5. **Two-Stream Non-Local Spatiotemporal Residual Convolution Neural Network**

This method (Qian et al. 2024) combines **3-D Convolutional Neural Network** (3-D CNN) and **Two-Stream Convolutional Neural Network** (TS CNN) to construct a channel pruning based **Two-Stream Non-Local Spatiotemporal Residual Convolutional Neural Network** (TNLST ResCNN).

This network adopts a dual stream architecture, including a temporal stream subnetwork and a spatial stream subnetwork. These two subnetworks separately use **Spatial–Temporal Residual Convolutional Neural Networks** (ST ResCNN). Finally, the mean fusion algorithm is used to fuse the recognition results of the two subnetworks. The overall architecture of the network is shown in Fig. 5.18a, where the structures of the non-residual convolutional layer is shown in Fig. 5.18b, the

Table 5.7 Comparison of different methods on NTU RGB+D 120 database

Method (reference)	X-Sub%	X-Set%	Parameter/M
MS-G3D Net (Liu et al. 2020b)	86.9	88.4	6.38
Dynamic-GCN (Ye et al. 2020)	**87.3**	88.6	14.40
Shift-GCN (Cheng et al. 2020)	85.9	87.6	2.76
ST-TR (Plizzari et al. 2021)	84.3	86.7	12.10
2 s MST-GCN (Chen et al. 2021)	87.0	88.3	6.0
TaCNN + (Xu et al. 2022)	86.7	87.3	4.4
STFE-GCN (Cao et al. 2023)	84.1	86.3	—
MSSTNet (Cheng et al. 2023)	85.3	86.0	39.60
STCTrans (Lu et al. 2024)	87.2	**89.3**	4.34

residual convolutional layer is shown in Fig. 5.18c, the structures of the residual block in the residual convolutional layer is shown in Fig. 5.18d, and the spatiotemporal convolutional layer in the residual blocks is shown in Fig. 5.18e. The optical flow network in the figure is a **Pyramid, Warping, and Cost volume network** (PWC net) (Sun et al. 2018), where BN represents **batch normalization** and LR represents **leaky Rectifier Linear Unit** (leaky ReLU).

In order to reduce the complexity of the network, a channel pruning scheme for spatiotemporal residual convolutional neural networks (Qian et al. 2024) was adopted to compress the model while maintaining its recognition accuracy. In order to enable the compressed network to better learn the long-range spatiotemporal dependencies of human behavior changes in the input video, a non-local module is introduced

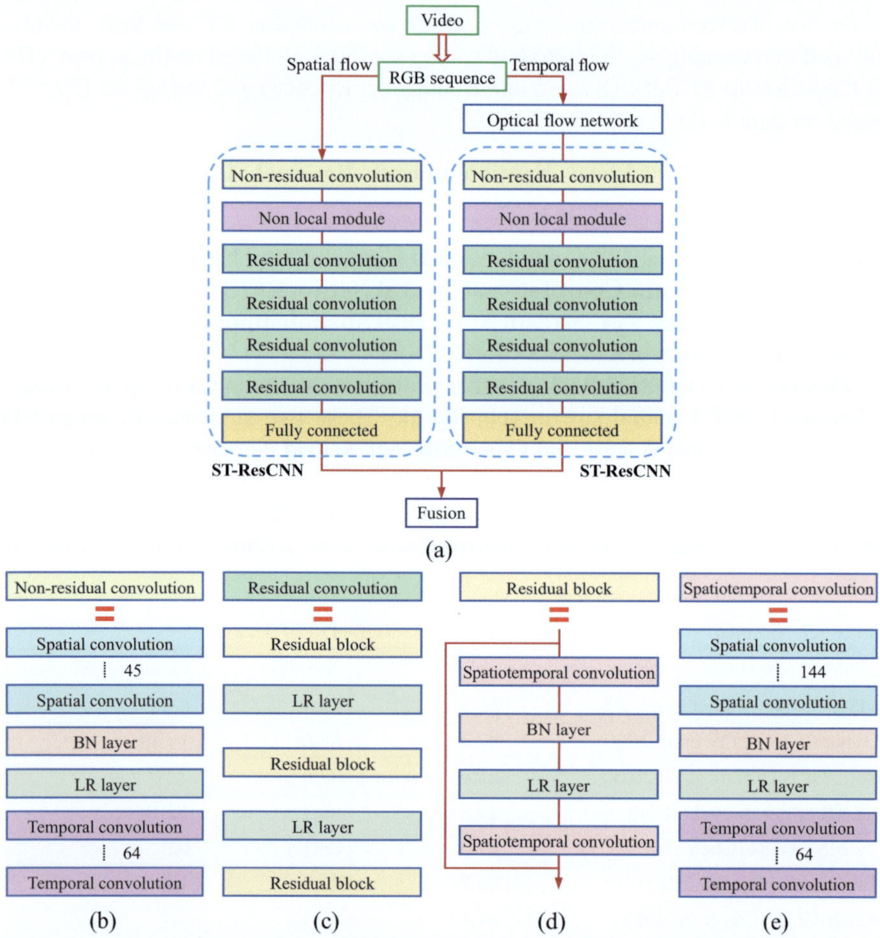

Fig. 5.18 Two-stream non-local spatiotemporal residual convolution neural network

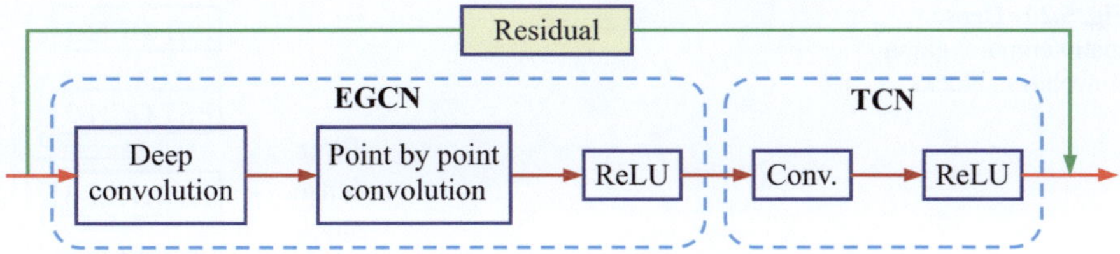

Fig. 5.19 Enhanced spatiotemporal graph convolutional network

before the first residual spatiotemporal convolution block of the pruned network to improve the recognition accuracy of the network, as shown in Fig. 5.18a.

6. **Improved Spatiotemporal Graph Convolutional Network**

This method (Lei et al. 2024) improves the traditional **Spatial–Temporal Graph Convolutional Network** (ST-GCN) in three aspects: ① Adopting an Enhanced Spatiotemporal Graph Convolutional Network (EST-GCN) to improve the network's ability to represent information between nodes; ② Introducing single-mode skeleton data into cascaded dense spatiotemporal graph convolution blocks to obtain rich spatiotemporal feature information and improve feature reuse rate; ③ A motion feature factor was introduced to measure the importance of different joints in the limbs, in order to improve the recognition performance of the model.

(1) Enhanced spatiotemporal graph convolutional network

The traditional ST-GCN utilizes both **Graph Convolutional Network** (GCN) and **Temporal Convolutional Network** (TCN) to simultaneously perform spatiotemporal feature sampling. GCN uses point by point convolution to sample individual nodes, taking into account the information of the nodes themselves, but ignoring the internal connections with other joints. **Enhanced Spatiotemporal Graph Convolutional Network** (EST-GCN) replaces GCN with **Enhanced Graph Convolutional Network** (EGCN) to complete spatial sampling of human joint information. EGCN uses depth-wise separable convolution, including depth-wise convolution and point-wise convolution. Deep convolution completes independent convolution on each channel, and the point by point convolution generates new feature maps using spatial position feature information. The enhanced spatiotemporal graph convolutional network is shown in Fig. 5.19, where the same TCN is still used in the time domain as ST-GCN, but EGCN and TCN are connected using residuals.

(2) Dense spatiotemporal graph convolution blocks

The traditional Spatiotemporal Graph Convolutional Network (ST-GCN) is composed of 10 layers of spatiotemporal graph convolution units cascaded together. The increase in model depth can enable the network to obtain high-level semantic information, but it ignores the rich features of lower levels. Dense connections attach low-level features to the back of the current layer features through concatenation, ensuring that each feature is reused, which can compensate for this drawback and improve the learning efficiency of the network for features.

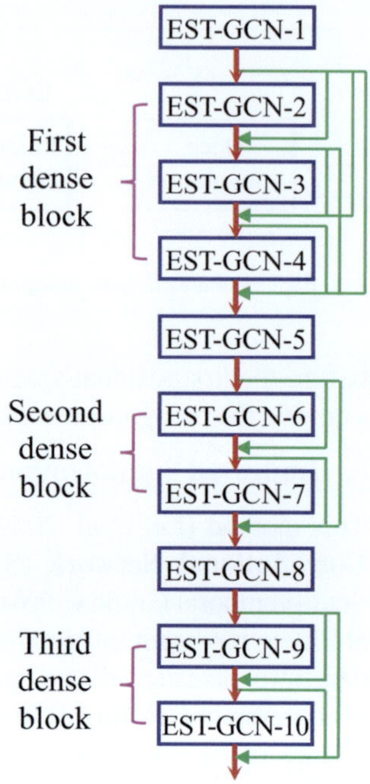

Fig. 5.20 Dense spatiotemporal graph convolution blocks

Referring to Fig. 5.20, a skip dense connection is used to divide the 10 layers of EST-GCN into 3 dense spatiotemporal graph convolution blocks, with dense connections only performed inside each dense block. Use an EST-GCN between two dense blocks to avoid increasing the number of channels and complete the down-sampling operation, so that each dense block still contains information from all previous layers. In Fig. 5.20, the first EST-GCN layer is the input layer, the second to fourth layers are the first dense block, the fifth layer is the transition layer, the sixth to seventh layers are the second dense block, the eighth layer is the transition layer, and the ninth to tenth layers are the third dense block.

(3) Motion feature factor

In practical applications, the degree of motion of each joint is different, and its contribution to motion recognition is also different. For this reason, different divisions can be performed on the joint points (including unique division, distance-based division, spatial configuration division, etc.) to obtain subsets with different characteristics. Next, different subsets are given different attentions based on their motion amplitudes using motion feature factors to help the network obtaining more accurate and favorable information.

References

Abu-Bakar S A R. Advances in human action recognition: An updated survey. IET Image Processing, 13(13): 2381-2394 (2019).

Caetano C, Bremond F, Schwartz W R. Skeleton image representation for 3D action recognition based on tree structure and reference joints. SIBGRAPI Conference on Graphics, Patterns and Images, 16–23 (2019a).

Caetano C, Sena J, Bremond F, *et al.* SkeleMotion: A new representation of skeleton joint sequences based on motion information for 3D action recognition. Proc. Advanced Video and Signal Based Surveillance, 1–8 (2019b).

Cao Z, Simon T, Wei S E, *et al.* Realtime multi-person 2D pose estimation using part affinity fields. Proc. CVPR, 1302–1310 (2017).

Cao Y, Wu W G, Li P, *et al.* Skeleton action recognition based on spatiotemporal feature enhanced graph convolutional network. Journal of Electronics & Information Technology, 45(8): 3022-3031 (2023).

Chen Y X, Zhang Z Q, Yuan C F, *et al.* Channel-wise topology refinement graph convolution for skeleton-based action recognition. Proc. ICCV, 13339–13348 (2021).

Cheng K, Zhang Y F, He X Y, *et al.* Skeleton based action recognition with shift graph convolutional network. Proc. CVPR, 180–189 (2020).

Cheng K Y, Wu J X, Wang W S, *et al.* multi-person interaction action recognition based on spatiotemporal graph convolution. Journal of Image and Graphics, 26(7): 1681-1691 (2021).

Cheng Q, Cheng J, Ren Z L, *et al.* Multiscale spatial-temporal convolutional neural network for skeleton-based action recognition. Pattern Analysis and Applications, 26(3): 1303-1315 (2023).

Dahou A, Al-qaness M A A, Abd Elaziz M, *et al.* Ensemble learning with temporal fusion for human activity recognition using model-based augmentation. Biomedical Signal Processing and Control, 110(A): 108168. https://doi.org/10.1016/j.bspc.2025.108168 (2025).

Du S L, Yuan Z, Ikenaga T. Kinematics-aware spatial-temporal feature transform for 3D human pose estimation. Pattern Recognition, 150, 110316 (2024).

Du S L, Ikenaga T. Human Pose Analysis: Deep Learning Meets Human Kinematics in Video, Springer Nature, Singapore (2025).

Forsyth D, Ponce J. Computer Vision: A Modern Approach, 2nd Ed. Prentice Hall (2012).

Gayathri T, Mamatha H R. How to improve video analytics with action recognition: A survey. ACM Computing Surveys, 57(1), https://doi.org/10.1145/3679011 (2025).

Gao J L, He T, Zhou X, *et al.* Focusing and diffusion: Bidirectional attentive graph convolutional networks for skeleton-based action recognition. arXiv: 1912.11521 (2019).

Hassan A A R, Feizi-Derakhshi M R. ResCBAR-FusionNet: A hybrid CNN-BiGRU-attention model for human activity recognition. Signal, Image and Video Processing, 19(8): 675. https://doi.org/10.1007/s11760-025-04286-2 (2025).

Host K, Ivasic-Kos M. An overview of human action recognition in sports based on computer vision. HELIYON, 8(6), https://doi.org/10.1016/j.heliyon.2022.e09633 (2022).

Hu G Y, Cui B, Yu S. Skeleton-based action recognition with synchronous local and non-local spatiotemporal learning and frequency attention. Proc. Multimedia and Expo, 1216–1221 (2019).

Ji X F, Qin L L, Wang Y Y. Human interaction recognition based on RGB and skeleton data fusion model. Journal of Computer Applications, 39(11): 3349-3354 (2019).

Jiang J H, Xia N, Li C W, *et al.* Ivasic-Kos M. Keypoint Detection Method for Single Person Gymnastics Actions Based on Multi-Scale Incremental Learning. Acta Electronica Sinica, 52(5): 1730–1742 (2024).

Karthika S, Jane Y N, Nehemiah H K. Spatiotemporal 3D skeleton kinematic joint point classification model for human activity recognition. Journal of Visual Communication and Image Representation, 110, 104471. https://doi.org/10.1016/j.jvcir.2025.104471 (2025).

Ke Q H, Bennamoun M, An S J, *et al.* A new representation of skeleton sequences for 3D action recognition. Proc. CVPR, 4570–4579 (2017).

Kumar P, Chauhan S, Awasthi L K. Human activity recognition (HAR) using deep learning: Review, methodologies, progress and future research directions. Archives of Computational Methods in Engineering, 31(1): 179-219 (2024).
Lei J S, Liu S G, Liu Q S, *et al.* Human Interaction Behavior recognition based on improved spatial temporal graph convolution network. Computer Applications and Software, 41(4): 151-158 (2024).
Li M S, Chen S H, Chen X, *et al.* Actional-structural graph convolutional networks for skeleton-based action recognition. Proc. CVPR, 3595–3603 (2019a).
LI M S, CHEN S H, CHEN X, *et al.* Symbiotic graph neural networks for 3D skeleton-based human action recognition and motion prediction. arXiv: 1910.02212 (2019b).
Li Y S, Xia R J, Liu X, *et al.* Learning shape motion representations from geometric algebra spatiotemporal model for skeleton-based action recognition. Proc. Multimedia and Expo, 1066–1071 (2019c).
Li J N, Wang D K, Zhang S L. Deep-learning-based 2D human pose estimation. Chinese Journal of Computers, 47(1): 231-250 (2024).
Liu J, Shahroudy A, Xu D, *et al.* Skeleton-based action recognition using spatiotemporal LSTM network with trust gates. IEEE Trans. PAMI, 40(12): 3007-3021 (2017a).
Liu J, Wang G, Hu P, *et al.* Global context-ware attention LSTM networks for 3D action recognition. Proc. CVPR, 1647–1656 (2017b).
Liu J, Wang G, Duan L Y, *et al.* Skeleton-based human action recognition with global context-aware attention LSTM networks. IEEE Trans. IP, 27(4): 1586-1599 (2018).
Liu J, Shahroudy A, Perez M, *et al.* NTU RGB+D 120: A large scale benchmark for 3D human activity understanding. IEEE T-PAMI, 42(10): 2684-2701 (2020a).
Liu Z Y, Zhang H W, Chen Z H, *et al.* Disentangling and unifying graph convolutions for skeleton-based action recognition. Proc. CVPR, 140–149 (2020b).
Liu Y, Xue P P, Li H, *et al.* A review of action recognition using joints based on deep learning. Journal of Electronics & Information Technology, 43(6): 1789-1802 (2021).
Lu X L, Yang J Q. Space-time-correlated transformer for skeleton-based action recognition. Signal Processing, 40(4): 766-775 (2024).
Luo S W. The Perception Computing of Visual Information. Beijing: Science Press (2010).
Maley C J. Computation for cognitive science: Analog versus digital. Wiley Interdisciplinary Reviews-Cognitive Science, 15(4). https://doi.org/10.1002/wcs.1679 (2024).
Ming Y M. Dynamic Temporal Graph Convolutional Network for Skeleton-Based Action Recognition (Dissertation). Beijing, Tsinghua University (2022).
Miranda L, Viterbo J, Bernardini F. A survey on the use of machine learning methods in context-aware middlewares for human activity recognition. Artificial Intelligence Review, 55(1): 3369-3400 (2022).
Peng W, Hong XP, Chen H Y, *et al.* Learning graph convolutional network for skeleton-based human action recognition by neural searching. arXiv: 1911.04131 (2019).
Plizzari C, Cannici M, Matteucci M. Skeleton based action recognition via spatial and temporal transformer networks. Computer Vision and Image Understanding, 208: #103219 (2021).
Qian H M, Chen S, Huangpu X Y. Human Activities Recognition Based on Two-stream NonLocal Spatial Temporal Residual Convolution Neural Network. Journal of Electronics & Information Technology, 46(3): 1100-1108 (2024).
Saha A, Rajak S, Saha J, *et al.* A survey of machine learning and meta-heuristics Approaches for sensor-based human activity recognition systems. Journal of Ambient Intelligence and Humanized Computing, 15(1): 29-56 (2024).
Shi L, Zhang Y F, Cheng J, *et al.* Skeleton-based action recognition with directed graph neural networks. Proc. CVPR, 7912–7921 (2019).
Shi H Y, Hou Z J, Chao X, *et al.* Multimodal spatial-temporal feature representation and its application in action recognition. Journal of Image and Graphics, 28(4): 1041-1055 (2023).
Shih K J, Singh S, Hoiem D. Where to look: Focus regions for visual question answering. CVPR, 4613–4621 (2016).

Si C Y, Chen W T, Wang W, *et al.* An attention enhanced graph convolutional LSTM network for skeleton-based action recognition. Proc. CVPR, 1227–1236 (2019).

Sun D Q, Yang X D, Liu M Y, *et al.* PWC-net: CNNs for optical flow using pyramid, warping, and cost volume. Proc. CVPR, 8934–8943 (2018).

Turaga P, Chellappa R, Subrahmanian V S, *et al.* Machine recognition of human activities: A survey. IEEE-CSVT, 18(11): 1473-1488 (2008).

Veličković P, Cucurull G, Casanova A, *et al.* Graph attention networks. Proc. ICLR, 1254–1263 (2018).

Wang Q L, Wu B G, Zhu P F, *et al.* ECA-Net: Efficient channel attention for deep convolutional neural networks. https://doi.org/10.48550/arXiv.1910.03151 (2019).

Wu Q, Teney D, Wang P, *et al.* Visual question answering: A survey of methods and datasets. CVIU, 163: 21-40 (2017).

Wu C, Wu X J, Kittler J. Spatial residual layer and dense connection block enhanced spatial temporal graph convolutional network for skeleton-based action recognition. Proc. ICCV Workshop, 1–5 (2019).

Xu C L, Hsieh S H, Xiong C M, *et al.* Can humans fly? Action understanding with multiple classes of actors. Proc. CVPR, 2264–2273 (2015).

Xu C L, Corso J J. Actor-action semantic segmentation with grouping process models. Proc. CVPR, 3083–3092 (2016).

Xu K L, Ye F F, Zhong Q Y, *et al.* Topology-aware convolutional neural network for efficient skeleton-based action recognition. Proc. AAAI, 36(3): 2866-2874 (2022).

Xu L H, Zhao L, Sun X X, *et al.* A comprehensive review of progress in deep-learning-based occluded human pose estimation. Journal of Image and Graphics, 29(12): 3529-3542 (2024).

Yan S J, Xiong Y J, Lin D H. Spatial temporal graph convolutional networks for skeleton-based action recognition. Proc. 32nd AAAI, 7444–7452 (2018).

Yan A, Wang Y L, Li Z F, *et al.* PA3D: Pose-action 3D machine for video recognition. Proc. CVPR, 7922–7931 (2019).

Yan R, Ge X J, Huang P, *et al.* A survey of group activity Recognition Based on Deep Learning. Chinese Journal of Computers, 47(11): 2552-2578 (2024).

Yang H Y, Gu Y Z, Zhu J C, *et al.* PGCNTCA: Pseudo graph convolutional network with temporal and channel-wise attention for skeleton-based action recognition. IEEE Access, 8: 10040-10047 (2020).

Ye F F, Pu S L, Zhong Q Y, *et al.* Dynamic GCN: Context-enriched topology learning for skeleton-based action recognition. Proc. ACM ICM, 55–63 (2020).

Zhang P F, Lan C L, Xing J L, *et al.* View adaptive neural networks for high performance skeleton-based human action recognition. IEEE Trans. PAMI, 41(8): 1963-1978 (2019).

Zhang P F, Lan C L, Zeng W J, *et al.* Semantics-guided neural networks for efficient skeleton-based human action recognition. Proc. CVPR, 1109–1118 (2020).

Zhang J X, Liu R H, Jin C X, *et al.* Skeleton-based action recognition on spatiotemporal attention mechanism and adaptive graph convolutional network. Signal Processing, 37(7): 1226-1237 (2021).

Zhang T Y, Min W Q, Han X Y, *et al.* A survey on future action anticipation in videos. Chinese Journal of Computers, 46(6): 1315-1338 (2023).

Zhang Y-J. Image Engineering (V.2): Image Analysis (5th Edition). Beijing: Tsinghua University Press (2024a).

Zhang Y-J. Image Engineering (V.3): Image Understanding (5th Edition). Beijing: Tsinghua University Press (2024b).

Zheng W, Li L, Zhang Z X, *et al.* Relational network for skeleton-based action recognition. Proc. Multimedia and Expo, 826–831 (2019).

Chapter 6
Detection of Human-Object Interaction Activity

Human-Object Interaction (HOI) is a special activity that reflects the mutual relationship between human and objects in a specific application scenario (Wang et al. 2024). Human object interaction is a common behavior, and the initiator generally has a clear purpose (Han et al. 2025).

Human-object interaction detection aims to finely locate individuals who produce specific action behaviors in images or videos, as well as objects that interact with them (Lee et al. 2024), in order to understand and analyze human behavior by recognizing the action relationships between humans and objects (Leonardi et al. 2024), and can also help identify group behavior (Liu et al. 2022).

The detection of human-object interaction is a task of locating humans and objects in a scene and predicting their interactions (Indermun et al. 2024). It can also be seen as using images or videos as input to detect humans and objects with interactive behaviors and their interactions (Parasa et al. 2024).

The sections of this chapter are arranged as follows.

Section 6.1 introduces both two-stage and single-stage methods for detecting human-object interaction relationships.

Section 6.2 analyzes the detection methods of human-object interaction relationship based on transformer and attention mechanism.

Section 6.3 introduces several other typical detection methods for human-object interaction relationships with distinctive features.

Section 6.4 introduces some databases used for detecting human-object interaction relationships and several evaluation indicators for the performance evaluation of detection methods.

Y.-J. Zhang, *Spatiotemporal Image Understanding*,
https://doi.org/10.1007/978-981-95-7130-7_6

6.1 Two-Stage and Single-Stage Methods

From the perspective of implementing interaction detection techniques, existing methods can be divided into two-stage methods and single-stage methods (Hakala and Hakkinen 2022).

6.1.1 Two-Stage Methods

Two-stage human-object interaction detection is an instance guided, bottom-up deep learning method that first detects instances of the target human (H) and object (O) in the image; then the instances of humans and objects are associated to determine the corresponding interaction relationship (I). This two-stage process is shown in Fig. 6.1.

1. **Basic Architecture**

The two-stage method generally consists of two serial modules: the target detection (also known as instance detection) module and the interaction association (also known as interaction prediction or interaction inference) module.

For example, the **Cascaded Parsing of Human-Object Interaction** (CP-HOI) network can achieve multi-stage, structured HOI detection (Zhou et al. 2022). At each cascading stage, the target detection module gradually refines the HOI recommendations and provides them to the structured interaction prediction module. The structured interaction prediction module is built on the basis of **Graph Parsing Neural Network** (GPNN), which integrates learning and inference, iteratively parsing the HOI structure and inferring the HOI representation (i.e. targets and relational features).

Figure 6.2 shows the process architecture of a typical two-stage HOI detection method (Antoun and Asmar 2023). In the first stage, all targets (including humans and objects) are first detected from the original image. Then, considering possible interactions of human-object pairs, the bounding boxes of humans and objects are cropped, and these boxes are provided to a **Convolutional Neural Network** (CNN). In the second stage, CNN is used to extract features from images of possible interactions of human-object pairs, such as appearance, spatial, posture, semantic, and graph features, etc., which can be connected in different ways to predict or classify interactions between candidate human-object pairs.

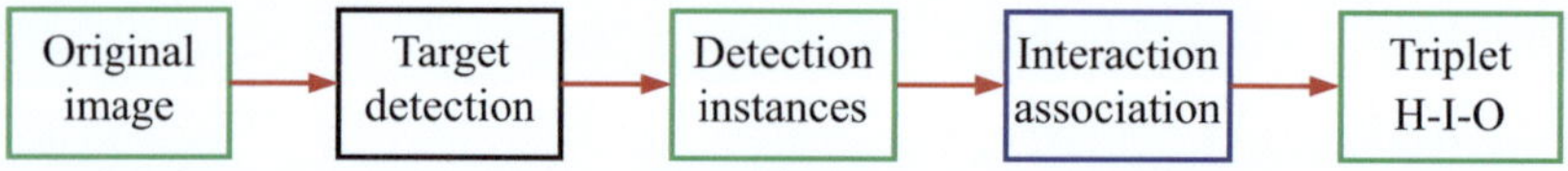

Fig. 6.1 Two-stage human-object interaction detection

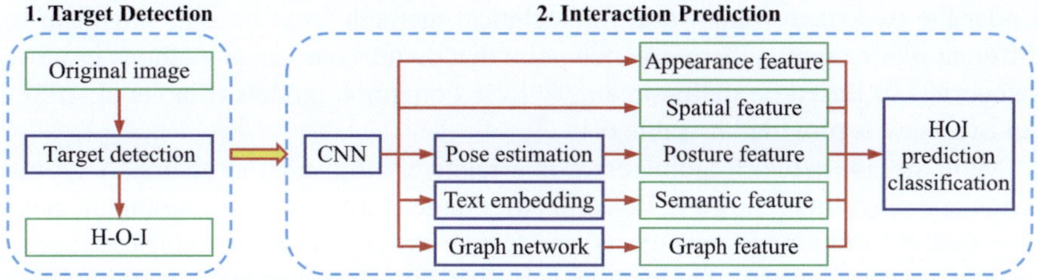

Fig. 6.2 Two-stage human-object interaction detection process architecture

Most two-stage methods use existing target detection models and mainly focus on the architecture of interaction prediction models. Among them, the extraction of various image features is also a key focus and affects the specific form of the architecture.

Appearance features are the most commonly used features in interaction detection. Deep learning techniques are often used to directly extract apparent features from the entire image, providing context about the interaction scene. In addition, appearance features are usually extracted separately for each pair of human-object interaction, where the appearance features of humans provide information about the action subject, while the appearance features of objects provide information about the action object. In the two-stage approach, the main utilization includes appearance features from individuals and objects alone, sometimes including their combined appearance features as well as appearance features from the entire image.

Spatial features can be extracted from the bounding boxes of detected humans and objects. It is generally difficult to estimate the true distance between interaction pairs from 2-D images. But the spatial relative relationship between interaction pairs can be encoded using the relationship between the bounding boxes of humans and objects.

The introduction of posture features can assist with appearance and spatial features, thereby enhancing the predictive classification of HOI. However, because a human may be obscured by another human or object, their posture and body parts cannot always be determined in the image (and may also be cropped from the image). Therefore, it is usually not possible to predict classification HOI solely based on posture features.

Semantic features often come from the embedding of semantic words, which is the process of using semantic words to represent detected targets or actions. Typical examples include image captioning (annotation) and visual Q&A. Semantic word embedding features are considered semantic features because they often generalize to the same type of targets (such as players, balls, drivers, cars, etc.). Therefore, semantically similar objects can lead to similar interactions.

Graph features can come from different **Graph Neural Networks** (GNNs). Below, the relevant features will be introduced separately with different methods.

2. **Two Types of Two-Stage Methods**

Under the two-stage framework, the technical methods used in each stage can be different. For example, there is a viewpoint that divides two-stage methods into two categories: ① Based on multi-stream, ② Based on graph models (Liao et al. 2022). An overview is provided in Table 6.1.

Multi-stream network architecture is a relatively universal structure. A typical schematic diagram is shown in Fig. 6.3. After target detection (determining the position, size, etc. of humans and objects) and feature extraction (determining the appearance, characteristics, etc. of humans and objects), the original image is combined with the network to construct three streams: ① Human flow: information of the initiator of the action; ② Object flow: information about the object of action; ③ Pair flow: information about human-object pairs. By integrating all information, the detection results of human-object interaction can be obtained.

The multi-stream network structure can combine the characteristics of different modalities. For example, the centroid motion path relaxation algorithm (Shi et al. 2023) represents spatiotemporal features based on the characteristics of different modal data, including the changing characteristics of dynamic parts of the image, the synergy of various parts of the human body in motion, and local saliency features. In summary, this algorithm extracts three different human action features based on two types of modal information: ① Extracting centroid motion features based on depth image information, which has good temporal and spatial characteristics; ② Establishing a spatial geometric human body model based on skeleton diagram information, which is oriented towards skeleton data, and obtain the characteristics of the human body and spatial plane direction changes, with good global motion direction description ability; ③ Extracting features of upper limb motion directions

Table 6.1 Overview of two types of two-stage methods (Liao et al. 2022)

Method category	Principle and process
Based on multi-stream	In the first stage, a target detector is used to obtain detection results of humans and objects, and they are paired one by one to form a series of candidate pairs of human- object. In the second stage, an interactive relationship classification network is used to extract and model features of visual objects and interactive relationships in multiple streams/branches, and then the classification results are fused
Based on graph models	Define humans and objects using nodes in graph networks, encode interaction relationships using edges connecting nodes, and explicitly model the structure of human-object interaction relationships using adjacency matrices

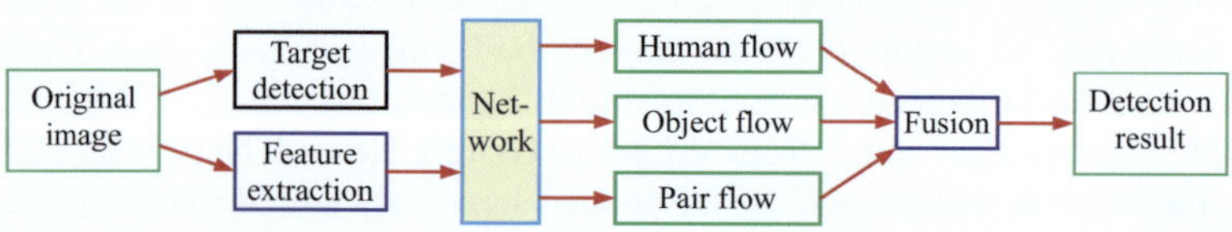

Fig. 6.3 Example of multi-stream network structure

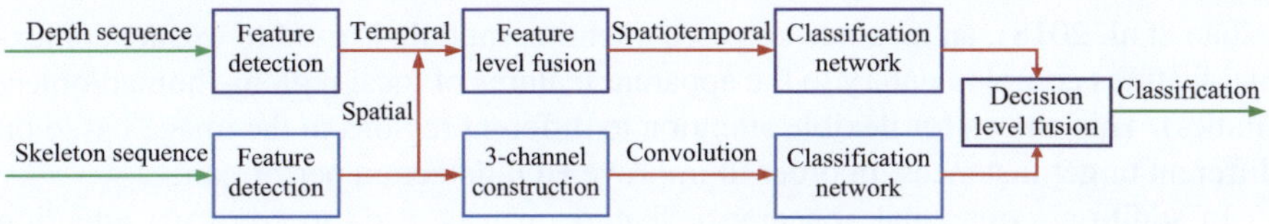

Fig. 6.4 A two stream network architecture diagram

with high participation based on skeleton diagram information having good motion sensitivity.

The overall framework of the network structure is shown in Fig. 6.4. The overall framework consists of two streams, namely spatiotemporal feature stream and spatial feature stream. In the spatiotemporal feature flow section, temporal and spatial features are extracted separately from the depth sequence and skeleton sequence, and feature level fusion is performed to generate spatiotemporal feature vectors. Then, the spatiotemporal feature vectors input into the classification network to calculate the prediction score. In the spatial feature flow section, a three-channel spatial feature map is first constructed using the skeleton sequence, and then inputs into the convolutional network layer to extract spatial features. Next, the feature vectors input into the classification network to calculate the prediction score. Finally, the predicted scores of the two streams are fused at the decision level to generate the final predicted scores for classification.

The multi-stream network model requires processing each instance of human-object pair one by one, which has a relatively high time complexity. In order to avoid this problem and comprehensively consider the correlation between different human-object pairs, graph network structures have received more attention (as shown below).

3. **Three Types of Two-Stage Methods**

There are other ways to classify two-stage methods, such as combining attention, combining graph models, as well as combining posture and body parts (Ruan et al. 2022).

(1) Methods combining attention

Combining attention can be done in different ways, such as in a joint probability model, **Box Attention Relational CNN** (BAR-CNN) for detecting visual relationships (Kolesnikov et al. 2019), which uses chain rules to decompose the probability model into two simpler models. The first model locates all targets in the input image. For each detected target, the second model detects all other targets that interacts with it. Here, attention mechanism is used to enhance the ability of the second model, enabling it to focus on the target located by the first detection model.

Another example, in the **Instance-Centric Attention Network for Human-Object Interaction Detection** (ICAN-HOID) (Gao et al. 2018), on the basis of the **Human-Object Region-based Convolutional Neural Network** (HO-RCNN)

(Chao et al. 2018), an instance centered attention module is used to extract contextual features complementary to the apparent features of local regions (human/object frames). This allows for flexible attention to different regions in the image based on different target instances, in order to improve HOI detection performance.

In addition, contextual appearance features can be used to construct attention maps, and the attention maps can be focused on relevant regions that may contain human-object interactions (Wang et al. 2019a). The attention module suppresses background noise generated by the global context on one hand, and highlights image regions that may contain human-object interactions on the other hand.

(2) Methods combining graph model

The graph model has strong reasoning ability, which is very helpful for HOI detection. The basic method for HOI detection based on graph models is to use nodes to represent humans and objects, and to use edges to represent the interaction between humans and objects. The stronger the interaction correlation between humans and objects, the stronger the edge strength. For example, **Graph Parsing Neural Network** (GPNN) (Qi et al. 2018) inherits the learning ability of neural networks and the representation ability of graph models, introducing an important connection function to solve the problem of graph structure learning. It infers the adjacency matrix in an end-to-end manner, thus enabling the inference of a parsing graph that clearly explains the HOI relationship and outputs it in a message passing manner.

Another example is **Visual Semantic Graph Attention Networks** (VS GATs) (Liang et al. 2020b), that is a two-graph attention network that aggregates in parallel visual spatial and semantic information. It utilizes attention mechanisms to effectively and dynamically aggregate contextual visual, spatial, and semantic information from primary human-object relationships and semantic relationships.

Still another example is the **Visual Spatial-Graph Network** (VSGNet) (Ulutan et al. 2020), that utilizes visual branches to extract humans, objects, and contextual features from human-object pairs. It refines visual features using spatial branches configured with human-object pairs, and connects branches using graph convolution structures and uses interaction suggestion scores as edge strengths between human-object nodes.

The **Spatial-Attention Graph Network** (SAGNet) (Zhang et al. 2020) integrates various appearance and spatial features into a graph model, using them to jointly infer interactions and allowing interaction predictions based on two forms (information influence and adjacent nodes), thereby eliminating ambiguity between visually similar but spatially different interactions.

(3) Methods combining posture and body parts

In human-object interaction, humans usually only use certain parts of their body to interact with objects, and the interaction situation varies when using different postures. This indicates the need for further analysis of specific interaction sites and the relativity of different parts of the body. For this purpose, a paired body part attention model (Fang et al. 2018) can be considered, which can focus on key parts in interaction and their correlations through learning, and can use paired regions of

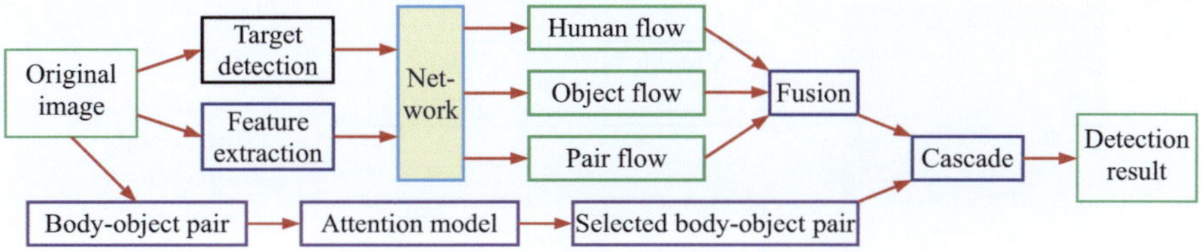

Fig. 6.5 Multi-stream network structure of the attention model combined into pairs

interest pooling to utilize the joint features of paired body parts while discarding the features of other body parts, as shown in Fig. 6.5 (where "body" represents the parts of the human body involved in interaction). This diagram is an improvement on the previous Fig. 6.3 (multi stream diagram).

Considering the differences in human-object appearance and spatial configuration, the **Posture-aware Multi-level Feature Network** (PMFNet) (Wan et al. 2019) directly utilizes human pose cues to capture the global spatial configuration of relationships. It specifically uses a multi-branch deep network to learn posture enhanced relationship representations at three semantic levels, including interactive context, target features, and detailed local clues.

In addition, the **Pose-based Modular Network** (PMN) (Liang et al. 2020a) designed a module consisting of a branch that processes the relative spatial pose features of each joint independently and another branch that uses graph convolution to update the absolute pose features of each joint. The fused features can be fed into the action classifier for classification.

A simple comparison of the advantages and disadvantages of the above three methods is shown in Table 6.2 (Ruan et al. 2022).

4. **Two Types of Graph Network-Based Methods**

Graph Neural Networks (GNNs) can be used to model scene relationships and knowledge structures through graphs (Qiao et al. 2025). A graph G is composed

Table 6.2 Comparison of three types of two-stage methods (Ruan et al. 2022)

Method category	Advantage	Disadvantage
Based on attention model	Can effectively extract contextual information	Only utilizing visual and spatial information
Based on graph model	Can simultaneously predict all interaction pairs in the image, eliminating pairing ambiguity	Only utilizing visual and spatial information, with high hardware requirements
Based on posture and body parts	Can effectively integrate information on human body parts or body posture with high accuracy	Large computational load and high hardware requirements

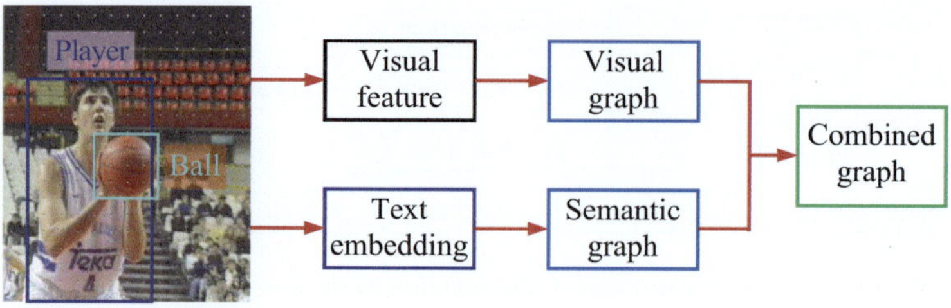

Fig. 6.6 A graph network constructed based on the detected humans and objects in the image (Zhang 2023)

Table 6.3 Advantages and disadvantages of different types of graph networks (Antoun and Asmar 2023)

Graph networks	Advantage	Disadvantage
Visual graph	Can help extract contextual clues	Seemingly reasonable spatial configuration can confuse the model
Semantic graph	Can assist in detection in different scenarios	Failed to integrate visual and spatial cues
Visual semantic combination graph	Can provide richer example representations	Visual and semantic cues may be unrelated to each other

of nodes N connected to edges E. GNN learns the latent features of nodes by iteratively propagating messages from adjacent nodes and updating hidden states through embedding functions, as shown in Fig. 6.6.

In Fig. 6.6, different types of graphs can be used for HOI prediction: visual graph, semantic graph, and visual semantic combination graph. In a visual graph, nodes are represented by visual features. In the semantic graph, these nodes are represented by their text embedding. In the combination graph, the outputs of the visual and semantic graphs are combined and connected to represent nodes. Table 6.3 presents the advantages and disadvantages of different types of graph networks (Antoun and Asmar 2023).

6.1.2 *Single-Stage Methods*

In the single-stage HOI method, both human-object pairs and interactions are detected simultaneously, and two parallel branches are used to estimate the interaction triplet. In the first branch, image feature maps are used to identify interaction points or regions, and to find corresponding interactions. In the second branch, object detection is performed to find human-object pairs. Finally, use these two branches for regression offset and match the interaction class with the detected instances.

1. **Two Types of Single-Stage Methods**

Single-stage methods can be divided into point-based methods and anchor-based methods (Antoun and Asmar 2023).

(1) Point-based methods

The point-based method infers at each determined interaction key point (including points representing humans, objects, and interaction points, or the midpoint of the corresponding human-object pair). The key to point-based methods is interaction point detection. For example, Hourglass-104 (Zhou et al. 2019b) can be used to extract apparent features for estimating the center points of each human, each object, and their corresponding sizes (width and height), while also considering local offsets. The interaction points detected in this way provide context and regularization basis for the detection boxes of humans and objects, and can be used in point matching branches. Next, generate an interaction triplet (human-interaction-object) by matching each interaction point with a human point and an object point.

The **Glance and Gaze Network** (GGNet) is a point-based method (Zhong et al. 2021). It uses two steps to predict interactions. The first step is to identify whether each input image pixel in the feature map is a possible interaction point. The second step is to use possible interaction points to explain the feature map generated in the first step, in order to find a precise set of action points. Finally, refined action point features are used to infer the interaction category at the interaction point. In addition to identifying interaction points, a unique position regress operator can be assigned to each interaction category to enhance the matching method of human-object interaction pairs. In this way, the impact of interaction categories on human-object spatial layout can be reduced.

(2) Anchor-based methods

The anchor-based method predicts interactions based on anchor boxes (regions with certain semantic meanings) rather than interaction points.

For example, **UnionDet** is an anchor box-based HOI detection method (Kim et al. 2020). It can detect the union bounding boxes of human-object pairs and these pairs can be used to extract comprehensive features. It uses a joint level detection framework to directly capture interaction regions and employs instance level detectors to perform object detection and action classification. In order to achieve more accurate instance level localization, it combines union level detectors and instance level detectors in parallel.

The **Dense Interaction Region Voting** (DIRV) framework is also an anchor box-based HOI detection method (Fang et al. 2021). This framework focuses on the interaction regions between humans and objects. Here, the interaction region represents the minimum region that covers humans and objects that are crucial for identifying interactions, without the need to cover the entire range of humans and objects. To specify the interaction region, thresholds need to be set on the bounding boxes of humans, objects, anchor boxes, and their union regions.

The advantages and disadvantages of the above two methods are shown in Table 6.4.

Table 6.4 Advantages and disadvantages of two types of single-stage methods (Antoun and Asmar 2023)

Method category	Advantage	Disadvantage
Point-based	Detect interaction based on a set of interaction point pairs	Visual mode has no obvious features
Anchor-based	Directly detect the interaction region	Not direct, sensitive to occlusion

2. **Three Types of Single-Stage Methods**

Single-stage methods can also be divided into relation point-based methods, box-based methods, and query-based methods (Liao et al. 2022). Among them, the relation point-based methods are related to the point-based method mentioned above, while the box-based method is basically the same as the anchor-based method mentioned above. The query-based method mainly utilizes a transformer network to obtain global information of images, and adaptively aggregates contextual information to enhance the robustness of human-object interaction triplet features, alleviating problems caused by target overlap and interaction ambiguity (more discussion will be provided in the next section). The overview of these three types of single-stage methods is shown in Table 6.5.

3. **Compared to Two-Stage Methods**

Single-stage methods generally have fast detection speed, high accuracy, and are easy to deploy. However, the construction and training of its model are relatively

Table 6.5 Overview of three types of single-stage methods (Liao et al. 2022)

Method	Principle and Process
Relation point-based	The detection boxes for humans and objects are represented by the center points, width, and height. The relationship between humans and objects is represented by the midpoint of the line connecting the center points of the two detection boxes as the center point of the relationship. The center point detection branch predicts the width, height, and relationship among the center points of the human center point, object center point, and corresponding detection boxes. The relationship matching branch predicts the positions of humans and objects, as well as the relative relationships between their positions, starting from the relationship center points
Box-based	Using neural networks to detect humans and objects in images, while parallel predicting bounding boxes that may have interactive relationships. By associating the humans and objects contained in the bounding boxes, a human-interaction-object triplet is formed
Query-based	Using convolutional neural networks and shared encoders to extract image features and encode global information, the instance decoder detects the target interaction relationship category based on the target query. By matching with the instance features in the instance decoder, the target position category and interaction relationship are associated, forming a human-interaction-object triplet

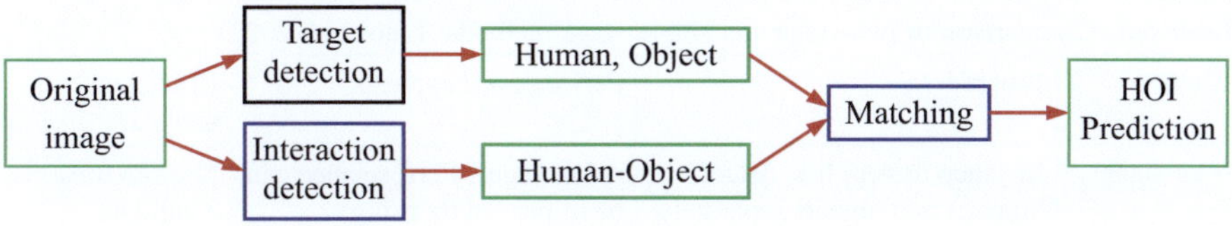

Fig. 6.7 Synchronization of target detection and interaction detection in single-stage HOI detection

complex. The single-stage method is more suitable for applications that require high real-time and accuracy, while the two-stage method is more suitable for applications with sufficient training samples, high hardware computing power, and low real-time requirements.

The single-stage method breaks the inherent separation paradigm of the two-stage method and can directly predict interaction relationships end-to-end. The two-stage method requires two independent and unrelated steps, and its performance is limited by the quality of the results from the first stage. In addition, even when considering the combination of humans and objects, two-stage methods often ignore contextual features in the image. In fact, features from bounding boxes that connect humans and objects contain some contextual information, but they also contain interference information that may come from backgrounds or other targets present in these boxes. The single-stage method captures contextual information from images by pairing humans and objects in the early stages of feature extraction and extracting comprehensive features (rather than processing targets separately), as shown in Fig. 6.7 (Antoun and Asmar 2023), where the interaction triplet prediction can be obtained by matching the instances detected by the targets with the interaction detection results.

The existing single-stage methods have significantly improved both efficiency and accuracy compared to the two-stage methods. The improvement in efficiency mainly comes from the design of end-to-end models, which do not require additional object detectors and can detect all interaction relationships at once. The improvement in accuracy can be attributed to its top-down structure, which can directly locate relationship points, focus on related human-object interaction pairs, and avoid interference from negative samples and unrelated human-object pairs as much as possible.

The current single-stage methods generally adopt a multi-task collaborative learning approach, where features are shared between different tasks. However, there may be significant differences in the features and optimization directions that target detection and relationship prediction focus on, which could lead to interference between different tasks in multi-task collaborative learning and may not achieve optimal results.

A comparison between two-stage and single-stage methods is shown in Table 6.6 (Liao et al. 2022).

Table 6.6 Comparison of two-stage and single-stage methods (Liao et al. 2022)

Method	Process	Performance analysis	Efficiency analysis
Two-stage	Instance driven, first detect humans and objects separately, and then predict interaction relationships	Advantages: Performance can be improved by using different features Disadvantages: Large search space and interference from a large number of negative samples	Need to traverse candidate humans and objects one by one Low efficiency
Single-stage	Relationship driven, directly predicting relationships and further linking humans and objects	Advantages: Directly locate relationships, reducing search space Disadvantage: Both association detection and relationship understanding interfere with performance	Directly detecting interaction relationship triplets High efficiency

6.2 Transformer-Based Approaches

Transformer is an encoder-decoder architecture composed entirely of attention mechanisms. Its **self-attention** mechanism and **cross-attention** mechanism can model all paired interactions between elements in a sequence, making it suitable for HOI detection (Jiang et al. 2025).

6.2.1 Two-Stage Methods Using Transformer

In the two-stage methods, the transformer can be used to decode and locate the target through learning queries. In the first stage, the input image is processed by CNN and then encoded and decoded by the detection transformer (Carion et al. 2020) to generate new features for a fixed number of learnable target queries. Next, use a **Multi-Layer Perceptron** (MLP) to decode these queries into target classification scores, bounding boxes, and interactivity scores (Zhang et al. 2021). In the second stage, the target query from the first stage provides prior knowledge for interactive classification; The **instance decoder** outputs the interactive query results and inputs them into the **interaction decoder**, and finally MLP is used to predict the final action class score. The entire process is shown in Fig. 6.8.

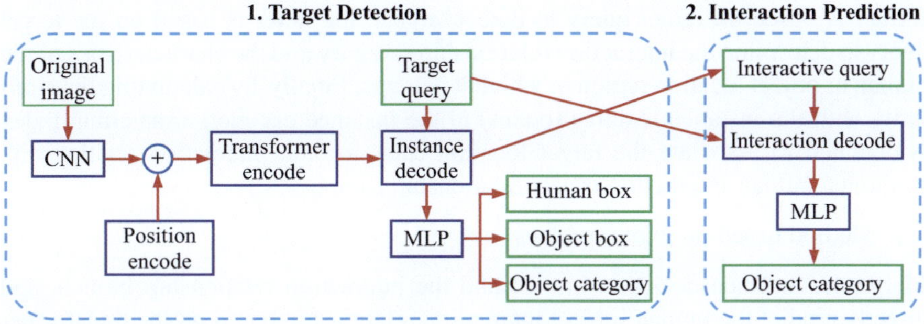

Fig. 6.8 HOI detection process based on two-stage transformer

6.2.2 *Single-Stage Methods Using Transformer*

When using a transformer, one can better predict the set of HOI triplets by leveraging the contextual relationships and interactions between humans and objects. The basic framework diagram of the end-to-end method based on transformers is shown in Fig. 6.9. First, the CNN backbone network is used to extract visual features from the original image. These features are then reduced in the channel dimension, flattened in the spatial dimension, and supplemented by positional encoding. Encoding with a transformer is to generate global storage features, decoding with a transform is to convert the learned positional embedding into output embedding. Finally, multiple **Feed-Forward Networks** (FFNs) are used to simultaneously predict four HOI instances.

On the basis of the above basic framework, there are many different specific implementation methods, including:

(1) Method based on decoding instances

One method defines the human-object interaction relationship as a set and use a **Human Object interaction TRansformer** (HOTR) network consisting of convolutional neural networks, shared encoders, and parallel decoders to detect it (Kim et al. 2021). Among them, convolutional neural networks and shared encoders extract image features and encode global information. The decoder includes an **instance decoder** and an **interaction decoder**, forming a parallel prediction structure. The

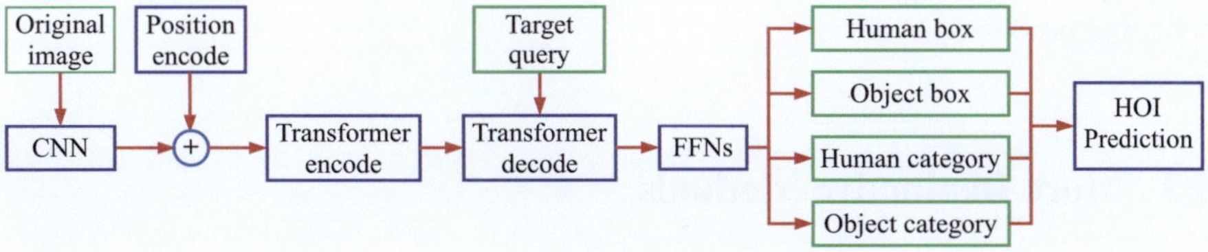

Fig. 6.9 Framework diagram of end-to-end method based on transformer

former is based on target query to detect targets; the latter is based on the target query to determine the interaction relationship category and the characteristics of the human or object location region to which it belongs. Finally, by calculating the similarity with the instance features (boxes) in the instance decoder, a matching index is obtained to associate the target location category and interaction relationship, forming a human-interaction-object relationship triplet.

(2) Method based on joint instances

Merge the instance detection branch and the interaction relationship branch, and directly predict the human -object interaction relationship based on the transformer network (Zou et al. 2021). Unlike HOTR networks, the decoding of the decoder here includes target queries for each human-object interaction relationship feature, detecting humans, objects, and their corresponding interaction relationships through a **Multi-Layer Perceptron** (MLP) with shared weights. The use of joint instances can reduce the computational complexity of redundant two-stage methods. Due to the abandonment of artificially designed post-processing strategies in decoding, the overall framework is made more concise and intuitive. Due to the fact that the target query for each human-object interaction feature is only responsible for one set of human-object interaction relationships, an additional background class needs to be set and the Softmax function needs to be used to obtain the relationship classification score when performing relationship classification.

(3) Method based on multimodal learning

Combining different modalities can improve the performance of detecting human-object interaction relationships. For example, Phrase HOI (Li et al. 2022) combines multi-task learning methods of phrase learning and label construction, utilizing language prior knowledge to jointly optimize human-object interaction relationship detection tasks and phrase learning tasks. It includes a human-object interaction relationship detection branch and a phrase branch. The former detects interaction targets and interaction relationship categories, while the latter outputs semantic vectors used to describe interaction relationships. Finally, using distillation loss and triplet loss, text knowledge is distilled through the phrase branch to the human-object interaction relationship detection branch, thereby expanding the shared knowledge space and improving detection performance.

In addition, on the basis of the transformer, a query-based detection module (Tamura et al. 2021) can be added to selectively aggregate contextual information within the image range to avoid the mixing of multiple instance features during the decoding process.

6.3 More Distinctive Methods

As research deepens, more diverse methods have been proposed. Below are some distinctive methods.

6.3.1 *Zero-Shot Learning*

Zero Shot Learning (ZSL) (Lampert et al. 2009), also known as **zero knowledge learning**, includes learning methods such as **metric learning**, **attribute recognition**, and **domain transfer-based learning**. In addition to being widely used in basic visual tasks such as image classification and object detection, it is also gradually being applied to human-object interaction detection tasks.

Zero shot learning can use the feature attributes of existing sample categories in the training set to predict the labels of unseen categories by sharing the semantic attributes of both categories. As shown in Fig. 6.10, it utilizes the processed already seen category database to assist other instances in obtaining effective feature representations, and then combines representations based on the attribute descriptions of HOI classes. This representation can be seen as a pseudo feature level instance description of unseen and seen categories.

Zero knowledge human-object interaction relationship detection can be divided into four categories, as shown in Table 6.7 (Liao et al. 2022).

Here are some typical examples.

By independently representing interaction relationships and objects, unseen human-object interaction relationships can be combined and generated during reasoning (Shen et al. 2018). The proposed HOI decomposition model consists of a set of visual feature extraction layers, verb separation networks, and object detection networks. This model can model both verbs and targets separately, and can use these

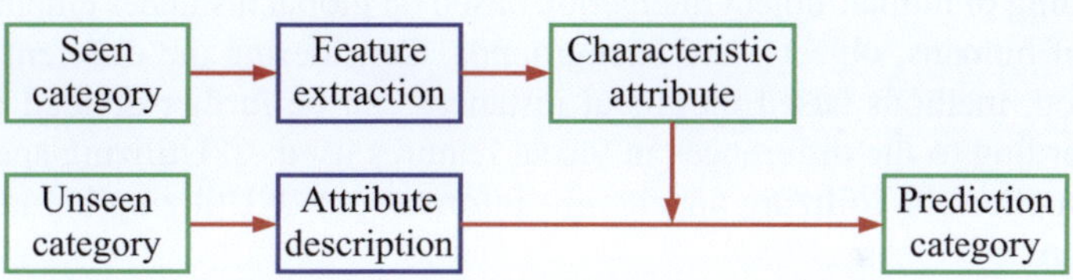

Fig. 6.10 Flow chart of zero shot learning

Table 6.7 Overview of four types of zero knowledge human-object interaction relationship detection (Liao et al. 2022)

Type	In application
Interactive	There are already annotations for object and action categories in the database, and it is necessary to detect interaction combination categories that have not appeared in the database
Object	It is needed to discover and detect new categories of objects that have not yet appeared in the database
Action	The object does not have a new category, but it is needed to infer its relationship with the new action category generated by humans
Open	It is needed to detect new object categories, action categories, and interaction relationships to cope with new open scenarios

networks to identify new human-object pairs based on verb or object instances of existing categories during detection.

Zero shot learning based on the transfer between attribute categories can embed semantic information into the local region occupied by foreground targets, so that the semantic and spatial attributes of the targets are jointly embedded into the visual input stream (Eum and Kwon 2019).

Based on the assumption that functionally similar objects participate in similar interactions with humans, (Bansal et al. 2020a) proposed a functional generalization module in which semantic features are used to represent the characteristics of humans and objects.

ConsNet uses both **Graph Neural Networks** (GNN) and language models to learn explicit and implicit knowledge of HOI from consistency graphs and word embedding (Liu et al. 2020).

6.3.2 Methods Based on Global and Local Instances

Considering the different strategies adopted for instance targets in the interaction detection stage, HOI detection methods can be divided into global instance-based and local instance-based methods (Gong et al. 2022).

1. **Global Instance Based Methods**

The modeling of human-object interaction based on global instances emphasizes the integrity of humans, objects, and backgrounds. Considering the different information utilized, methods based on global instances can be further divided into three types according to the differences in visual features used: ① Utilizing spatial position information; ② Utilizing appearance information; ③ Utilizing human posture information.

(1) Utilizing spatial position information

After the object detector obtains the human frames and object frames, their relative spatial layout can provide important prior information for HOI detection. The spatial distribution of human frames and object frames varies with the type of interaction. By using spatial location information, less likely classifications during prediction can be excluded, so as to improve the accuracy of determining interaction categories.

For example, the **spatial priming model** (Bansal et al. 2020b) includes visual channels and layout channels that share visual context at multiple stages (as shown in Fig. 6.11). In the visual channel, multiple convolutional layers are used to extract the layout features of humans, and combined with the semantic representation of objects, the joint box of humans and objects is output. In the layout channel, multiple residual blocks are combined with the global features extracted from the average pooling layer. By aggregating the results of two channels and combining human and physical features, the final prediction result can be jointly output.

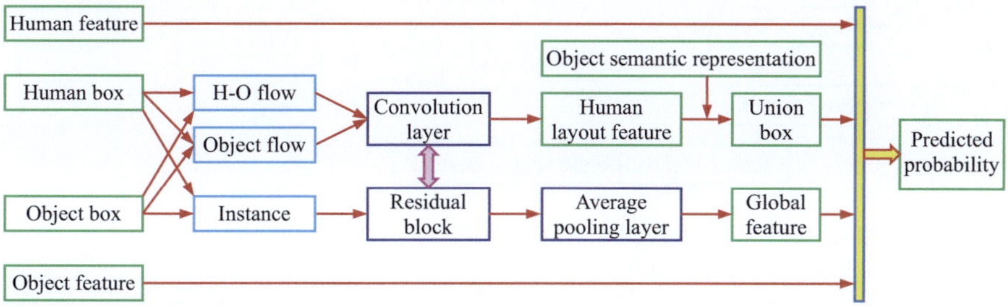

Fig. 6.11 Flow chart of spatial priming model

(2) Utilizing appearance information

In human-object interaction detection, the obtained appearance information of humans and objects (including human frames and object frames) mainly describes the external contours and positions of humans and objects.

For example, in a two-stage appearance encoding method (Gupta et al. 2019), the first stage constructs a set of candidate boxes for each human and object in the image, and then it pairs the human candidate boxes with the object candidate boxes to form a human-object candidate box pair. In the second stage, a decomposition model is used to score candidate box pairs, and the scoring results are passed through by parameters between different interaction categories to reduce the false detection rate of human-object interaction detection. This method separates the generation of target candidate boxes from interaction detection, which has a certain impact on real-time performance. In addition, the pairing and decomposition of human and object boxes also increase computational complexity.

The single-stage **Parallel Point Detection and Matching** (PPDM) model (Liao et al. 2020) attempts to overcome these problems. It consists of two branches, the point detection branch estimates the positions of human body points, interaction points, and object points; the point matching branch considers human body points and object points originating from the same interaction point as matching pairs. This approach only requires filtering out a small number of candidate interaction points, saving computational costs and improving real-time performance. This method also uses two key-point heat-map prediction networks, **Deep Layer Aggregation** (DLA) (Yu et al. 2018) and Hourglass (Law and Dend 2018), to expand the receptive field of interaction points and displacement prediction values, in order to extract higher-level semantic features.

(3) Utilizing human posture information

By utilizing human postures to connect humans and objects more accurately and closely, the performance of human-object interaction detection will be improved. Several examples of this type of method have been provided in Sect. 6.1.1. Similarly, based on the **Human-Object Region-based Convolutional Neural Network** (HO-RCNN) (Chao et al. 2018), the pose estimation network (Li et al. et al. 2019a) and the human skeleton branch have been used to extract human pose features (Li

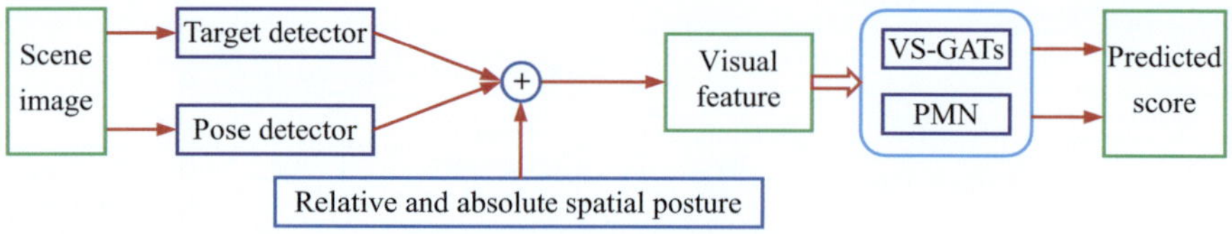

Fig. 6.12 Graph modular network integrating visual-semantic-pose information

et al. et al. 2019b). The interactive discrimination between skeleton branches and the network composed of "human-object pair flow" enables the model to learn interactive knowledge, thereby bringing more effective supervision constraints to solve the training difficulty problems caused by rare categories due to information scarcity.

In addition, the **Visual-Semantic-Pose Graph Modular Network** (VSP-GMN) (Liang et al. 2020b) utilizes **Graph Neural Networks** (GNNs) to combine multiple cues to reduce ambiguity between scene understanding and intrinsic semantic rules. As shown in Fig. 6.12, connecting the various joints of the human body to the center of the object is taken as the relative spatial pose feature, and is input into the **Pose-based Modular Network** (PMN) and **Visual Semantic Graph Attention Network** (VS GATs) separately with absolute spatial pose feature and visual feature. Combining the scores of the two networks, the predicted score of the human-interaction-object relationship triple is obtained.

2. **Local Instance Based Methods**

The modeling of human-object interaction based on local instances emphasizes the local characteristics of humans, objects, and background, with finer granularity compared to global instances. In addition, there are more interaction pairs and more association patterns.

When considering different parts of the human body, it is often possible to rely on human joints or skeleton points. The **Relation Parsing Neural Network** (RPNN) (Zhou and Chi 2019a) uses Detectron (Girshick et al. 2020) and Mask RCNN (He et al. 2017) to detect human frames, object frames, and human skeleton points. It also constructs local features of four human body parts, namely the head, hands, buttocks, and legs by using human skeleton point information to enhance the representation ability of local human body features. Finally, **Graph Parsing Neural Network** (GPNN) (Qi et al. 2018) integrates local information to construct a graph structure.

The correlation between different parts of the human body and interaction behavior varies, and their contributions to interaction detection are also different. The **Multi-level Pairwise Feature Network** (MPFNet) (Liu et al. 2021a) utilized a constructed database (see Sect. 6.4) called the **Human Activity Knowledge Engine** (HAKE). This database contains data on body parts that refine each interaction action into multiple local interaction actions. Fine grained information about the state of human body parts can be extracted from it, and efficiency can be improved through synthesis.

Human-object interaction often involves multiple different action perception points, and the **Glance and Gaze Network** (GGNet) (Zhong et al. 2021) can adaptively model a set of action perception points in single-stage human-object interaction detection through two steps: scanning and gazing. The gazing step utilizes the feature map generated by the scanning step to progressively infer the action perception points around each pixel, and aggregates their features for interactive prediction to improve detection performance.

6.3.3 Spatiotemporal Human-Object Interaction Detection

The **spatiotemporal human object interaction detection** also takes into account temporal factors on the basis of space. In other words, it is necessary to detect human-object interaction relationships in space–time. In practice, it usually refers to the time period during which all human-object interaction relationships appearing in a video need to be located, and to the detection of human-object interaction triplets in each frame during that time period (Baek and Choe 2025).

In order to identify the human-object interaction relationship in videos, different networks have been constructed, and Table 6.8 provides some examples (Liao et al. 2022).

In the real world, there are many types of human-object interactions and their relationships are also complex. These issues are particularly evident in the video. From the perspective of neural network modeling, what is relatively scarce is data that has a large number of annotations for each category. The data usually presents a long tail distribution of labels (which can also be understood as data statistical skewness), and it is worth paying attention to how to achieve better performance in rare categories. **SkEw Robust VideO Human-Object Interaction** (SERVO-HOI) network (Agarwal et al. 2023) is an end-to-end framework. It places multiple image representations in context and trains them to explicitly address data skew issues, thereby improving tail labels.

In HOI detection of videos, it can be considered to initially perform HOI detection of still images in the first frame, and then track them in subsequent frames. In order to detect the current HOI and predict future HOI in the video, human gaze information can be used, as people usually stare at the target and continue to stare before interacting with it. These gaze features can be fused with the visual appearance of the human-object pairs and background in the scene through a spatiotemporal transformer.

A specific video based HOI detection and prediction framework is shown in Fig. 6.13 (Ni et al. 2023). It mainly consists of three modules. Firstly, object detection and human head detection based on the input video are performed. In the object module, by tracking and grasping the trajectory of the object, the object can be labeled with text through recognition, thus obtaining comprehensive object features. In the gaze module, based on human head detection, gaze tracking is achieved by leveraging the association between the human and the head. By inputting complete

Table 6.8 Some networks for detecting human-object interaction relationships through video (Liao et al. 2022)

Network	Principle and process	References
Spatiotemporal graph parsing network	Encode videos using graph sequences and learn the evolution of spatiotemporal relationships in the temporal domain and spatial graph topology to identify human-object interaction relationships	Wang et al. (2019b)
Multi stream integrated network	Combining action recognition, behavior prediction, and feature localization, focusing on special regions (hotspots) highly correlated with human-object interaction, and directly learning object attributes from videos	Nagarajan et al. (2019)
Learning interactive graphs and hierarchical temporal networks	Modeling local interaction information between humans and objects at frame granularity, using embedded vectors at frame granularity and modeling with graph structure, learning interaction relationships between humans and objects as graph nodes in the scene	Sunkesula et al. (2020)
Human-object interaction relationship transformation network	First, detect visual cues present in static images, and then decode these visual cues through a changing network to detect targets with interactive relationships and their interactions with each other	Ji et al. (2021)
Spatial–Temporal HOI (ST-HOI) detector network	Using temporal information such as trajectory and posture of humans and objects to compensate for the bias introduced by inconsistent features, and then using a 3-D network to generate spatiotemporal human-object interaction results at key-frame granularity	Chiou et al. (2021)

human-object information into the spatiotemporal module, encoding it separately in space and time, and combining them, appropriate predictions can be made for the head.

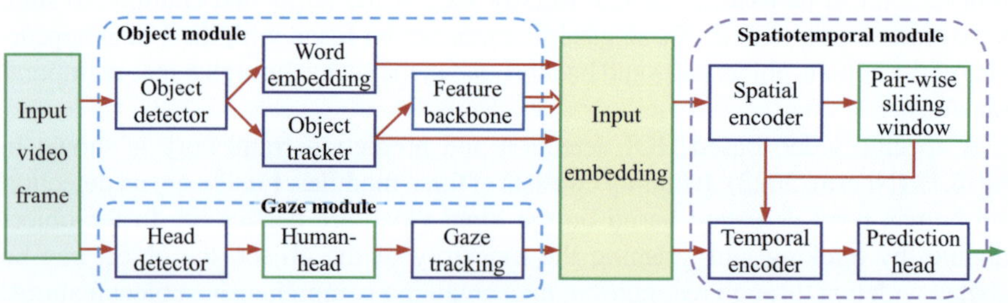

Fig. 6.13 Video based HOI detection and prediction framework

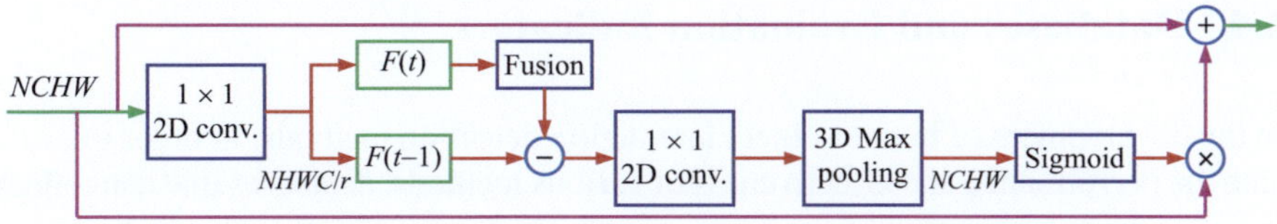

Fig. 6.14 Motion module for obtaining inter frame difference feature attention weights

This framework is a multimodal framework that utilizes gaze cues in a cross-attention mechanism and employs a target tracker to enable the time encoder to separately focus on the temporal evolution of each human-object pair, in order to detect and predict HOI from third person videos.

In human-object interaction, the human hand is often the initiating part of an action. To detect human-object interaction actions, a system architecture that simultaneously detects hands and objects in the scene can be adopted (Benavent-Lledo et al. 2022). This is equivalent to transforming human-object interaction detection into hand-object interaction detection. Considering the speed and accuracy of inference, the detection of hands and objects is carried out using the YOLO series. After obtaining the bounding boxes of the hand and object, the object that the hand is most likely to interact with can be selected based on their distance from each other. By recognizing the scene and obtaining a set of target and global actions, the most likely appropriate action in each context can be determined.

Video data has complex and redundant information in the spatiotemporal dimension. To address this issue, a spatiotemporal feature-based motion module can be used to obtain contextual relationships and calculate spatiotemporal differences between pixel features (Shi and Zhao 2024). Here, let the input feature $\boldsymbol{F} = [N, T, C, H, W]$, where N represents the number of input images at one time; T and C represent the numbers of time dimension and feature channel, respectively; H and W correspond to the spatial dimensions of the video. The overall flowchart of the motion module is shown in Fig. 6.14.

For a given time input, the convolution operation to reduce the number of feature channels (which can reduce both parameter count and computational complexity; r is the reduction ratio) is first performed. Then, the subtle dynamic changes between frames are obtained by leveraging the differences between adjacent frames. Next, 3-D max pooling is used to aggregate the spatiotemporal information of inter frame difference features, in order to identify the most prominent contextual features from a larger spatiotemporal receptive field. Finally, the attention weights of inter frame difference features are obtained using the Sigmoid function to better identify interactive actions in the video.

6.4 Databases and Evaluation Indicators

In the development of human-object interaction detection methods, in order to evaluate the performance and effectiveness of various methods, databases that can reflect various interaction scenarios are often needed. Especially with the increasing use of deep learning and neural network methods, the support of large-scale, annotated databases is becoming increasingly important for training models.

Evaluating the performance of different methods requires the use of various indicators, and several commonly used evaluation indicators for human-object interaction detection will be introduced later.

6.4.1 *Databases with Different Annotation Granularities*

From the perspective of annotation granularity, the human-object interaction detection databases can be divided into three levels: **instance level database**, **part level database**, and **pixel level database**.

1. **Instance Level Database**

Instance level annotation refers to the annotation of human and object frames in an image (often also annotating the relationship between humans and objects). Instance level annotation is a relatively low-cost annotation method that can meet the basic needs of human-object interaction detection tasks. Due to its low annotation cost and multiple data sources, it is the most widely used.

The overview of several typical instance level databases is shown in Table 6.9.

The **Verbs in COCO** (V-COCO) database (Gupta and Malik 2015) selected 10,346 images (2533 in the training set, 2867 in the validation set, and 4946 in the testing set) from the **Common Objects in COntext** (COCO) database (Lin et al. 2014) for interactive relationship annotation. Among them, the categories of interactive objects are 80, and the categories of interaction relationships are 29 (of which 4 categories are generally not considered due to the absence of interactive objects in the action). For annotation, instance segmentation was performed for individual targets in each category, and 5 textual descriptions (Verbs, the origin of V in the database name) were provided for each image. Instance boxes were used for the target to better

Table 6.9 Overview of several instance level databases

Database	Number of images	Type of objects	Type of relationships
V-COCO	10346	80	29
HICO-DET	47776	80	117
HCVRD	52855	1824	927
HOI-A	38688	11	10

estimate its location in the region. Human-object interaction is described in the form of < actions, objects > .

The **Humans Interacting with Common Objects Detection** (HICO-DET) database (Chao et al. 2018) collected 47,776 commercially licensed images (38,118 in the training set and 9658 in the testing set) from Flickr, as well as a series of keywords with human subjects and action types. HICO-DET has annotated 117 types of actions and 80 types of objects (consistent with the V-COCO database), and the combination of these actions and objects constitutes 600 different types of human-object interaction relationships. These 600 interaction relationships are divided into 462 common/no rare (including 10 or more samples) and 138 rare (including less than 10 samples). By using undirected edges as labels for interaction classes, the human box is connected to the object box, providing a total of 150,000 annotated instances of human-object interaction. Each instance box is represented by a class label between the human box and the object box.

The **Human Centered Visual Relationship Detection** (HCVRD) database (Zhuang et al. 2018) has a large scale, with 788,160 images and 9852 types of interactive actions. This database not only cares about the interaction action relationship, but also considers the relative positional relationship between humans and objects.

The images in the **Human-Object Interaction for Application** (HOI-A) database (Liao et al. 2020) are all from real scenes, covering images with different appearance types, low resolution, and severe occlusion. Therefore, although there are few categories of objects and human-object relationship categories, their detection and recognition are still difficult.

2. **Part Level Database**

On the basis of instance level annotation, part level annotation further annotates human body parts at a finer granularity. In the same time, the interaction relationship between human body parts and objects is also annotated. Part level annotation mainly focuses on more accurately locating human body parts that interact with objects, and is useful in considering the interaction detection between different parts of the human body (local instances) and objects, or in considering the interaction detection of human body posture. Part level annotation of human-object interaction relationships can improve the model's understanding of behavior, reduce the difficulty of learning imbalanced data, and enhance detection performance.

The **Human Activity Knowledge Engine** (HAKE) is a database based on the state of human body parts (Li et al. 2020), which combines instance level activity annotation and part level activity annotation. The database annotated nearly 120,000 images, including over 280,000 instances of individuals, approximately 250,000 instances of objects, and approximately 720,000 human-object interaction pairs with human body part states.

For the work of human-object interaction detection, some annotated data was extracted and a **Part State Network for Human-Object Interaction** (PaStaNet HOI) database for human-object interaction was constructed (Li et al. 2020). This database contains approximately 110,000 annotated images, with 77,260 images as the training set, 11,298 images as the validation set, and 22,156 images as the test set. This database includes 116 interaction relationships and 80 object categories, comprising 520 categories of human-object interaction relationships. This database uses part state labels to infer the state of human body parts, covering a total of 247,000 human body instances, 220,000 object instances, and 7,000,000 local action labels.

3. **Pixel Level Database**

Pixel level annotation is more refined than part level annotation. It not only distinguishes the parts of each human body, but also provides very fine-grained category annotation for each pixel on the human body, object, and scene.

Instance level annotation and part level annotation often use regular bounding boxes to mark the range and position of humans and objects. If there are severe occlusion situations in the scene, it is difficult to achieve clear and unambiguous labeling. In addition, there may be interactions between people and scenes in reality, and irregular scenes are difficult to annotate with regular boxes. Finally, factors such as age and gender can also have an impact on the way people interact with objects. Fine grained labeling of individuals (adults/children, men/women) can improve the effectiveness of HOI detection.

The **Person in Context** (PIC) database (Liu et al. 2021b) has pixel level annotation for human body parts and objects, thus avoiding the problems caused by regular boxes and making the annotation of humans and objects clearer in occlusion situations. The database collected 17,122 high-resolution images centered around humans online, including 12,339 in the training set, 1916 in the validation set, and 2867 in the test set. The database densely annotated the images, labeling 25 component categories and 16 body key-points for each person. This database includes 141 object categories, 23 relational categories, and 25 semantic human body parts. There are 14 types of human-object positional relationships and 9 types of action relationships marked.

The pixel level human-object interaction detection database requires precise segmentation of human body parts and scenes, and has high requirements for HOI detection methods. An example of performing fine-grained pixel by pixel relationship segmentation uses the network of **Cascaded Parsing of Human-Object Interaction** (CP-HOI) (Zhou et al. 2022).

6.4.2 Special Databases

There are also some databases closely related to human-object interaction detection, but each with its own characteristics.

1. **Human–Machine Interaction Database**

Human–machine interaction is a special case of human-object interaction. A new database for human–machine interaction with synchronized hand, body, and object manipulation data (Kang et al. 2023) is built for this type of work. It includes synchronized human pose data from the **Inertial Measurement Unit** (IMU) sensor network, hand pose data from intelligent data gloves, and object position and pose information obtained from motion capture systems, while the subjects move and interact with screwdrivers, hammers, wrenches, drills, and rectangular work-pieces. This is a body-hand-object database (body for human) that includes data on the position and movement of objects held and manipulated by humans with their hands.

2. **Database of Daily Life Activities**

HOIsim is a simulator focused on human-object interaction in 3-D activities (Zakour et al. 2021), with the aim of correctly understanding human activities and enabling robots to provide meaningful assistance in daily life. With the help of HOIsim, a program generated synthetic database of two daily life activities, lunch and breakfast, was constructed. This database contains directly usable truth annotations for human and object pose forms, as well as truth activity labels. By utilizing meaningful randomization of activity flows and environmental topology, a large number of random variants of these activities can be quickly generated. Based on the abstraction of low-level pose data in the form of HOI spatiotemporal graph, the lunch database generated using two deep learning models for activity recognition was evaluated. Among them, the accuracy based on recursive neural network model reached 87%, while the accuracy based on the transformer network model reached 94.7%.

3. **Database for Studying Model Generalization**

In real-world scenarios, it is necessary to systematically generalize the HOI detection model to handle new combinations of human-object interaction relationships. In practice, training data typically only covers a limited portion of all possible combinations in the real world. In order to evaluate the system generalization performance of the HOI detection model, two new HOI detection databases named **HICO-DET-SG** and **V-CO-SG** were created based on the HICO-DET and V-COCO databases, respectively (Takemoto et al. 2023). The experimental results show that many representative HOI detection models perform much worse on the new database than on the original database, indicating that system generalization is a challenging goal in HOI detection. By analyzing and evaluating the results, possible research directions for improving the system's generalization performance have also been further clarified.

4. **Synthetic Database**

In order to solve the problem of **Egocentric Human Computer Interaction** (EHOI) detection in industrial environments, a new multimodal database called **Egocentric Industrial Synthetic Multimodal dataset for Human-Object Interaction detection** (EgoISM HOI) has been constructed (Leonardi et al. 2024). The images in this database are synthesized according to industrial environments, along with other related data (such as depth maps or segmentation masks), all of which have rich annotations for hands and objects.

The database, source code, and pre-trained model can be found on https://iplab.dmi.unict.it/egoism-hoi.

6.4.3 Evaluation Indicators

From the perspective of (interactive) detection, if the true situation is true and the detection result is also true, it is called **True Positive** (TP); If the true situation is false and the test result is also false, it is called **True Negative** (TN); If the true situation is false but the test result is true, it is called **False Positive** (FP); If the true situation is true but the test result is false, it is called **False Negative** (FN).

With the help of the various detection results mentioned above, the **precision** (*P*) can be further calculated, which represents the proportion of correctly detected true samples among all samples whose HOI detection is true:

$$P = \frac{\mathrm{T_P}}{\mathrm{T_P} + \mathrm{F_P}} \tag{6.1}$$

It is also possible to further calculate the **recall** (*R*), which represents the proportion of HOI correctly detected true samples among all true samples:

$$R = \frac{\mathrm{T_P}}{\mathrm{T_P} + \mathrm{F_N}} \tag{6.2}$$

For the detection of a single (interactive) category, the **Average Precision** (AP) can be defined based on precision (*P*) and recall (*R*):

$$\mathrm{AP} = \int_0^1 P(R)\mathrm{d}R \tag{6.3}$$

where $P(R)$ is a function with *R* as a parameter. The integral value of AP (also known as the accumulated value of the product of *P* and *R*) is the area under the PR curve (accuracy-recall curve), and the larger the value, the better the HOI detection effect.

Finally, in order to evaluate the superiority or inferiority of the detection method, considering the detection of all (interaction) categories, the average accuracy (also known as average precision) of all classes can be used, which is the average value of the average precision (AP), called the **mean Average Precision** (mAP):

$$\mathrm{mAP} = \frac{\mathrm{AP}}{C} \tag{6.4}$$

where *C* is the number of categories detected by HOI.

Considering the characteristics of HOI detection, if the human frame and object frame are accurately located, that is, the **Intersection over Union** (IoU) ratio of the overlapping part between the predicted box and the true value box is greater than 0.5, and the interaction category is correctly predicted, it can be considered True Positive (TP), otherwise it is False Positive (FP). In other words, TP require: ① The IoU between the predicted human frame and its true frame is greater than or equal to 0.5; ② The IoU between the predicted object frame and its true frame is greater than or equal to 0.5; ③ The predicted human-object interaction actions are consistent with the true actions. It can be represented as follows:

$$\mathrm{HOI}_{\mathrm{detection}} = \begin{cases} \mathrm{TP} \quad \mathrm{If} \begin{cases} \text{IoU (Prediction box, True value box)} \geq 0.5 \\ \text{Interaction Prediction = Ture} \end{cases} \\ \mathrm{FP} \quad \text{Otherwise} \end{cases} \tag{6.5}$$

It should be noted that for specific databases, the calculation of evaluation indicators often needs to be adjusted appropriately (with some variations). Here are some points to note regarding the widely used databases V-COCO and HICO-DET.

In the V-COCO database, some HOIs without target labels are defined. To cope with this situation, according to the standard evaluation scheme of V-COCO, performance evaluation can be divided into two situations. In the first scenario, the detector needs to report the absence of a target; while in the second scenario, the detector can ignore the prediction of the target bounding box.

For the HICO-DET database, mAP has two modes, namely default (DT) mode and known target (KO) mode. In DT mode, each HOI category should be evaluated for all test images. In KO mode, HOI only needs to be evaluated on images that contain their relevant target categories. MAP is reported on three different category sets: ① For all 600 HOI categories in HICO (complete); ② Conduct analysis on 462 HOI categories (common/no rare) in HICO that contain 10 or more samples; ③ Conduct a study on 138 HOI categories (rare) in HICO that contain less than 10 samples.

References

Agarwal A, Dabral R, Jain A, *et al.* Skew-robust human-object interactions in videos. Proc. WACV, 5087–5096 (2023).

Antoun M, Asmar D. Human object interaction detection: Design and survey. Image and Vision Computing, 130, #104617 (2023).

Baek D, Choe J. VHOIP: Video-based human-object interaction recognition with CLIP prior knowledge. Pattern Recognition, 190: 133–140. https://doi.org/10.1016/j.patrec.2025.02.014 (2025).

Bansal S S, Rambhatla A, Shrivastava R, *et al.* Detecting human-object interactions via functional generalization. Proc. AAAI, 10460–10469 (2020a).

Bansal S S, Rambhatla A, Shrivastava R, *et al.* Spatial priming for detecting human-object interactions. https://arxiv.org/abs/2004.04851 (2020b).

Benavent-Lledo M, Oprea S, Castro-Vargas J A, *et al.* Predicting human-object interactions in egocentric videos. Proc. IJCNN, 1–7 (2022).

Carion N, Massa F, Synnaeve G, *et al.* End-to-end object detection with transformers. Proc. ECCV 213–229. (2020)

Chao Y W, Liu Y, Liu X, *et al.* Learning to detect human object interactions. Proc. WACV, 381–389 (2018).

Chiou M J, Liao C Y, Wang L W, *et al.* ST-HOI: A spatial-temporal baseline for human-object interaction detection in videos. Proc. ACM-WICDAR, 9–17 (2021).

Eum S, Kwon H. Semantics to space (S2S): Embedding semantics into spatial space for zero-shot verb-object query inferencing. https://arxiv.org/abs/1906.05894 (2019).

Fang H S, Cao J K, Tai Y W, *et al.* Pairwise body-part attention for recognizing human object interactions. Proc. ECCV, 51–67 (2018).

Fang H S, Xie Y C, Shao D A, *et al.* DIRV: Dense interaction region voting for end-to-end human-object interaction detection. Proc. 35AAAI, 35, 1291–1299 (2021).

Gao C, Zou Y, Huang J B. ICAN: instance-centric attention network for human-object interaction detection. arXiv:1808.10437 (2018).

Girshick R, Radosavovic I, Gkioxari G, et al. Detectron. https://github.com/facebookresearch/detectron (2020).

Gong X, Zhang Z Y, Liu L, *et al.* A survey of human-object interaction detection. Journal of Southwest Jiaotong University, 57(4): 693–704 (2022).

Gupta S, Malik J. Visual semantic role labeling. https://arxiv.org/pdf/1505.04474. pdf (2015)

Gupta T, Schwing A, Hoiem D. No-frills human object interaction detection: factorization, layout encodings, and training techniques. Proc. ICCV, 9677–9685 (2019)

Han G, Zhao J C, Zhang L L, *et al.* A survey of human-object interaction detection with deep learning. IEEE Transactions on Emerging Topics in Computational Intelligence, 9(1): 3–26 (2025).

Hakala J, Hakkinen J. A method for measuring contact points in human-object interaction utilizing infrared cameras. Frontiers in Robotics and AI, 8, #800131, https://doi.org/10.3389/frobt.2021.800131 (2022).

He K, Gkioxari G, Dollár P, et al. Mask RCNN. Proc. ICCV, 2961–2969 (2017).

Indermun S, Schreve K, Weber T, *et al.* Dynamic human-object interaction detection for feature exclusion in visual simultaneous localization and mapping (SLAM). International Journal of Advanced Robotic Systems, 21(5), https://doi.org/10.1177/17298806241279782 (2024).

Ji J W, Desai R, Niebles J C. Detecting human-object relationships in videos. Proc. ICCV, 8086–8096 (2021).

Jiang W B, Ren W H, Tian J D, *et al.* Interaction-aware transformer network for human-object interaction detection. IEEE Trans. Cybernetics. https://doi.org/10.1109/TCYB.2025.3587037 (2025).

Kang P Q, Zhu K Z, Jiang S, *et al.* HBOD: A novel dataset with synchronized hand, body, and object manipulation data for human-robot interaction. Proc. BSN, https://doi.org/10.1109/BSN58485.2023.10330940 (2023)

Kim B, Choi T, Kang J, *et al.* UnionDet: Union-level detector towards real-time human-object interaction detection. Proc. ECCV, 498–514 (2020).

Kim B, Lee J, Kang J, et al. HOTR: end-to-end human-object interaction detection with transformers. Proc. CVPR, 74–83 (2021).

Kolesnikov A, Kuznetsova A, Lampert C H, *et al.* Detecting visual relationships using box attention. Proc. ICCVW, 1749–1753 (2019).

Lampert C H, Nickisch H, Harmeling S. Learning to detect unseen object classes by between class attribute transfer. Proc. CVPR,951–958 (2009).

Law H, Dend J. Cornernet: Detecting objects as paired keypoints. Proc. ECCV, 734–750 (2018).

Leonardi R, Ragusa F, Furnari A, *et al.* Exploiting multimodal synthetic data for egocentric human-object interaction detection in an industrial scenario. Computer Vision and Image Understanding, 242, https://doi.org/10.1016/j.cviu.2024.103984 (2024).

Lee H, Kang D, Park H, *et al.* Enhanced human object interaction detection via maximum IoU partitioning and chunk block attention. IEEE Access, 12: 182310–182321 (2024).

Li J, Wang C, Zhu H, *et al.* Crowdpose: Efficient crowded scenes pose estimation and a new benchmark. Proc. CVPR, 10863–10872 (2019a).

Li Y L, Zhou S. Huang X, *et al.* Transferable interactiveness knowledge for human-object interaction detection. Proc. CVPR, 3585–3594 (2019b).

Li Y L, Xu L, Liu X, *et al.* PastaNet: Toward human activity knowledge engine. Proc. CVPR, 379–388 (2020)

Li Z M, Zou C, Zhao Y, *et al.* Improving human-object interaction detection via phrase learning and label composition. Proc. AAAI, 36(2): 1509–1517 (2022).

Liang Z J, Liu J F, *et al.* Pose-based modular network for human-object interaction detection. https://arxiv.org/abs/2008.02042 (2020a).

Liang Z J, Rojas J, Liu J F, *et al.* Visual-semantic graph attention networks for human- object interaction detection. https://arxiv.org/abs/2001.02302 (2020b).

Liao Y, Liu S, Wang F, *et al.* PPDM: Parallel point detection and matching for real-time human-object interaction detection. Proc. CVPR, 479–487 (2020).

Liao Y, Li Z M, Liu C. A review of deep learning-based human-object interaction detection. Journal of Image and Graphics, 27(9): 2611–2618 (2022).

Lin T Y, Maire M, Belongie S J, *et al.* Microsoft COCO: common objects in context. Proc. ECCV, 740–755 (2014).

Liu Y, Yuan J S, Chen C W. ConsNet: Learning consistency graph for zero-shot human-object interaction detection. Proc. 28th ACM International Conference on Multimedia, 4235–4243 (2020).

Liu H C, Mu T J, Huang X L. Detecting human object interaction with multi-level pairwise feature network. Computational Visual Media, 7(2): 229–239 (2021a).

Liu S, Wang Z T, Gao Y L, *et al.* Human-centric relation segmentation: dataset and solution. IEEE Trans-PAMI, 44(9): 4987–5001 (2021b).

Liu J C, Liu Y, Ma J X. Group activity recognition based on relationship network and core person modeling. Journal of Qingdao University of Science and Technology (Natural Science Edition), 43(3): 98–106 (2022).

Nagarajan T, Feichtenhofer C, Grauman K. Grounded human object interaction hotspots from video. Proc. ICCV, 8687–8696 (2019).

Ni Z F, Mascaró E V, Ahn H, et al. Human–object interaction prediction in videos through gaze following. Computer Vision and Image Understanding, 233, #103741 (https://doi.org/10.1016/j.cviu.2023. 103741) (2023).

Parasa A, Gugulothu H, Penmetsa S S P, *et al.* NeuroRobo: Bridging the emotional gap in human-robot interaction with facial sentiment analysis, object detection, and behavior prediction. Lecture Notes of the Institute for Computer Sciences, Social Informatics and Telecommunications Engineering (537), 162–72 (2024).

Qi S Y, Wang W G, Jia B X, *et al.* Learning human object interactions by graph parsing neural networks. Proc. ECCV, 407–423 (2018).

Qiao T Q, Li R C, Li F W B, *et al.* Geometric visual fusion graph neural networks for multi-person human-object interaction recognition in videos. Expert Systems with Applications, 290: 128344. https://doi.org/10.1016/j.eswa.2025.128344 (2025).

Ruan C Z, Zhang X S, Liu K, *et al.* Progress on human-object interaction detection of deep learning. Journal of Frontiers of Computer Science and Technology, 16(2): 323–336 (2022).

Shen L, Yeung S, Hoffman J, *et al.* Scaling human-object interaction recognition through zero-shot learning. Proc. WACV, 1568–1576 (2018).

Shi H Y, Hou Z J, Chao X, *et al.* Multimodal spatial-temporal feature representation and its application in action recognition. Journal of Image and Graphics, 28(4): 1041–1055 (2023).

Shi Y Q, Zhao F. Video behavior recognition based on dynamic spatiotemporal information fusion. Computer Applications and Software, 41(4): 179–184 (2024).

Sunkesula S P R, Dabral R, Ramakrishnan G. LIGHTEN: Learning interactions with graph and hierarchical temporal networks for HOI in videos. Proc. ACM-ICM, 691–699 (2020).

Takemoto K, Yamada M, Sasaki T, *et al.* HICO-DET-SG and V-COCO-SG: New data splits for evaluating the systematic generalization performance of human-object interaction detection models. arXiv, May 17 (2023).

Tamura M, Ohashi H, Yoshinaga T. QPIC: Query-based pairwise human-object interaction detection with image-wide contextual information. Proc. CVPR, 10410–10419 (2021).

Ulutan O, Iftekhar A S M, Manjunath B S. VSGNet: spatial attention network for detecting human object interactions using graph convolutions. Proc. CVPR, 13614–13623 (2020).

Wan B, Zhou D S, Liu Y F, *et al.* Pose-aware multi-level feature network for human object interaction detection. Proc. ICCV, 9468–9477 (2019).

Wang T C, Anwer R M, Khan M H, *et al.* Deep contextual attention for human-object interaction detection. Proc. ICCV, 5694–5702 (2019a).

Wang T C, Zhu G M, Zhang L, *et al.* Spatiotemporal interaction graph parsing networks for human-object interaction recognition. Proc. ACM-ICM, 4985–4993 (2019b).

Wang J, Shuai H H, Li Y H, *et al.* Human-object interaction detection: An overview. IEEE Consumer Electronics Magazine, 13(6): 56–72 (2024).

Yu F, Wang D, Sheihamer E, *et al.* Deep layer aggregation. Proc. CVPR, 2403–2412 (2018).

Zakour M, Mellouli A, Chaudhari R. HOIsim: Synthesizing realistic 3D human-object interaction data for human activity recognition. Proc. RHIC, 1124–1131 (2021).

Zhang F Z, Campbell D, Gould S. Spatio-attentive graphs for human object interaction detection. arXiv: 2012.06060 (2020).

Zhang A, Liao Y, Liu S, *et al.* Mining the benefits of two-stage and one-stage HOI detection. Proc. NEURIPS, 21, 17209–17220 (2021).

Zhang Y-J. A Selection of Image Understanding Techniques: From Fundamentals to Research Front. CRC Press, England (2023).

Zhong X, Qu Zhong, Ding C, *et al.* Glance and gaze: Inferring action-aware points for one-stage human-object interaction detection, Proc. CVPR, 13229–13238 (2021).

Zhou P, Chi M. Relation parsing neural network for human-object interaction detection. Proc. ICCV, 843–851 (2019a).

Zhou X, Wang D, Krähenbühl P. Objects as points, in: arXiv preprint arXiv: 1904.07850 (2019b).

Zhou T F, Qi S Y, Wang W G, *et al.* Cascaded parsing of human-object interaction recognition. IEEE Trans. PAMI, 44(6): 2827–2840 (2022).

Zhuang B, Wu Q, Shen C, *et al.* HCVRD: A benchmark for large-scale human-centered visual relationship detection. Proc. AAAI, https://ojs.aaai.org/index.php/AAAI/article/view/12260 (2018).

Zou C, Wang B H, Hu Y, *et al.* End-to-end human object interaction detection with HOI transformer. Proc. CVPR, 11820–11829 (2021).

Chapter 7
Behavior Recognition Networks

Behavior refers not only to a combination of actions performed by the subject/initiator, but also to a series of actions taken by the subject/initiator and driven by certain subjective intentions. It can also be said that behavior is an activity that involves both objective and subjective factors.

Behavior is semantically higher-level and at a more abstract level. The recognition of behavior requires not only the detection of actions, but also the analysis of the relationship between the actors and actions, and the establishment of the connection between activities and the environment.

From a technical perspective, behavior recognition often requires the integration of various spatiotemporal information, such as human body information, action information, environmental information, scene structure and various change/evolution information.

Recently, there have been many research works related to behavior recognition that mainly combine neural network and deep learning techniques, such as (Dong et al. 2025; Jiang et al. 2025; Yu et al. 2026; Zhang et al. 2024; Zhou et al. 2024; Zhou et al. 2025; Zhu et al. 2024), etc.

The sections of this chapter are arranged as follows.

Section 7.1 introduces a network method that combines motion information and contextual information.

Section 7.2 discusses a network that samples videos in sequential segments to obtain information on motion changes over a long period of time.

Section 7.3 analyzes a graph convolutional network for activity and behavior recognition, as well as some improvements made to it.

Y.-J. Zhang, *Spatiotemporal Image Understanding*,
https://doi.org/10.1007/978-981-95-7130-7_7

7.1 Networks Combining Motion and Context

The **Two-Stream Convolutional Network** (TSCN) (Simonyan 2014a) combines the spatial convolutional network for processing single frame images with the temporal convolutional network for processing multi-frame optical flow images (utilizing both spatial and temporal motion information), and is commonly used for motion and behavior recognition. If the shallow convolutional network is replaced with the deep convolutional network VGGNet (Simonyan 2014b), a **Very Deep Two-Stream Convolutional Network** (VD-TSCN) can be constructed, which will have better recognition performance for motion behavior (Wang et al. 2015). The following introduces a method for further distinguishing between the motion information provided by the moving target and the scene information provided by the context. It uses a two-stream convolutional network to recognize the motion region and context information, respectively, and further fuses the recognition results of the two to obtain the final behavior recognition result (Chen et al. 2016).

7.1.1 Network Model Framework

The behavior recognition framework based on motion convolution and context convolution network models is shown in Fig. 7.1, which can be divided into two threads: motion convolution and context convolution. The final recognition result is obtained by fusing the results of the two threads.

(1) Motion convolution

This thread consists of two networks: a **Spatial Convolutional Network** (SCN) responsible for identifying the apparent information of moving targets, and a **Temporal Convolutional Network** (TCN) responsible for identifying the motion information of moving targets. The input of the spatial convolutional network is a 3-frame (RGB) color image. The input of the temporal convolutional network is a 2

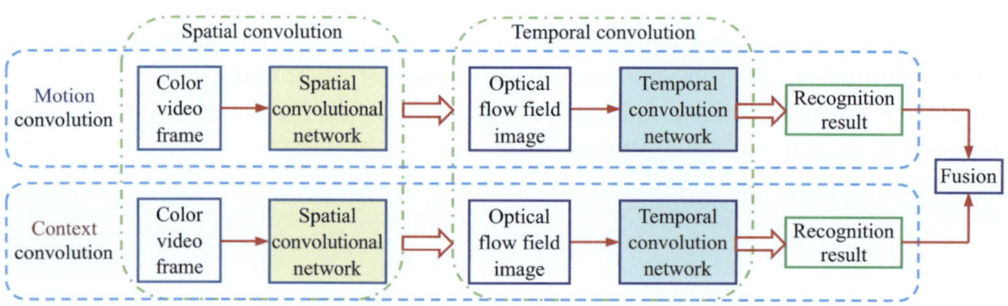

Fig. 7.1 Behavior recognition framework based on motion and context convolutional network model

L frame (e.g. $L = 10$) stacked optical flow field image (considering both horizontal and vertical directions).

(2) Context convolution

This thread includes also two networks: a spatial convolutional network and temporal convolutional network (similar as in the motion convolution thread). The input of the spatial convolutional network is the entire video sequence frame image. The input of the temporal convolutional network is the stacked optical flow field image of L frames (e.g. $L = 10$).

(3) Fusion of recognition results

After obtaining separately the network recognition results of motion convolution and context convolution, these results can be fused together by weighted average:

$$R(V) = p_{\mathrm{m}}R_{\mathrm{m}}(\mathbf{V}) + p_{\mathrm{c}}R_{\mathrm{c}}(\mathbf{V}) \tag{7.1}$$

$$R_{\mathrm{m}}(V) = q_{\mathrm{ms}}R_{\mathrm{ms}}(\mathbf{V}) + q_{\mathrm{mt}}R_{\mathrm{mt}}(\mathbf{V}) \tag{7.2}$$

$$R_{\mathrm{c}}(V) = q_{\mathrm{cs}}R_{\mathrm{cs}}(\mathbf{V}) + q_{\mathrm{ct}}R_{\mathrm{ct}}(\mathbf{V}) \tag{7.3}$$

where $\boldsymbol{V}$ represents the input video; $R_{\mathrm{m}}(V)$ and $R_{\mathrm{c}}(V)$ represent the recognition results of motion convolution and context convolution, respectively; p_{m} and p_{c} are corresponding weighting coefficients; $R_{\mathrm{ms}}(V)$, $R_{\mathrm{mt}}(V)$ and $R_{\mathrm{cs}}(V)$, $R_{\mathrm{ct}}(V)$ respectively represent the recognition results of spatial and temporal convolutional networks in motion convolution, as well as spatial and temporal convolutional networks in context convolution; q_{ms}, q_{mt}, q_{cs}, q_{ct} are the weighting coefficients corresponding to these recognition results, respectively. After experimentation, $p_{\mathrm{m}} = p_{\mathrm{c}} = 1$ was selected because the recognition performances of motion convolution and context convolution are basically the same. The $p_{\mathrm{ms}} = p_{\mathrm{cs}} = 1$ and $p_{\mathrm{mt}} = p_{\mathrm{ct}} = 2$ are selected because the recognition results of temporal convolutional networks are better than those of spatial convolutional networks, and giving greater weights to temporal convolutional networks can improve the fusion effect.

7.1.2 Camera Motion Estimation and Compensation

In the above discussion, the network directly utilized the raw input video for motion detection and behavior recognition. In practice, the motion of the camera can also be considered, and some preprocessing can be performed on the input video before proceeding with subsequent work.

The motion information in the scene may come from both foreground motion caused by freely moving targets (such as the human body) and background motion caused by freely moving cameras. The motion information in the scene is the result of the combination of these two types of motion. In order to estimate human motion based on **homography transformation**, it is necessary to eliminate the influence of camera motion. To achieve this, it is possible to first determine the feature matching pairs between adjacent frames in the video that correspond to camera motion (such as using **Histogram of Oriented Gradient** (HOG) to describe features).

After obtaining the set of feature matching pairs $\boldsymbol{M}_{t,t+1}$ caused by camera motion in adjacent video frames I_t and I_{t+1}, the **RANdom SAmple Consensus** (RANSAC) algorithm (Fischler and Bolles 1981) can be used to estimate the homography transformation matrix $\boldsymbol{H}$ from $\boldsymbol{M}_{t,t+1}$. Next, the inverse transformation matrix $\boldsymbol{H}^{-1}$ is used to correct camera motion in the second frame I_{t+1}. Then, the optical flow of the motion corrected video frames is recalculated to obtain the motion compensated optical flow field $\boldsymbol{F}$ at time t corresponding to I_t, which mainly reflects the motion information of the human body. Finally, calculate the optical flow field $\boldsymbol{F}_\mathrm{c}$ after motion compensation:

$$\mathbf{F}_\mathrm{c} = O\{[\mathbf{H}^{-1}(M_{t,t+1})]I_{t+1}, I_t\} \tag{7.4}$$

In order to study the behavior of motion targets, it is often necessary to separate them from the background area/contextual scene. This can be achieved by utilizing the information obtained from motion compensated optical flow field. This process mainly includes: ① Median filtering the optical flow field after camera motion compensation to eliminate the influence of isolated noise points; ② Detecting the maximum connected component in the optical flow field after median filtering, and calculating its integral map to accelerate the subsequent calculation of the average optical flow intensity; ③ Performing sliding window detection on the optical flow field after median filtering; ④ Using **Non-Maximum Suppression** (NMS) technique, the motion candidate regions are selected based on the results of sliding window detection.

7.1.3 Experimental Results and Analysis

The corresponding experimental setups for evaluating the method introduced in the previous subsection are as follows. Two datasets: HMDB51 database and UCF101 database are used in experiments. Their statistical information is shown in Table 7.1.

Table 7.1 Some statistical data of HMDB51 database and UCF101 database

Statistics	HMDB51	UCF101
Video sample source	YouTube + film	YouTube
Total number of video samples	6766	13320
Test set size	1530	3700
Total number of behavior categories	51	101

The evaluation indicator used is accuracy. Both databases contain 3 splits each, and experiments need to be conducted on each of the 3 data splits. The accuracy results of the 3 splits will be averaged to obtain the final evaluation result.

In the experiments, the motion candidate regions are first input into the spatial convolutional network according to Fig. 7.1, and the motion compensated optical flow field is input into the temporal convolutional network to learn motion information. The entire video frames are input into the spatial convolutional network. By using the temporal convolutional network, the optical flow field without camera motion compensation is used to learn contextual information. Finally, using Eq. (7.2), the recognition results of motion and context are fused to obtain experimental results. Below are three experiments and their results.

(1) Motion and contextual information in HMDB51 database

For the HMDB51 database, three scenarios were considered: ① Using only motion information, ② Using only contextual information, ③ Combining motion and contextual information. The results are shown in Table 7.2 (bold numbers indicate the best).

As shown in Table 7.2, the performance of using only motion information is worse than that using only contextual information. The spatial convolutional network is 1.7% worse, while the temporal convolutional network is 5.6% worse. The reason here should be related to the wide range of video data sources in the HMDB51 database, including videos from movies and YouTube video websites. At this point, there are certain difficulties in estimating camera motion, resulting in poor results based on optical flow fields and affecting subsequent motion region detection as well as behavior recognition results.

As shown in Table 7.2, combining motion information and contextual information yields better results than that only using motion information or contextual information separately. Specifically, the combined average performance improved by 8.5% compared to that using only motion information and 1.6% compared to that using only contextual information. If viewed from a network perspective, the average performance of spatial convolutional networks has improved by 2.8% compared to that using only motion information, and by 1.1% compared to that using only contextual information. The average performance of temporal convolutional networks improved by 8.4% compared to that using only motion information and 2.8% compared to that using only contextual information.

(2) Motion and contextual information in UCF101 database

For the UCF101 database, three scenarios were also considered: ① Using only motion information, ② Using only contextual information, ③ Combining motion and contextual information. The results obtained are shown in Table 7.3 (bold numbers indicate the best).

As shown in Table 7.3, the performance of using only motion information is just slightly worse than that using only contextual information. The spatial convolutional network is basically the same, while the temporal convolutional network is about 1.0% worse. The reasons for this can be attributed to two aspects. On the one hand,

Table 7.2 Behavior recognition results of motion and contextual information in HMDB51 database (Chen et al. 2016)

Information	Spatial convolutional network (%)				Temporal convolutional network (%)				Two-stream convolutional network (%)			
	Split 1	Split 2	Split 3	Average	Split 1	Split 2	Split 3	Average	Split 1	Split 2	Split 3	Average
Only motion	46.7	43.9	41.8	44.1	54.6	53.4	54.0	54.0	59.0	58.2	58.1	58.4
Only context	48.3	46.4	42.8	45.8	61.8	58.4	58.5	59.6	67.2	64.5	64.3	65.3
Motion + context	49.5	47.5	43.7	46.9	64.3	61.3	61.6	62.4	68.2	66.4	66.0	66.9

Table 7.3 Behavior recognition results of motion and contextual information in HCF101 database (Chen et al. 2016)

Information	Spatial convolutional network (%)				Temporal convolutional network (%)				Two-stream convolutional network (%)			
	Split 1	Split 2	Split 3	Average	Split 1	Split 2	Split 3	Average	Split 1	Split 2	Split 3	Average
Only motion	79.9	76.9	77.5	78.1	84.7	86.3	86.7	85.9	90.5	90.3	90.9	90.6
Only context	79.7	77.2	77.3	78.1	85.8	87.7	87.3	86.9	90.8	91.9	91.3	91.3
Motion + context	82.2	80.3	80.6	81.0	88.1	90.5	90.1	89.6	92.4	92.8	92.6	92.6

using only a single homography transformation to estimate camera motion is not accurate enough, resulting in the optical flow field after camera motion compensation still containing optical flow caused by non-human motion. On the other hand, the optical flow after motion compensation mainly reflects the movement of the human body, corresponding to a smaller area of the optical flow field. Compared to the scene change information provided by the context optical flow field, deep convolutional networks are more prone to overfitting when trained on motion compensated optical flow field data.

As can be seen from Table 7.3, the results obtained by combining motion information and contextual information are better than that only using motion information or contextual information separately. Specifically, the combined average performance improved by 2.0% compared to that using only motion information and 1.3% compared to that using only contextual information. If viewed from a network perspective, the average performance of spatial convolutional networks has improved by nearly 3.0% compared to that using only motion information, and has also improved by nearly 3.0% compared to that using only contextual information. The average performance of time-domain convolutional networks has improved by about 3.7% compared to that using only motion information, and by about 2.7% compared to that using only contextual information.

(3) Comparison with some related methods

The network method that combines motion information with contextual information was experimentally compared with some other related methods. These methods include: **Two-Stream Convolutional Network** (TSCN) (Simonyan 2014a), Combination of TSCN and LSTM (Ng et al. 2015), **Very Deep Two-Stream Convolutional Network** (VD-TSCN) (Wang et al. 2015), Long-term temporal convolutional network (Varol et al. 2016). The comparison results of these five methods on the same two databases are shown in Table 7.4 (bold numbers indicate the best).

As shown in Table 7.4, combining motion information with contextual information can indeed effectively improve the performance of behavior recognition methods. This method, which combines motion and contextual information, outperforms other methods in motion behavior recognition on two large-scale universal video databases.

Table 7.4 Comparison with some related methods on two databases (Chen et al. 2016)

Methods	HMDB51	UCF101
Two-stream (TSCN)	59.4	88.0
Two-stream + LSTM	–	88.6
VD-TSCN	–	91.4
Long-term temporal convolution	64.8	91.7
Motion + context	66.9	92.6

7.2 Sequential Segment Network Utilizing Structural Information

The actual activity and behavior may involve many stages of actions over a long period of time. Some similar activities or behaviors may contain partially similar actions. If only a single moment or short-term data in the video is randomly sampled for training and recognition, without utilizing the long-term motion change information in the video, it may not be possible to effectively distinguish behaviors with similar actions.

In the method introduced in Sect. 7.1, the spatial convolutional network only processes one frame of RGB image at a time, while the temporal convolutional network only processes 10 consecutive frames of optical flow field at a time. In this way, only short-term motion information can be learned, which could not meet the needs of a wider range of applications.

The following introduces a method of segmenting and sampling videos according to their temporal sequence to obtain long-term motion change information of the entire video (Chen and Zhang 2017).

7.2.1 Sequential Segments

For each complete video $\boldsymbol{V}$, divide it into N equally spaced parts on the timeline: $\boldsymbol{V} = \{\boldsymbol{P}_1, \boldsymbol{P}_2, \ldots; \boldsymbol{P}_N\}$. For each part $\boldsymbol{P}_n$, randomly select a segment p_n from it, and combine all sampled segments into a sequence: $\{p_1, p_2, \ldots, p_N\}$. Through this sequence, the global content of video $\boldsymbol{V}$ can be learned while preserving the sequential structural relationship between each sampled segment.

By learning the video content of each segment, the output vector $\boldsymbol{S}$ ($\boldsymbol{S} \in \mathrm{R}^K$) that represents the global structural information of the video is obtained:

$$\mathbf{S} = L\big[\mathbf{f}(p_1, \mathbf{W}),\ \mathbf{f}(p_2, \mathbf{W}),\ \cdots,\ \mathbf{f}(p_N, \mathbf{W})\big] \tag{7.5}$$

where $\boldsymbol{f}(p_n, \boldsymbol{W}) \in \mathrm{R}^K$ represents the output vector of the fully connected layer of the convolutional network processing the video sampling segment p_n; $\boldsymbol{W}$ represents the parameters of the convolutional network; K represents the number of behavior categories that need to be identified; $L(\cdot)$ represents a function that learns information from each sampling segment.

The function $L(\cdot)$ can take different forms. For example, in the **Temporal Segment Network** (TSN) model (Wang et al. 2016), the average pooling function was chosen to learn the statistical information of each sampling segment:

$$\mathbf{S} = \frac{1}{N}\sum_{n=1}^{N}\mathbf{f}(p_n, \mathbf{W}) \tag{7.6}$$

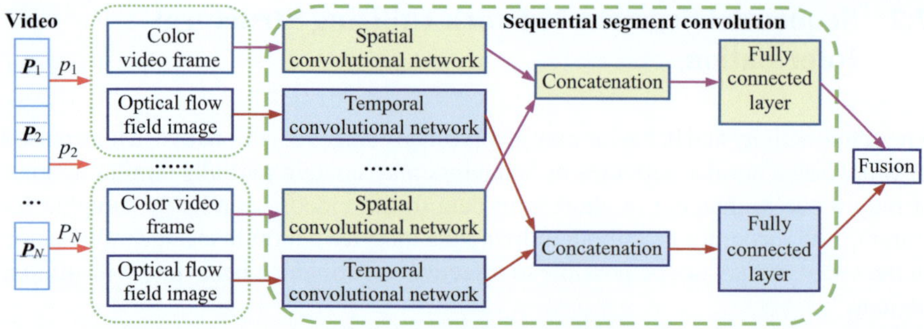

Fig. 7.2 Sequential segment convolutional network model diagram

However, this function only utilizes the internal information of each sampling segment, ignoring the sequential relationship among each sampling segment.

In the **Sequential Segment Network** (SSN), the temporal order relationship between each sampling segment is preserved. This can be seen from the end-to-end model diagram of sequential segmented convolutional network shown in Fig. 7.2.

In Fig. 7.2, the input of the network is a sequence of segments $\{p_1, p_2, \ldots, p_N\}$, sampled sequentially from N parts divided from the video. In practical applications, each segment of data includes one frame of RGB image and multiple consecutive frames of optical flow field images. In the convolution stage, the data of each segment is processed through a two-stream convolutional network to obtain the corresponding output vectors $\boldsymbol{f}_{\mathrm{s}}(p_n, \boldsymbol{W}) \in \mathrm{R}^K$ and $\boldsymbol{f}_{\mathrm{t}}(p_n, \boldsymbol{W}) \in \mathrm{R}^K$. Then, these output vectors are concatenated (cascaded) in the pooling layer of the network to form the total convolutional output vector $\boldsymbol{f}_{\mathrm{cs}} = [\boldsymbol{f}_{\mathrm{s}}(p_1, \boldsymbol{W}), \boldsymbol{f}_{\mathrm{s}}(p_2, \boldsymbol{W}), \ldots, \boldsymbol{f}_{\mathrm{s}}(p_n, \boldsymbol{W})] \in \mathrm{R}^{NK}$ and $\boldsymbol{f}_{\mathrm{ct}} = [\boldsymbol{f}_{\mathrm{t}}(p_1, \boldsymbol{W}), \boldsymbol{f}_{\mathrm{t}}(p_2, \boldsymbol{W}), \ldots, \boldsymbol{f}_{\mathrm{t}}(p_n, \boldsymbol{W})] \in \mathrm{R}^{NK}$. Finally, input $\boldsymbol{f}_{\mathrm{cs}}$ and $\boldsymbol{f}_{\mathrm{ct}}$ separately into the fully connected layer and fuse them to obtain the entire video output vector $\boldsymbol{S} \in \mathrm{R}^K$. This output vector can be written as:

$$\mathbf{S} = \mathbf{W}_{f_c}\mathbf{f}_c = \mathbf{W}_{f_c}\left[\mathbf{f}_c(p_1, \mathbf{W}),\ \mathbf{f}_c(p_2, \mathbf{W}),\ \cdots,\ \mathbf{f}_c(p_N, \mathbf{W})\right] \tag{7.7}$$

where $\boldsymbol{W}_{fc} \in \mathrm{R}^{KNK}$ represents the parameters of the fully connected network layer. As shown in Eq. (7.7), each sampled segment is arranged in the order they appear in the video.

The learning function of the sequential segment model will degenerate into average pooling under specific conditions, where $\boldsymbol{W}_{fc}$ satisfies the following equation:

$$\mathbf{W}_{f_c} = \begin{bmatrix} 1/N & 0 & \cdots & 0 & 1/N & 0 & \cdots & 0 & \cdots & 1/N & 0 & \cdots & 0 \\ 0 & 1/N & \cdots & 0 & 0 & 1/N & \cdots & 0 & \cdots & 0 & 1/N & \cdots & 0 \\ \vdots & \vdots & \ddots & \vdots & \vdots & \vdots & \ddots & \vdots & \vdots & \vdots & \vdots & \ddots & \vdots \\ 0 & 0 & \cdots & 1/N & 0 & 0 & \cdots & 1/N & \cdots & 0 & 0 & \cdots & 1/N \end{bmatrix} \tag{7.8}$$

At this point, the fully connected layer is equivalent to an average pooling layer, and the sequential segment model degenerates into a temporal segment model. From this, it can be seen that the temporal segment model is a special case of the sequential segment model. Or in other words, the sequential segment model is an extension of the temporal segment model.

7.2.2 Experimental Results and Analysis

The above sequential segment convolutional network has been tested. Again, the two databases: HMDB51 database and UCF101 database, as shown in Table 7.1 were used, and all three data splits of these databases were used. The evaluation indicator used is still accuracy, which is the average value of accuracies computed from the three data splits.

In the following, three experiments are presented and the results are discussed, both the segment models and segment divisions are considered.

(1) Comparison between sequential segment model and temporal segment model

The comparison of these two models is actually a comparison of two learning functions. The sequential segment model cascades the output vectors of each segment, while the temporal segment model averages the output vectors of each segment.

The comparison results of the two models on the HMDB51 database are shown in Table 7.5, and the comparison results of the two models on the UCF101 database are shown in Table 7.6 (bold numbers indicate the best).

As shown in Tables 7.5 and 7.6, the sequential segment model performs better than the temporal segment model on both databases. This indicates that maintaining the sequential relationship of each segment is still meaningful, consistent with the previous analysis.

(2) Comparison of the numbers of equal divisions

The sequential segment model first divides the video into equal parts as input, and then randomly samples a moment from each part to input into the convolutional network

Table 7.5 Behavior recognition results of sequential segment model and temporal segment model in HMDB51 database (Chen and Zhang 2017)

Models	Spatial convolutional network (%)				Temporal convolutional network (%)				Two-stream convolutional network (%)			
	Split 1	Split 2	Split 3	Average	Split 1	Split 2	Split 3	Average	Split 1	Split 2	Split 3	Average
Temporal segment	57.8	53.1	52.0	54.3	62.7	62.9	64.0	63.2	71.3	69.0	69.2	69.8
Sequential segment	62.2	58.7	59.2	60.0	64.5	64.6	65.8	65.0	75.6	72.8	72.9	73.8

Table 7.6 Behavior recognition results of sequential segment model and Temporal segment model in UCF101 database (Chen and Zhang 2017)

Models	Spatial convolutional network (%)				Temporal convolutional network (%)				Two-stream convolutional network (%)			
	Split 1	Split 2	Split 3	Average	Split 1	Split 2	Split 3	Average	Split 1	Split 2	Split 3	Average
Temporal segment	85.2	83.9	84.3	84.5	86.5	89.1	89.0	88.2	93.4	94.5	93.6	93.8
Sequential segment	87.1	86.2	87.0	86.8	87.2	89.6	89.7	88.8	93.9	95.5	95.1	94.8

for recognition. For this purpose, experiments were conducted on the sequential segment model using the UCF101 database Split 1, dividing the video into 3, 6, and 12 parts, respectively. The experimental results are shown in Table 7.7 (bold numbers indicate the best).

As shown in Table 7.7, the numbers of equal divisions of video have a certain impact on the performance (recognition results) of the model. When the number of equal divisions is 3 and 6, the performances of the spatial convolutional network and the temporal convolutional network are reversed, but the results of the fusion of the dual stream convolutional network are still the best, especially when the number of equal divisions is 6. When the number of equal divisions is 12, the performance of all three networks decreases. There are two reasons for this: ① The average duration of videos in the database is about 7 s, and dividing them into 12 equal parts is somewhat excessive (each part is shorter); ② As the number of equal divisions increases, the vector dimension after cascading increases, resulting in an increase in the parameters of subsequent fully connected network layers, thereby increasing the risk of overfitting in network training.

(3) Comparison with some related methods

The sequential segment network method was compared with some other related methods, including: ① The method combining sequence inputs based on Fisher vector representation with **Recurrent Neural Networks** (RNNs), and integrating the RNN-FV + IDT method with **Improved Dense Trajectory** (IDT) features (Wang and Schmid 2013) that are robust to camera motion performance (Lev et al. 2016);

Table 7.7 Comparison of sequential segment models with different numbers of equal divisions on UCF101 database Split 1 (Chen and Zhang 2017)

Numbers of equal divisions	Spatial convolutional network (%)	Temporal convolutional network (%)	Two-stream convolutional network (%)
3	87.0	87.4	**93.7**
6	87.1	87.2	**93.9**
12	86.5	85.1	**93.5**

Table 7.8 Comparison of some related methods on two databases (%) (Chen and Zhang 2017)

Methods	HMDB51	UCF101
RNN-FV+IDT	67.7	94.0
Fusion+IDT	69.2	93.5
Hybrid	70.4	92.5
SSN	73.8	94.8

②The Fusion + IDT method fusing spatiotemporal information in the convolution process based on the two-stream model with an IDT method (Feichtenhofer et al. 2016); ③ Hybrid method combining unsupervised video representation based on manually designed features with supervised deep networks (Souza et al. 2016). The comparison results of these methods are shown in Table 7.8 (bold numbers indicate the best).

As shown in Table 7.8, compared to some methods that combine different features, the sequential segment model still has certain advantages.

(4) Integrating SSN into motion and context based convolutional network model

The Sequential Segment Network (SSN) can be integrated into the motion and context based convolutional network model in Sect. 7.1. Specifically, the spatial convolutional network in Fig. 7.1 can be replaced with a sequentially segmented spatial convolutional network, and the temporal convolutional network in Fig. 7.1 can be replaced with a sequentially segmented temporal convolutional network. Table 7.9 shows the experimental results of the model network combined in this way on the HMDB51 database, and Table 7.10 shows the experimental results of the model network combined in this way on the UCF101 database (bold numbers indicate the best).

Comparing Tables 7.9 and 7.10 with Tables 7.2 and 7.3, respectively, it can be seen that the combination of sequential segment networks improves the recognition performance of various modalities (using only motion information, using only contextual

Table 7.9 Behavior recognition results of combined models in HMDB51 database (Chen and Zhang 2017)

Information	Spatial convolutional network (%)			Temporal convolutional network (%)			Two-stream convolutional network (%)			
	Split 1	Split 2	Split 3	Split 1	Split 2	Split 3	Split 1	Split 2	Split 3	Average
Only motion	59.7	56.3	57.9	60.6	59.4	61.1	68.3	67.5	67.3	67.7
Only context	62.2	58.7	59.2	64.5	64.6	65.8	75.6	72.8	72.9	73.8
Motion + context	63.3	60.1	60.5	66.1	65.5	66.7	76.1	73.9	74.3	74.8

Table 7.10 Behavior recognition results of combined models in UCF101 database (Chen and Zhang 2017)

Information	Spatial convolutional network (%)			Temporal convolutional network (%)			Two-stream convolutional network (%)			
	Split 1	Split 2	Split 3	Split 1	Split 2	Split 3	Split 1	Split 2	Split 3	Average
Only motion	85.9	84.7	85.6	86.1	88.3	88.5	92.4	93.7	93.5	93.2
Only context	87.1	86.2	87.0	87.2	89.6	89.7	93.9	95.5	95.1	94.8
Motion + context	88.0	87.2	87.7	88.9	91.3	90.9	94.3	95.7	95.5	95.1

information, and combining motion information and contextual information). This indicates that the sequential segment strategy has certain universality.

7.3 Graph Convolutional Network for Activity and Behavior

The recognition of various sports activities and behaviors is a branch of behavior recognition that has received early attention. In order to identify sports activities, athletes' skeletons are usually used to determine their movements and postures.

The human **skeleton** can be represented as a graph with skeleton joints as nodes and bones as edges. This graph can be denoted as $G = (V, E, X)$, where $V = \{v_1, v_2, \ldots, v_N\}$ is a set of N nodes; E is the set of all edges, which can be formulated as the adjacency matrix $\boldsymbol{A} \in \mathrm{R}^{N \times N}$, and its element a_{ij} reflects the strength of the correlation between nodes v_i and v_j. The neighborhood of v_i can be represented as $N(v_i) = \{v_j | a_{ij} \neq 0\}$. X is a feature set of N nodes, which can be formulated as a matrix $\boldsymbol{X} \in \mathrm{R}^{N \times C}$, where C represents the number of channels. The feature of node v_i can be represented as $\boldsymbol{x}_i \in \mathrm{R}^C$.

The use of skeleton data for action recognition has several advantages. Firstly, skeleton data is a 3-D coordinate sequence of multiple skeleton joints, so its topological structure can be modeled using prior knowledge. In addition, compared with RGB data, it has better robustness not only to external noise such as lighting and occlusion, but also to changes in human scale or viewing angle. Finally, due to the fact that the number of human joints in the skeleton data is generally much smaller than the number of pixels in the image, it can improve the computational efficiency of the model.

Traditional activity recognition often uses color (RGB) images and videos. On the basis of RGB data, depth (D) data has also been widely used in recent years. Compared to RGB data, RGBD data has multiple advantages (Shaikh et al. 2021), including: RGBD data can provide more structural information than RGB data (mainly including color information and texture information), which makes detection and segmentation of bones and joints easier; RGBD data is not sensitive to changes in lighting, which improves the reliability of activity recognition under poor lighting conditions.

Behavior recognition based on RGBD data can be divided into depth sequences based and skeleton sequences based according to the type of data used. In RGBD videos, depth sequence based methods mainly describe actions based on changes in depth information in human depth maps, such as calculating the difference between adjacent frames in depth videos and overlaying them to form a depth action map. The skeleton sequence based method can robustly describe various spatial actions and activities due to the fact that skeleton data itself carries a lot of human body topology information.

Graph Convolutional Networks (GCN) have shown excellent performance in skeleton joint-based behavior recognition (Wu et al. 2024; Liu et al. 2025). It considers modeling the topology of the graph (the connection relationships between nodes in the graph). According to whether the topology is dynamically adjusted during the inference process, graph convolutional network methods can be divided into static methods and dynamic methods. The former has a fixed topology structure, while the topology of the latter will be dynamically adjusted.

In the convolution of topology shared graphs, feature transformation is performed using weight $\boldsymbol{W}$, and the representation of adjacent nodes of v_i is aggregated through a_{ij} to update its representation z_i:

$$z_i = \sum_{v_j \in N(v_i)} a_{ij} \mathbf{x}_j \mathbf{W} \tag{7.9}$$

For static methods, a_{ij} is manually defined or set as trainable parameters. For dynamic methods, a_{ij} is usually generated by the model based on input samples. The input data is a 3-D skeleton, which can be represented as $\boldsymbol{X} \in \mathrm{R}^{C \times T \times N}$, where C represents the 3-D coordinates of the skeleton joint points, T represents the number of video frames, and N represents the number of skeleton joint points.

7.3.1 Channel-Wise Topology Refinement Modeling

Channel-wise topology models the similarity of each channel by calculating the difference in features on the basis of shared topology, also known as channel based topology. The overall framework of **Channel-wise Topology Refinement Graph Convolution** (CTR-GC) is shown in Fig. 7.3 (Chen et al. 2021), which serves as the basis for the corresponding graph convolutional network (see next sub-section). Firstly, the input features are transformed into high-level features, and then the channel topology is dynamically inferred to capture pairwise correlations between input sample joints under different types of motion features. The features in each channel are aggregated with the corresponding topology to obtain the final output.

Specifically, CTR-GC consists of three modules: ① Feature transformation: It is completed by the transformation function $T(\cdot)$; ② Channel-wise topology modeling: It is completed by the relevant modeling function $M(\cdot)$ and refinement function $R(\cdot)$; ③ Channel-wise aggregation: It is completed by the aggregation function $A(\cdot)$. Given the input feature $\boldsymbol{X} \in \mathrm{R}^{N\times C}$, the output $\mathbf{Z} \in \mathrm{R}^{N\times C'}$ of CTR-GC is

$$\mathbf{Z} = A\{T(\mathbf{X}), R[M(\mathbf{X}), \mathbf{A}]\} \tag{7.10}$$

where $\boldsymbol{A} \in \mathrm{R}^{N\times N}$ is a learnable shared topology.

(1) Feature transformation: As shown in the lower left area (dashed box) of Fig. 7.3, feature transformation aims to convert input features into high-level representations through $T(\cdot)$. Here, a simple linear transformation can be used as the topology shared graph convolution, and its formula is

$$\tilde{\mathbf{X}} = T(\mathbf{X}) = \mathbf{X}\mathbf{W} \tag{7.11}$$

where $\tilde{\mathbf{X}} \in \mathrm{R}^{N\times C'}$ is the transformed feature, and $\boldsymbol{W} \in \mathrm{R}^{C\times C'}$ is the weight matrix.

(2) Channel-wise topology modeling: As shown in the upper left area (dashed box) of Fig. 7.3, the adjacency matrix is used as a shared topology for all channels and is learned through backpropagation. In addition, it is necessary to first learn the channel specific correlation $\boldsymbol{Q} \in \mathrm{R}^{N\times N\times C}$ to model the specific relationships between nodes in the C' channel. Then, using $\boldsymbol{Q}$ to refine the shared topology $\boldsymbol{A}$, the channel topology $\boldsymbol{R} \in \mathrm{R}^{N\times N\times C}$ is obtained.

Specifically, the relevant modeling function $M(\cdot)$ is first used to model the channel correlation between nodes. In order to reduce computational costs, two linear transformations ϕ and ψ are used to reduce the feature dimensionality before sending the input features to $M(\cdot)$. Given a pair of nodes (v_i, v_j) and their corresponding features (x_i, x_j), two simple and effective correlation modeling functions can be designed.

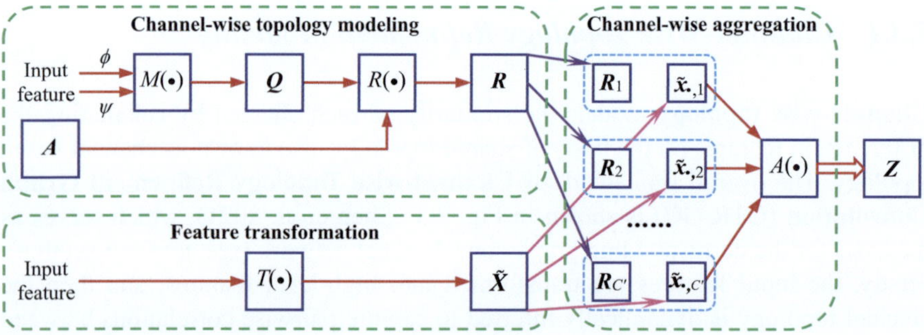

Fig. 7.3 Overall framework of channel-wise topology refinement graph convolution

The first related modeling function $M_1(\cdot)$ is

$$M_1\left[\psi(\mathbf{x}_i), \phi(\mathbf{x}_j)\right] = \sigma\left[\psi(\mathbf{x}_i) - \phi(\mathbf{x}_j)\right] \tag{7.12}$$

where, $\sigma(\cdot)$ is the activation function. $M_1(\cdot)$ essentially calculates the distance between $\psi(x_i)$ and $\phi(x_j)$ along the channel dimension, and uses the nonlinear transformation of these distances as the topological relationship of a specific channel between v_i and v_j. The second related modeling function $M_2(\cdot)$ is

$$M_2\left[\psi(\mathbf{x}_i), \phi(\mathbf{x}_j)\right] = \text{MLP}\left[\psi(\mathbf{x}_\text{i})|| - \phi(\mathbf{x}_\text{j})\right] \tag{7.13}$$

where || represents concatenation operation; MLP is a multi-layer perceptron with excellent fitting ability.

Based on the relevant modeling functions and by using linear transformation L to increase the channel dimension, the correlation $\boldsymbol{Q} \in \text{R}^{N\times N\times C'}$ of a specific channel can be obtained:

$$\mathbf{q}_{ij} = L\{M\left[\psi(\mathbf{x}_i), \phi(\mathbf{x}_j)\right]\} \quad i, j \in \{1,\ 2,\ \ldots,\ N\} \tag{7.14}$$

where $\boldsymbol{q}_{ij} \in \text{R}^{C'}$ is a vector in $\boldsymbol{Q}$, representing the topological relationship of a specific channel between v_i and v_j. It should be noted that $\boldsymbol{Q}$ is not necessarily symmetrical, i.e. $\boldsymbol{q}_{ij} \neq \boldsymbol{q}_{ji}$, which can increase the flexibility of related modeling.

Finally, by refining the shared topology $\boldsymbol{A}$ with specific channel correlation $\boldsymbol{Q}$, the channel topology $\boldsymbol{R} \in \text{R}^{N\times N\times C}$ is obtained:

$$\mathbf{R} = R(\mathbf{Q}, \mathbf{A}) = \mathbf{A} + \alpha\mathbf{Q} \tag{7.15}$$

where α is a trainable scalar used to adjust the refinement strength and needs to be added to each channel.

(3) Channel-wise aggregation: As shown in the right area (dashed box) of Fig. 7.3, given a refined channel topology $\boldsymbol{R}$ and high-level features $\tilde{\mathbf{X}}$, CTR-GC aggregates features in a channel-wise manner. Specifically, CTR-GC constructs a channel map for each channel, which has a corresponding refined topology $\boldsymbol{R}_c \in \text{R}^{N\times N}$ and feature $\tilde{\mathbf{x}}_{\cdot,c} \in \text{R}^{N\times 1}$, where $\boldsymbol{R}_c$ and $\tilde{\mathbf{x}}_{\cdot,c}$ are respectively from the c-th channel of $\boldsymbol{R}$ and $c \in \{1, 2, \ldots, C'\}$. Each channel diagram reflects the node relationships under specific types of motion features. Therefore, feature aggregation is performed on each channel graph, and the final output $\boldsymbol{Z}$ is obtained by connecting the output features of all channel graphs:

$$\mathbf{Z} = A(\tilde{\mathbf{X}}, \mathbf{R}) = \left[\mathbf{R}_1\tilde{\mathbf{x}}_{\cdot,1} \ || \ \mathbf{R}_2\tilde{\mathbf{x}}_{\cdot,2} \ || \ \cdots \mathbf{R}_{C'}\tilde{\mathbf{x}}_{\cdot,C'}\right] \tag{7.16}$$

where || represents concatenation operation. Throughout the entire process, the inference of specific channel correlations $\boldsymbol{Q}$ depends on the input samples, as shown in Eq. (7.14). Therefore, CTR-GC is a dynamic graph convolution that adapts to different input samples.

7.3.2 *Graph Convolutional Network for Activity Recognition*

Based on the aforementioned **Channel-wise Topology Refinement Graph Convolution** (CTR-GC), a corresponding **Channel-wise Topology Refinement Graph Convolutional Network** (CTR-GCN) can be constructed and used for skeleton joint-based activity recognition (Li and Li 2023).

Here, the neighborhood of each joint point is set as the whole human skeleton map. The entire network consists of 10 basic blocks, followed by global average pooling and a Softmax classifier for predicting action labels. The numbers of channels for the 10 blocks are 64, 64, 64, 128, 128, 128, 256, 256, 256, respectively. The time dimension is halved through stride time convolution in the 5-th and 8-th blocks. The basic modules of CTR-GCN are shown in Fig. 7.4a (Chen et al. 2021). Each module mainly includes spatial modeling and temporal modeling, as well as residual connections.

As shown in the upper part of Fig. 7.4a, three CTR-GCs were used in parallel to extract correlations between human joints in spatial modeling, and the results were summarized as output.

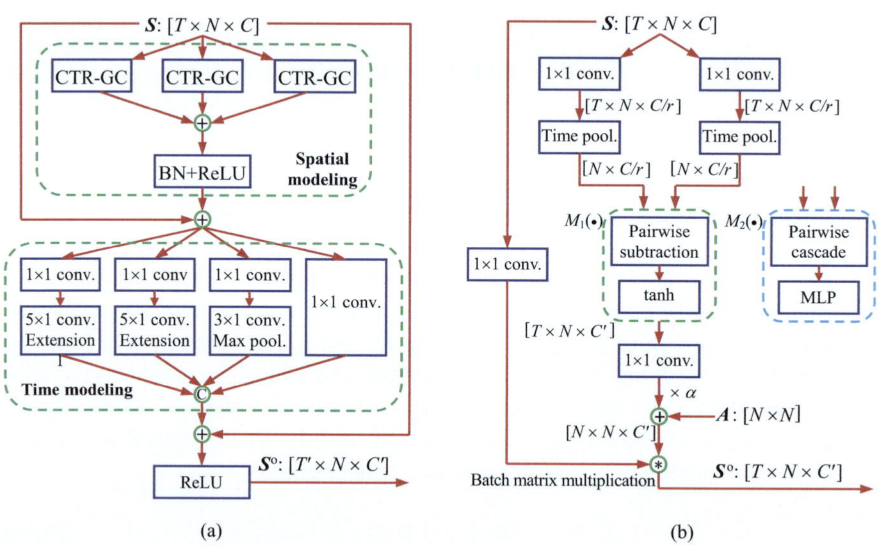

Fig. 7.4 Basic modules and related modeling functions of Channel Topology Refinement Graph Convolutional Network (CTR-GCN)

As shown in the lower part of Fig. 7.4a, a multi-scale time modeling module with fewer branches was designed to model actions of different durations in time modeling. This module consists of four branches, each containing a 1×1 convolution to reduce the channel dimension. The first three branches consist of two time convolutions with different extensions and one max pooling after a 1×1 convolution. The results of the four branches are connected to provide the output.

In Fig. 7.4b (Chen et al. 2021), taking CTR-GC with the relevant modeling function $M_1(\cdot)$ as an example ($M_2(\cdot)$ is also shown). CTR-GC is designed to extract features from graphs with input features $\boldsymbol{X} \in \mathrm{R}^{N \times C}$. In order to apply CTR-GC to the skeleton sequence $\boldsymbol{S} \in \mathrm{R}^{T \times N \times C}$, it is necessary to pool $\boldsymbol{S}$ along the time dimension and use pooling features to infer channel topology. Specifically, CTR-GC first utilizes ϕ and ψ with a reduction rate r to extract compact representations. Then time pooling is used to aggregate temporal features. Next, CTR-GC performs pairwise subtraction and activation according to Eq. (7.12). L is then used to increase the dimension of the activation channel to obtain the correlation of specific channels, which is used to refine the shared topology $\boldsymbol{A}$ to obtain the topology of sub-channels. Finally, channel-wise aggregation is performed in each skeleton graph (achieved through batch matrix multiplication) to obtain the output expression $\boldsymbol{S}^{\circ}$.

7.3.3 Scale Space and Dynamic Time Graph Convolution

There are still some further improvements to the convolutional network CTR-GCN. Below is an introduction to the work of graph convolution in spatial scale and dynamic time (Ming 2022).

1. **Scale Based Space**

In order to extract short-term and long-term features from action videos, CTR-GCN adopts a multi-scale mechanism (setting convolution kernels of different sizes). However, CTR-GCN directly concatenates multi-scale features and sends them from the current layer's GCN to the next layer's GCN. That is, in the current GCN layer, the multi-scale information (multi-scale features) obtained from the previous layer needs to be fused, or in other words, the current GCN layer will calculate potential correlations based on the multi-scale features of the previous layer and make updates. Since the multi-scale information obtained from the previous layer is processed in the current layer, more 1×1 convolutions are required to calculate the similarity and residual terms between joint points. In this way, there will be too many multi-scale feature fusion modules in GCN.

To reduce computational complexity, a **Scale Wise Graph Convolutional Network** (SW-GCN) can be used. In the GCN layer, the scale features are first preserved by updating them based on the spatial correlation of the current scale features, and then a 1×1 convolution module is used to fuse their multi-scale features. This operation is equivalent changing the original "fusing multi-scale features first, then taking spatial correlation" to "taking spatial correlation first, then fusing multi-scale features". The advantage of this new process is that it can effectively capture spatial correlations at all scales while significantly reduce its parameter and computational complexity. Specifically, if the input features contain K scale information, both the parameter and computational complexity can be reduced to $1/K$. This method reduces model complexity by only modifying the convolution algorithm without adding or removing any modules. This technique is easy to implement.

2. **Dynamic Time Convolutional Network**

The receptive field of time-domain convolution is limited. To capture global information using a single **Temporal Convolutional Network** (TCN), two methods are generally used: ① Using larger convolution kernels, but this makes it difficult to focus on short-term actions or local features, and requires larger number of parameters and greater computational complexity; ② Using more (stacking) layers, this will also lead to an increase in parameters and computational complexity. In multi-scale TCNs, in order to reduce the computational cost of each TCN, a 1×1 convolutional layer is passed through before entering each TCN, which means that corresponding dimensionality reduction operations need to be performed for feature extraction at each time scale.

To overcome the above problems, a **Dynamic Temporal Convolution** (D-TC) module can be constructed and utilized to update the feature for convolution kernel window size and channel separately. Specifically, the input features are first subjected to feature transformation, and the result of the feature transformation is subjected to average pooling operation on the channel. Then, the result of the average pooling operation is used as the input feature, and a 1×1 convolution is used to generate the adjacency matrix inside the convolution kernel window, for effectively capturing local temporal features.

3. **Network Model Framework**

The designed network model framework is shown in Fig. 7.5. The network still consists of 10 layers of graph convolution modules, but the networks used in each layer are different. The first layer includes the **Channel-wise Topology Refinement Graph Convolutional Network** (CTR-GCN) and the **Dynamic Temporal Convolutional Network** (D-TCN), which perform feature transformations on the input X based on the human body topology and extract multi-scale action features. The remaining nine layers are composed of a **Scale Wise Graph Convolutional Network** (SW-GCN) and a D-TCN. Finally, the network provides predicted action categories by passing the outputs of these 10 layers through **Global Average Pooling** (GAP) and **Fully Connected** (FC) layers.

This network model has two main improvements compared to CTR-GCN: ① SW-GCN are replaced with CTR-GCN in the last nine layers; ② TCN are replaced with D-TCN in all layers.

4. **Experiments and Results**

Fig. 7.5 Network Model Framework

In order to verify the effectiveness of the above improvements, two databases for behavior recognition based on skeleton were used in experiments.

(1) NTU-RGB + D

This database (Shahroudy et al. 2016) contains 56,578 skeleton sequences, 60 action categories, collected from 40 different persons (each frame of video contains 1 to 2 persons) and from 3 different camera perspectives. Use the samples collected from Camera 2 and Camera 3 as the training set, and the samples collected from Camera 1 for testing. Each skeleton diagram contains 25 body joints (see Sub-Sect. 5.3.1).

(2) NTU-RGB + D 120

This database (Liu et al. 2020) is an extension of NTU-RGB + D, containing 114,480 skeleton sequence, 120 action categories, collected from 106 different persons (aged from 10 to 57 years old), 155 different camera perspectives, and 96 different backgrounds with different lighting. Use samples collected from even numbered cameras as the training set and samples collected from odd numbered cameras for testing. The skeleton diagram used is the same as for NTU-RGB + D.

The following are the experimental results obtained by comparing the above four methods using the database NTU-RGB + D 120. Number the comparison methods (network model) as: (A) CTR-GCN; (B) SW-GCN; (C) D-TCN; (D) SW-GCN + D-TCN. The histograms in Fig. 7.6 show the comparison results of their performance, where Fig. 7.6a shows the recognition accuracy (Acc) of each method; Fig. 7.6b shows the model complexity of each method (GFLOPs = 10^9 FLOPs); Fig. 7.6c shows the number of model parameters (MPs = 10^6 parameters) for each method.

Compared with the baseline CTR-GCN, the recognition accuracy of SW-GCN + D-TCN has been improved (also improved compared to the other two methods) to

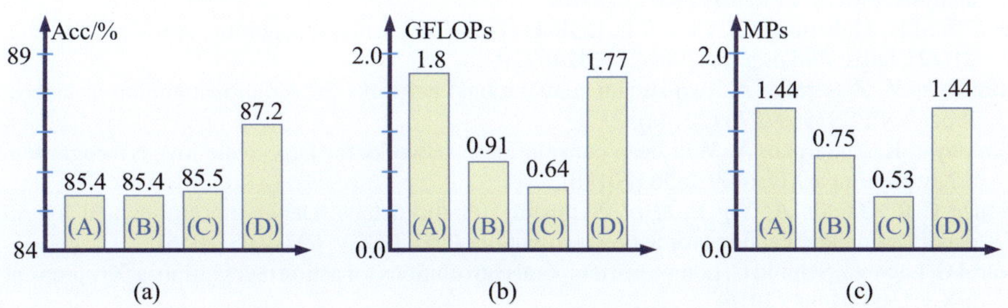

Fig. 7.6 Comparison results of four methods

some extents, the model complexity has been slightly reduced (more complex than the other two methods), and the number of model parameters remains unchanged (more than the other two methods).

References

Chen Q, Liu F, Li X, *et al.* Saliency-context two-stream convnets for action recognition. Proc. ICIP, 3076–3080 (2016).
Chen Q Q, Zhang Y-J. Sequential segment networks for action recognition. IEEE SPL, 24(5): 712–716 (2017).
Chen Y X, Zhang Z Q, Yuan C F, *et al.* Channel-wise topology refinement graph convolution for skeleton-based action recognition. Proc. ICCV, 13339–13348 (2021).
Dong C Y, Liu J, Xie S L. DMSA-Net: A deformable multiscale adaptive classroom behavior recognition network. Peerj Computer Science, 11, e2876. https://doi.org/10.7717/peerj-cs.2876 (2025).
Feichtenhofer C, Pinz A, Zisserman A. Convolutional two-stream network fusion for video action recognition. Proc. CVPR, 1933–1941 (2016).
Fischler M A, Bolles R C. Random sample consensus: a paradigm for model fitting with applications to image analysis and automated cartography. Communications of the ACM, 24(6):381–395 (1981).
Jiang J X, Liu J P, Kadzinski M, *et al.* A Bayesian network approach for dynamic behavior analysis: Real-time intention recognition. Information Fusion, 118: 102873 (2025). https://doi.org/10.1016/j.inffus.2024.102873.
Lev G, Sadeh G, Klein B, *et al.* RNN fisher vectors for action recognition and image annotation. Proc. ECCV, 833–850 (2016).
Li H X, Li X T. Improved graph convolutional network with channel topology refinement based on attention. Journal of Test and Measurement Technology, 37(2): 120–126 (2023).
Liu J, Shahroudy A, Perez M, *et al.* NTU RGB+D 120: A large-scale benchmark for 3D human activity understanding. IEEE Trans-PAMI, 42(10): 2684–2701 (2020).
Liu S L, Ding Y N, Zhang J R, *et al.* Multidimensional refinement graph convolutional network with robust decouple loss for fine-grained skeleton-based action recognition. IEEE Trans-NNLS, 36(4): 7615–7626 (2025).
Ming Y M. Time dynamic graph convolution behavior recognition method based on RGBD skeleton (Dissertation). Beijing, Tsinghua University (2022).
Ng J Y-H, Hausknecht M, Vijayanarasimhan S, *et al.* Beyond short snippets: Deep networks for video classification. Proc. CVPR, 4694–4702 (2015).
Shahroudy A, Liu J, Ng T-T, et al. NTU RGB+D: A large scale dataset for 3D human activity analysis. Proc. CVPR, 1010–1019 (2016).
Shaikh M B, Muhammad B, Chai D L. RGB-D Data-based action recognition: A review. Sensors, 21(12), https://doi.org/10.3390/s21124246 (2021).
Simonyan K, Zisserman A. Two-stream convolutional networks for action recognition in videos. Proc. ANIPSS, 568–576 (2014a).
Simonyan K, Zisserman A. Very deep convolutional networks for large-scale image recognition. arXiv preprint arXiv:1409.1556 (2014b).
Souza C R, Gaidon A, Vig E, *et al.* Sympathy for the details: Dense trajectories and hybrid classification architectures for action recognition. Proc. ECCV, 697–716 (2016).
Varol G, Laptev I, Schmid C. Long-term temporal convolutions for action recognition. arXiv preprint arXiv:1604.04494 (2016).
Wang H, Schmid C. Action recognition with improved trajectories. Proc. ICCV, 3551–3558 (2013).

Wang L, Xiong Y, Wang Z, *et al.* Towards good practices for very deep two-stream Convnets. arXiv preprint arXiv:1507.02159 (2015).

Wang L, Xiong Y, Wang Z, *et al.* Temporal segment networks: towards good practices for deep action recognition. Proc. ECCV, 20–36 (2016).

Wu Z Z, Chen S, Tan M, *et al.* Cross-channel feature-enhanced graph convolutional network for skeleton-based action recognition. Pattern Recognition and Artificial Intelligence, 37(8): 703–714 (2024).

Yu J Q, Zhou Y S, Pan R J, *et al.* Physics-environment interaction network for dense crowd behavior recognition. Pattern Recognition, 170: 112123. https://doi.org/10.1016/j.patcog.2025.112123.

Zhang Y, Zhang B B, Dong W, *et al.* Multi-modal video action recognition method based on language-visual contrastive learning. Acta Automatica Sinica, 50(2): 417–430 (2024).

Zhou Y, Wang J, Zhang J H. A multimodal image recognition system for student behavior analysis in smart classrooms in universities. Traitement du Signal, 41(6): 3285–3293 (2024).

Zhou L C, Liu X P, Guan X Q, *et al.* CSSA-YOLO: Cross-scale spatiotemporal attention network for fine-grained behavior recognition in classroom environments. Sensors, 25(10): 3132. https://doi.org/10.3390/s25103132 (2025).

Zhu L P, Wu Q L, Chen X H, *et al.* Group activity recognition under multi-scale sub-group interaction relationships. Journal of Electronics & Information Technology, 46(5): 2228–2236 (2024).

Chapter 8
Abnormal Event Detection

People often use events to describe special activities or behaviors. Abnormal events are actually events, but they emphasize that they are significantly different from normal and regular activities or behaviors, usually referring to activities or behaviors that are not expected to appear or occur, as can be seen in (Huang et al. 2024; Huang et al. 2025; Ji et al. 2024; Lin et al. 2025; Liu et al. 2024a; Liu and Sang 2024b; Lyu et al. 2026; Ma et al. 2025; Mao et al. 2024; Sun et al. 2024; Zhu et al. 2024). Abnormal activities or behaviors can involve both individuals and multiple persons, often in groups (Zhao et al. 2024). Recently, embedding-based methods have shown some state-of-the art results (Murakami et al. 2025).

From the perspective of time and space, abnormal events often do not occur frequently over time and may have certain degree of locality in space. From a statistical perspective, the probability of its occurrence should be relatively small.

From the perspective of detecting abnormal events, if neural networks are used and deep learning techniques are employed (Balakrishnan et al. 2024), the main problem encountered is that the probability of abnormal events is relatively small, and there are fewer samples available. Therefore, there are many methods that use normal samples for training, while considering the difference between the current situation and the normal situation during detection to determine the abnormality.

The sections of this chapter are arranged as follows.

Section 8.1 discusses the classification of abnormal event detection methods, taking into account the features used and the learning approach.

Section 8.2 introduces methods for abnormal event detection based on convolutional auto-encoders and one-class neural networks.

Section 8.3 adds local gradient structure information to traditional sparse auto-encoders to construct a gradient based sparse auto-encoder.

Section 8.4 introduces an LSTM auto-encoder network using both generative error metric and feature trajectory smoothing metric.

Section 8.5 introduces a depth generative model that considers both generative loss and temporal smoothing loss for abnormal event detection.

Y.-J. Zhang, *Spatiotemporal Image Understanding*,
https://doi.org/10.1007/978-981-95-7130-7_8

Section 8.6 introduces a scene content adapted semi-supervised deep generative model.

Section 8.7 analyzes a master-auxiliary aggregation strategy that combines different anomaly detectors for abnormal event detection, which has certain advantages.

8.1 Classification of Abnormal Event Detection Methods

Intuitively speaking, anomalies are comparative to normalcy. However, the normal definition can also or may change over time, environment, purpose, conditions, etc. It should be pointed out that both normal and abnormal are subjective concepts, and objective and quantitative abnormal events are usually difficult to define accurately.

The detection of abnormal events often relies on videos, such as (Balakrishnan et al. 2024; Lyu et al. 2026; Wang and Zhang 2020b; Wang et al. 2021a; Wang et al. 2021b; Zhu et al. 2024). It is commonly referred to as **Video Anomaly Detection** (VAD) or **Video Anomaly Detection and Localization** (VADL), the latter is to emphasize the need to not only detect abnormal events that occur in the video, but also determine their (spatiotemporal) location in the video.

Video abnormal event detection mainly includes two basic tasks: ① Video feature extraction; ② Establishment of abnormal event detection models. The commonly used video features are mainly divided into manually designed features and features extracted by deep models. The video abnormal event detection models are commonly divided into traditional probabilistic inference based models and deep learning based models. However, there are also various ways to classify methods for detecting abnormal events. In the following, two ways of abnormal event detection are considered: ① Dividing it into traditional machine learning based methods and deep learning based methods; ② Dividing it into methods using supervised learning, methods using unsupervised learning, and methods using semi-supervised learning.

1. **Traditional Machine Learning and Deep Learning**

From the development perspective of abnormal event detection methods, traditional machine learning based methods were commonly used in the early years, while deep learning-based methods have been used more recently (such as (Debbarma et al. 2025; Jin et al. 2025; Zhang et al. 2022)). In addition, there are some methods that combine these two (called hybrid learning). A classification result is shown in Table 8.1 (Wang and Zhang 2020b).

In Table 8.1, for each type of detection method, it can be further divided into four categories according to the input model: ① Point model, whose basic unit is a single video spatiotemporal block; ② Sequence model, whose basic unit is a continuous sequence of spatiotemporal block; ③ Graph model, whose basic unit is a set of interconnected spatiotemporal blocks; ④ Composite model, whose basic unit can be some unit combination of the first three models.

Table 8.1 Classification of abnormal event detection methods from a development perspective (Wang and Zhang 2020b)

Type of methods	Input Model	Discriminant criteria	Type of methods	Input Model	Discriminant criteria
Traditional machine learning	Point model	Cluster discrimination	Deep learning	Point model	Cluster discrimination
		Co-occurrence discrimination			Reconstruction discrimination
		Reconstruction discrimination			Joint discrimination
		Other discriminations		Sequence model	Prediction error discrimination
	Sequence model	Generative probability discrimination		Composite model	
	Graph model	Graph inference discrimination	Hybrid learning	Point model	Cluster discrimination
		Graph structure discrimination			Reconstruction discrimination
	Composite model				Other discriminations

For each model in Table 8.1, the discriminant **criteria used to distinguish anomalies are** also different.

(1) Point Model

There are mainly five criteria for anomaly discrimination: ① Cluster discrimination (based on the distribution of feature points in the feature space, points that are far from the cluster center, belong to small clusters, or have a low probability density of distribution, are all judged as anomalies); ② Co-occurrence discrimination (based on the probability of feature points appearing together with normal samples, feature points with a lower probability of appearing together with normal samples are judged as anomalies); ③ Reconstruction discrimination (describing the distribution of low dimensional subspaces/manifolds as feature points in the feature space, and then determining anomalies based on the distance between the feature points considered by the reconstruction error metric and the normal sample subspace/manifold); ④ Joint discrimination (the model uses two or more of the above three types of discrimination in combination); ⑤ Other discriminations (including hypothesis testing discrimination, semantic analysis discrimination, etc.).

(2) **Sequence Model**

It mainly includes two criteria for anomaly discrimination: ① Generative probability discrimination (the model outputs a probability value based on the input sequence, which describes the degree to which the input sequence follows the normal feature transition law, and judges samples with low output probabilities as anomalies); ②

Prediction error discrimination (the model predicts the feature values of the next time based on the input sequence, determines the degree to which the input sequence follows the normal transition law based on the prediction error, and identifies samples with larger prediction errors as anomalies).

(3) **Graph Model**

It mainly includes two criteria for anomaly discrimination: ① Graph inference discrimination (the model judges feature points that do not conform to the normal inference relationship based on the inference relationship between feature points on the graph as anomalies); ② Graph structure discrimination (the model identifies uncommon topological structures as anomalies based on the topological structure of the graph).

2. **Supervised Learning, Unsupervised Learning, and Semi-Supervised Learning.**

From the perspective of anomaly detection technology, if there is a clear boundary between normal and abnormal events and corresponding samples, **supervised learning** techniques can be used for classification. If there is a lack of prior knowledge about normal and abnormal events, and only the clustering distribution of each event sample is considered, **unsupervised learning** techniques are needed. If an abnormal event is defined as all events except for normal events, trained only with prior knowledge of normal events, and learned the patterns of normal events using normal samples, then all samples that do not follow the normal patterns are judged as anomalies, this is the **semi-supervised learning technique**. Of course, these technologies can also be combined at different levels, commonly referred to as integrated technologies. The classification results are shown in Table 8.2 (Wang 2022).

In Table 8.2, the division of semi-supervised learning techniques is relatively detailed. In fact, there are also more related studies on semi-supervised learning techniques. In practical applications, on the one hand, semi-supervised learning techniques are easier to use than supervised learning techniques because normal samples are easier to obtain than abnormal samples; on the other hand, due to the use of prior knowledge of normal events, semi-supervised learning techniques typically perform better than unsupervised learning techniques. Therefore, researchers pay more attention to semi-supervised learning techniques and conduct more research works.

8.2 Basic Detection Methods Based on Neural Networks

The basic methods for abnormal event detection include using convolutional autoencoders and using one-class neural networks.

Table 8.2 Classification of abnormal event detection methods from a technology perspective (Wang 2022)

Type of methods	Specific technology		Main means/ characteristics
Supervised learning	Binary classification		Support vector machine
	Multi-instance learning		Multiple networks
Unsupervised learning	Hypothesis testing method		Binary classifier
	Unmask method		Binary classifier
Semi-supervised learning	Traditional machine learning	Distance method	One-class method
			KNN method
		Probability method	Distribution probability
			Bayesian probability
		Reconstruction error method	Sparse coding
	Deep learning	Depth distance method	Deep one-class method
			Deep KNN method
		Depth probability method	Autoregressive network
			Variational Auto-encoder
			Generative Adversarial Networks
		Depth generated error method	Deep generative networks
Integrated learning	Weighted sum method		Multiple detectors
	Cascade method		Gaussian Classifier
	Ranking method		Multiple detectors

8.2.1 Block-Learning Based on Convolutional Auto-Encoder

The complete representation and description of video events often require multiple features. The fusion of multiple features has stronger representative power than a single feature. For example, in methods based on **convolutional auto-encoders** and **block-learning** (Li et al. 2021b), a combination of appearance features and motion features is used.

The flowchart of using convolutional auto-encoder for video abnormal event detection is shown in Fig. 8.1. The video frame image is first divided into non-overlapping small blocks, and then the **motion features** (such as **optical flow**) representing the motion state and **appearance features** (such as **Histogram of Orientation Gradient**, HOG) representing the existence of the target from them are extracted.

For each optical flow feature and HOG feature of a certain image block, an **Anomaly Detection Convolutional Auto-Encoder** (AD-ConvAE) is set up for

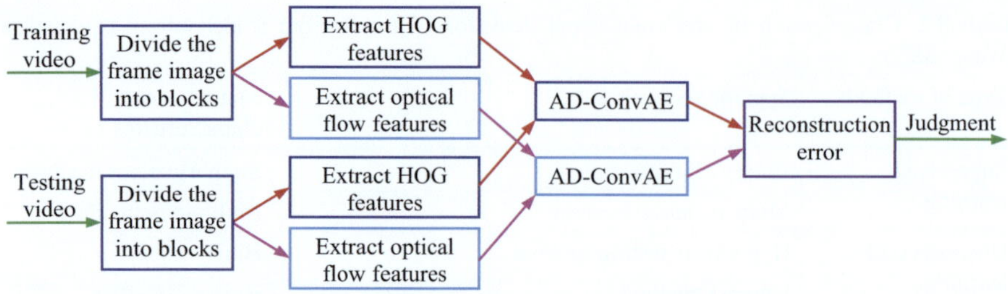

Fig. 8.1 Flowchart of video anomaly event detection using convolutional auto-encoder

training and testing. The AD-ConvAE of each block region in each frame image only focuses on the motion of that position region in the frame image, and using block-learning methods can more effectively learn local features. During the training process, the video only contains normal samples, and AD-ConvAE learns the normal motion pattern of a certain region through the optical flow and HOG features of blocks in the frame image. During the testing process, the optical flow and HOG features of the blocks in the test frame image are reconstructed using AD-ConvAE, and the weighted reconstruction error is calculated based on the optical flow reconstruction error and HOG reconstruction error. If the reconstruction error is large enough, it indicates the presence of abnormal events in the block. In this way, in addition to detecting abnormal events, the localization of abnormal events is also completed.

The network structure of AD-ConvAE includes two parts: encoding and decoding. In the encoding part, multiple pairs of convolutional and pooling layers are used to obtain deep features. In the decoding part, multiple pairs of convolution and up-sampling operations are used to reconstruct the depth representation of features, and finally output an image of the same size as the input image.

8.2.2 Detection Based on One-Class Neural Network

One-class Neural Network (ONN) is an extension of one-class classifiers in deep learning frameworks, also known as one-type neural network. **One-Class Support Vector Machine** (OC-SVM) is a widely used unsupervised anomaly detection method. In fact, it is a special form of SVM that can learn a hyperplane, separate all data points in the kernel Hilbert space from the origin, and maximize the distance from the hyperplane to the origin. In the OC-SVM model, all data outside the origin is labeled as positive samples, and the origin is labeled as negative sample.

ONN can be regarded as a neural network structure designed using the equivalent loss function of OC-SVM. In ONN, the data representation in the hidden layer is directly driven by ONN, so it can be designed for anomaly detection tasks and combined with feature extraction and anomaly detection stages for joint optimization. ONN combines the layer by layer data representation capability and one-class

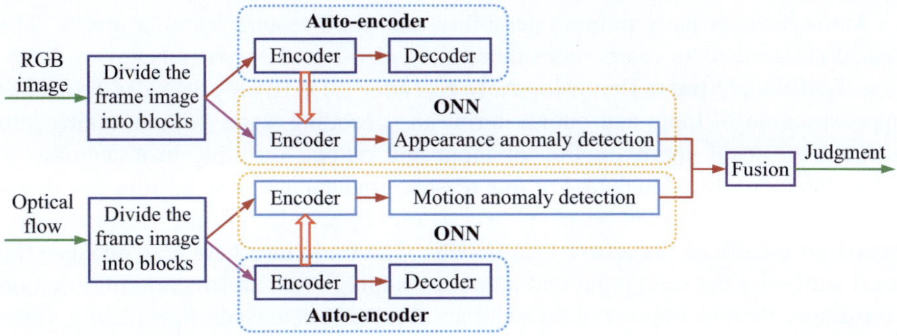

Fig. 8.2 Flow chart of video anomaly event detection using ONN

classification capability of auto-encoders, which can distinguish between all normal and abnormal samples.

There is a video anomaly event detection method using ONN (Jiang and Li 2021) that trains ONN separately on local blocks of video frame images and optical flow images of the same size to detect appearance and motion anomalies, and fuses these two to determine the final detection result. The flowchart of using ONN for video anomaly event detection is shown in Fig. 8.2. During the training phase, two auto-encoder networks are learned using the RGB images and optical flow images of the training samples, respectively. The encoder layer of the auto-encoder used for pre-training is combined with the ONN network to optimize parameters and learn an anomaly detection model. In the testing phase, the RGB image and optical flow image of the given testing region are input into the appearance anomaly detection model and motion anomaly detection model, respectively. Their output scores are fused, and a detection threshold is set to determine whether the region is abnormal.

8.3 Sparse Denoising Auto-Encoder and Gradient Structure Information

Many abnormal behavior detection methods require the use of a large amount of abnormal behavior data for training and learning, but it is often difficult to collect sufficient abnormal behavior samples in reality. One solution to this problem is to use sparse representation for modeling, specifically by constructing a sparse dictionary of normal behavior samples and detecting abnormal behavior through reconstructed error information. The principle here is that the sparsity and reconstruction error of the reconstruction coefficients obtained from normal behavior data reconstructed on a dictionary basis will be smaller than those obtained from abnormal behavior data reconstruction.

Auto-encoders have simple operability and good feature learning ability. The sparse auto-encoders can be considered for video-based anomaly behavior detection. Traditional **Sparse Denoising Auto Encoder** (SDAE) only consider the overall approximation of input and output during the decoding stage, without taking into account the local approximation of input and output, resulting in a decrease in the accuracy of decoded data. For this reason, gradient structure information (local gradient difference) could be added to construct **Sparse Denoising Auto Encoder-based on Gradient Structure** (SDAE-GS). The basic idea here is to enhance the local similarity between input and output by adding gradient structure information constraints, thereby improving the accuracy of reconstructed data. Specifically, video data containing normal behavior is first used as training samples. Based on traditional SDAE, an improved SDAE-GS model is obtained by adding constraints on data gradient structure information. Then the test sample data is input into the network, and the error between the input and output is compared. If the error is too large, the sample is judged as abnormal behavior, otherwise it can be considered as normal behavior.

Below, the method based on SDAE is first introduced, and then the improved method based on SDAE-GS is introduced.

8.3.1 SDAE-Based Method

Sparse Denoising Auto Encoder (SDAE) can improve the standard auto-encoder by first making some adjustments to the input data (adding Gaussian noise), and then encoding and decoding. Adding sparse constraints to neurons during the process of solving parameters is to improve robustness. The learning process of SDAE based video anomaly event detection is shown in Fig. 8.3 (Cong et al. 2013), which preprocesses the input video sequence and adds Gaussian noise. After superimposing Gaussian noise, detection is carried out using an auto-encoder, which sequentially passes through the input layer, hidden layer, and output layer. Finally, the learning outcomes are obtained.

In preprocessing, S sub-regions are randomly selected from the non-abnormal behavior video image input in frame T, with each sub-region having a size of $N \times N$. Then, for each sub-region, the following values are calculated: ① Original grayscale value (f); ② Horizontal grayscale gradient value (f_x); ③ Vertical grayscale gradient value (f_y); ④ Horizontal optical flow value (O_x); ⑤ Vertical optical flow value (O_y). After this calculation, $T \times S$ training samples $\boldsymbol{X} = [f, f_x, f_y, O_x, O_y]$ were obtained,

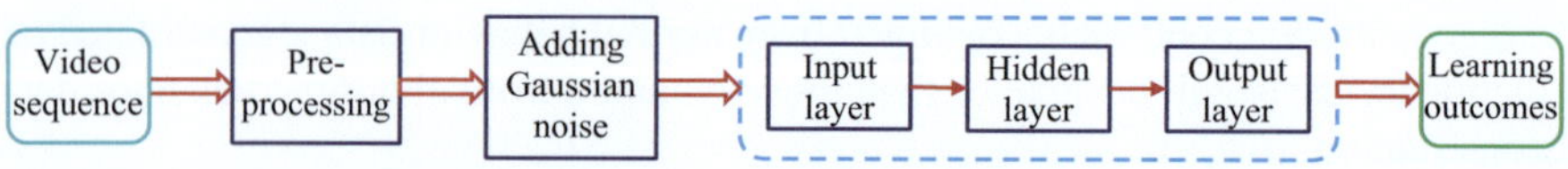

Fig. 8.3 Learning flowchart of video anomaly event detection based on SDAE

and the dimension of the entire input data is $N_d = N \times N \times 5$. Add Gaussian noise and normalize it to [0, 1] before using it as input data for the input layer.

During the encoding phase, the encoding function $\boldsymbol{h} = f(\boldsymbol{X})$ is used:

$$\mathbf{h} = f(\mathbf{X}) = \text{sigmoid}\left(\mathbf{W}^{(1)}\mathbf{X} + \mathbf{b}^{(1)}\right) \tag{8.1}$$

where $\boldsymbol{h} \in [0, 1]^M$, in which M is the number of neurons in the hidden layer; $\boldsymbol{W}^{(1)} \in \mathrm{R}^{N \times N}$ represents the weight matrix; $\boldsymbol{b}^{(1)} \in \mathrm{R}^N$ represents the bias vector of the hidden layer, and superscripts represent layers; Sigmoid(z) = 1/(1 + exp(−z)).

In the decoding stage, the decoding function $g(\boldsymbol{h})$ is used to obtain the output $\boldsymbol{Y}$:

$$\mathbf{Y} = g(\mathbf{h}) = \text{sigmoid}\left(\mathbf{W}^{(2)}\mathbf{X} + \mathbf{b}^{(2)}\right) \tag{8.2}$$

where $\boldsymbol{b}^{(2)} \in \mathrm{R}^N$ represents the bias vector of the output layer. If set $\boldsymbol{W} = [W^{(1)}, W^{(2)}]$, $\boldsymbol{b} = [\boldsymbol{b}^{(1)}, \boldsymbol{b}^{(2)}]$ as the parameters of the auto-encoder, then the output $\boldsymbol{Y} = H_{w,b}(\boldsymbol{X})$. The parameters $\boldsymbol{W}$ and $\boldsymbol{b}$ can be obtained by optimizing the following cost functions:

$$J(\mathbf{W}, \mathbf{b}) = \left\|\mathbf{X} - H_{w,b}(\mathbf{X})\right\|^2 + p\mathbf{W} + q\sum_{i=1}^{N} KL(s||a_i) \tag{8.3}$$

where on the right side of the equation, the first term is the error term, the second term is the regularization term, the third item is a sparse item, $a_i = \frac{1}{N}\sum_{k=1}^{N} h_i^{(1)} x_k$ is the average activation value of the i-th hidden layer neuron; s is a sparsity parameter close to 0, often taken as 0.05. The parameter $\boldsymbol{W}$ obtained in this way reflects the main features of normal video frames.

The testing process for detecting abnormal events based on SDAE is shown in Fig. 8.4. In the test video, a certain number of sub-regions are randomly selected from each frame of the image and input into SDAE. The output is obtained through forward propagation algorithm, and the reconstruction error between the input and output is used as the abnormal feature description value of the sub-region. Calculate and sum the abnormal feature description values for all sub-regions of each frame image to obtain the abnormal feature description value L of the frame image. Compare this value with the threshold T to determine whether there is abnormal behavior in the frame image. This final step can be expressed as ($D_a = 1$ represents abnormality, $D_a = 0$ represents normal):

$$D_a = \begin{cases} 1 & L \geq T \\ 0 & L < T \end{cases} \tag{8.4}$$

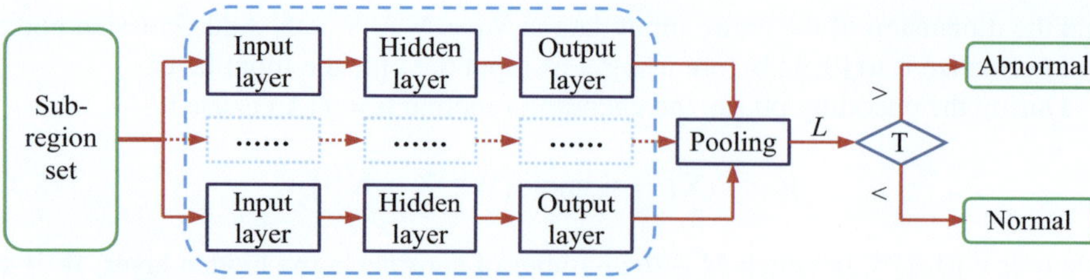

Fig. 8.4 Test flowchart for video anomaly event detection based on SDAE

8.3.2 SDAE-GS-Based Method

The SDAE-GS method incorporates gradient structure information on the basis of the SDAE method (Yuan and Zhang 2017). Specifically, the gradient difference $\boldsymbol{f}_{\mathrm{i}}$ between $\boldsymbol{f}_x$ and $\boldsymbol{f}_y$ is calculated at the input layer, and the gradient difference $\boldsymbol{f}_{\mathrm{o}}$ between $\boldsymbol{f}_x$ and $\boldsymbol{f}_y$ is calculated at the output layer. If $H(\cdot)$ is the operator for extracting horizontal grayscale gradients and $V(\cdot)$ is the operator for extracting vertical grayscale gradients, then $\boldsymbol{f}_{\mathrm{i}} = H(\boldsymbol{X}) - V(\boldsymbol{X}), \boldsymbol{f}_{\mathrm{o}} = H(\boldsymbol{Y}) - V(\boldsymbol{Y})$, where $\boldsymbol{Y} = H_{w,b}(\boldsymbol{X})$. The gradient structure information obtained from this is $(\boldsymbol{f}_{\mathrm{i}} - \boldsymbol{f}_{\mathrm{o}})^{\mathrm{T}}(\boldsymbol{f}_{\mathrm{i}} - \boldsymbol{f}_{\mathrm{o}})$. Furthermore, let matrix $\boldsymbol{A} = H(\cdot) - V(\cdot)$, then $(\boldsymbol{f}_{\mathrm{i}} - \boldsymbol{f}_{\mathrm{o}})^{\mathrm{T}}(\boldsymbol{f}_{\mathrm{i}} - \boldsymbol{f}_{\mathrm{o}})$ can be written as $\|\boldsymbol{AX} - \boldsymbol{AY}\|_2$, and the cost function can be represented as

$$J(\mathbf{W}, \mathbf{b}) = \left\|\mathbf{X} - H_{w,b}(\mathbf{X})\right\|^2 + p\mathbf{W} + q\sum_{i=1}^{N} KL(s||a_i) + r\|\mathbf{AX} - \mathbf{AY}\|^2 \tag{8.5}$$

Comparing with Eq. (8.3), the error term, regularization term, and sparsity term are all the same, except for the addition of a fourth term, which is the gradient structure information term. The gradient structure information term (denoted as $\boldsymbol{J}_{\mathrm{d}}$) for the gradient of each layer parameter can be represented as

$$\frac{\partial \mathbf{J}_{\mathrm{d}}}{\partial \mathbf{W}^{(2)}} = \left\{-r[\mathbf{A}^{\mathrm{T}}(\mathbf{AX} - \mathbf{AY})]\right\} \times f'(\mathbf{z}^3) s^{(2)^{\mathrm{T}}} \tag{8.6}$$

$$\frac{\partial \mathbf{J}_{\mathrm{d}}}{\partial \mathbf{W}^{(1)}} = \mathbf{W}^{(2)^{\mathrm{T}}}\left\{-r[\mathbf{A}^{\mathrm{T}}(\mathbf{AX} - \mathbf{AY})]\right\} \times f'(\mathbf{z}^3) \times f'(\mathbf{z}^2) s^{(1)^{\mathrm{T}}} \tag{8.7}$$

$$\frac{\partial \mathbf{J}_{\mathrm{d}}}{\partial \mathbf{b}^{(2)}} = \left\{-r[\mathbf{A}^{\mathrm{T}}(\mathbf{AX} - \mathbf{AY})]\right\} \times f'(\mathbf{z}^3) \tag{8.8}$$

$$\frac{\partial \mathbf{J}_{\mathrm{d}}}{\partial \mathbf{b}^{(1)}} = \mathbf{W}^{(2)^{\mathrm{T}}}\left\{-r[\mathbf{A}^{\mathrm{T}}(\mathbf{AX} - \mathbf{AY})]\right\} \times f'(\mathbf{z}^3) \times f'(\mathbf{z}^2) \tag{8.9}$$

where $\boldsymbol{a}^{(1)} = \boldsymbol{X}$, $z^{(2)} = \boldsymbol{W}^{(1)}\boldsymbol{X} + \boldsymbol{b}^{(1)}$, $\boldsymbol{a}^{(2)} = f(z^{(2)}) = \mathrm{Sigmoid}(\boldsymbol{W}^{(1)}\boldsymbol{X} + \boldsymbol{b}^{(1)})$, $z^{(3)} = \boldsymbol{W}^{(2)}\boldsymbol{X} + \boldsymbol{b}^{(2)}$, $\boldsymbol{Y} = H_{w,b}(\boldsymbol{X}) = f(z^{(3)}) = \mathrm{Sigmoid}(\boldsymbol{W}^{(2)}\boldsymbol{X} + \boldsymbol{b}^{(2)})$.

For each video clip C_t, the total generation loss of the TS-Unet model can be represented as a weighted sum (where each W represents the corresponding weight):

$$L_{\text{global}}^{t} = W_{\text{int}} L_{\text{int}}^{t}(I_t, J_t) + W_{\text{grad}} L_{\text{grad}}^{t}(I_t, J_t) + W_{\text{flow}} L_{\text{flow}}^{t}(I_t, J_t) + W_{\text{adv}} L_{\text{adv}}^{t}(J_t) \tag{8.10}$$

8.3.3 Comparison Between SDAE and SDAE-GS

An experimental comparison between the two methods was conducted using the University of Minnesota (UMN) database (Cong et al. 2013). The UMN database is a group-abnormal behavior databases released by the University of Minnesota, which includes videos from three different scenarios, each of which contains abnormal events of group escape. According to the requirements of the benchmark data, for each scene's video, the first 400 frames without abnormal events are taken as training data, of which 350 frames are used to train network parameters, 50 frames are used to estimate the threshold T, and the remaining frames are used as the test set.

The experimental indicators utilized are **Receiver Operating Characteristic** (ROC) curves. Detecting anomalies is based on a threshold, and the ROC curve can precisely reflect the impact of threshold changes on detection performance. Therefore, the **Area Under Curve** (AUC) of the ROC curve is used as the evaluation indicator.

The experimental results are shown in Table 8.3. It can be seen that adding gradient structure information enhances the local similarity between input and output data, and the detection effect is improved (the experiment also found that the detection stability is improved, but the computational complexity is increased) (Yuan and Zhang 2017).

8.4 LSTM Auto-Encoder Network Based on Feature Trajectory Smoothing

In semi-supervised anomaly detection based on deep learning, **Generative Error** (GE) is a commonly used metric (Luo et al. 2021). However, GE mainly considers only spatial positioning performance. In order to better detect anomalies in videos,

Table 8.3 Comparison of experimental results (Yuan and Zhang 2017)

Methods	Scene 1	Scene 2	Scene 3
SDAE	0.957	0.998	0.966
SDAE-GS	0.981	0.998	0.986

LSTM auto-encoder networks (Hasan et al. 2016) that can capture temporal patterns in videos and corresponding metrics can also be used.

The following introduces an anomaly detection method that utilizes an LSTM auto-encoder network, which combines the GE metric with the **Feature Trajectory Smoothing** (FTS) metric (Sun et al. 2023).

8.4.1 Overall Framework and Process

The overall framework and process of this method are shown in Fig. 8.5, which mainly includes two processes: training process and detection process. In the following, the entire network structure is first introduced, and then these two processes are presented separately.

1. **Network Structure**

The LSTM auto-encoder network mainly consists of three network modules: ① Encoder module; ② Convolutional LSTM module; ③ Decoder module.

(1) The encoder module extracts spatial features of the input video. It is composed of multiple 2-D spatial convolutional layers. Consider T consecutive input video frames $I = \{I_1, I_2, \ldots, I_T\}$. If E is used to represent the encoder, its output features are $\{f_1, f_2, \ldots, f_T\}$, that is, $f_t = E(I_t)$.
(2) The convolutional LSTM module aims to capture the temporal patterns of videos in the feature space. If H is used to represent the processing function of convolutional LSTM, then $\{h_1, h_2, \ldots, h_T\}$ can be obtained from $\{f_1, f_2, \ldots, f_T\}$, where the hidden state $h_t = H(f_t, h_{t-1})$.
(3) The decoder module functions as a generator. It can predict future frames for a given input frame $\{h_1, h_2, \ldots, h_T\}$. It consists of multiple 2-D spatial convolutional layers and 2-D spatial deconvolution layers. If D is used to represent the decoder, its prediction result for frame h_t is $\hat{I}_{t+1}$ (true value is I_{t+1}), that is, $\hat{I}_{t+1} = D(h_t)$.

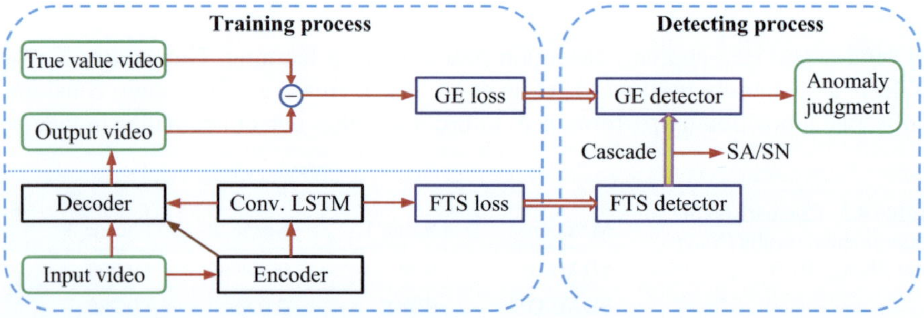

Fig. 8.5 Overall framework and process of LSTM auto-encoder network based on feature trajectory smoothing

2. **Training Process**

During the training process, GE loss and FTS loss are used to constrain the model to learn the normal regularity of the video.

(1) GE loss

The GE loss L_{GE} includes two parts: intensity loss L_{int} and gradient loss L_{grad}. They are in turn:

$$L_{\text{GE}} = L_{\text{int}} + L_{\text{grad}} \tag{8.11}$$

$$L_{\text{int}} = \sum_{t=1}^{T} \left\| \hat{I}_{t+1} - I_{t+1} \right\|_2 \tag{8.12}$$

$$L_{\text{grad}} = \sum_{t=1}^{T} \left[\left\| \nabla_x(\hat{I}_{t+1}) - \nabla_x(I_{t+1}) \right\|_1 + \left\| \nabla_y(\hat{I}_{t+1}) - \nabla_y(I_{t+1}) \right\|_1 \right] \tag{8.13}$$

The intensity loss L_{int} is used to penalize the loss in pixel intensity, while the gradient loss L_{grad} is used to penalize the loss in gradient between pixels.

The purpose of using GE loss is to enable the model to accurately generate normal samples. It cannot directly constrain the features of the video, as there is a decoder module between the feature space and GE loss. Therefore, the GE loss is not sufficient to force the features to maintain the temporal regularity of the video, and the convolutional LSTM module alone cannot accurately capture the temporal regularity of the video.

(2) FTS loss

In order to accurately capture the temporal regularity of the video, an FTS loss directly related to the temporal regularity of the video is used. The consideration here is that the content of video frames generally changes smoothly over time. Therefore, the features of video frames should also smoothly change in the feature space. The Euclidean distance can be used to measure the similarity between features, and the FTS loss can be formulated by accumulating the distances between all adjacent features at all times. That is, FTS loss can be represented as

$$L_{\text{FTS}} = \sum_{t=1}^{T} \| f_{t+1} - f_t \|_2 \tag{8.14}$$

(3) Global loss

Global loss is used during training, which is the weighted sum of GE loss and FTS loss (k is weight):

$$L_{\text{train}} = L_{\text{GE}} + k * L_{\text{FTS}} \tag{8.15}$$

3. **Detecting Process**

During the detection process, GE detectors designed on the basis of GE loss and FTS detectors designed on the basis of FTS loss were utilized separately, and these two detectors were cascaded to achieve faster and better anomaly detection.

(1) GE detector

Compared to the entire frame image, anomalies usually occur in local spatial regions, so GE detectors can use frame level generative errors in video frames to determine anomalies. Here, the L_{int} of the last frame in the video sequence can be used to calculate the generative error $e(t)$ at the frame block level using Eq. (8.11). In practical applications, the GE loss map of the entire frame image can be calculated first (p represents the number of channels in the video frame image):

$$\text{GE}_{\text{map}}(t) = \sum_{p} \left\| \hat{I}_{t+1} - I_{t+1} \right\|_2 \tag{8.16}$$

Then, the loss value within the largest loss block (block size b) in the GE loss map can be selected:

$$A_{\text{GE}}(t) = \max\{\text{mean}_b[\text{GE}_{\text{map}}(t)]\} \tag{8.17}$$

(2) FTS detector

FTS loss reflects the changes in feature trajectories. When an abnormal moving target appears, the feature trajectory will undergo significant changes. Compared to the entire video sequence, this is also local in time. Therefore, the FTS loss map between adjacent frame images in the video sequence can be calculated first (p represents the number of channels in the video frame image):

$$\text{FTS}_{\text{map}}(t) = \sum_{p} \|f_t - f_{t-1}\|_2 \tag{8.18}$$

Then, the maximum loss value from these FTS loss map can be selected as the abnormal score value for the video sequence:

$$A_{\text{FTS}}(t) = \max\left[\text{FTS}_{\text{map}}(t)\right] \tag{8.19}$$

(3) Cascade

The FTS detector operates relatively fast and is complementary to the GE detector. For this reason, the FTS detector can be cascaded with the GE detector for anomaly detection and to improve retrieval speed. The FTS detector can detect/distinguish strong abnormal (SA) samples and strong normal (SN) samples, but the threshold values TH_A and TH_N need to be set separately for them. With the help of training samples, they can be calculated as follows:

$$\mathrm{TH_A} = \max(A_{\mathrm{FTS}}) + [\max(A_{\mathrm{FTS}}) - \min(A_{\mathrm{FTS}})] * k_{\mathrm{A}} \tag{8.20}$$

$$\mathrm{TH_N} = \min(A_{\mathrm{FTS}}) + [\max(A_{\mathrm{FTS}}) - \min(A_{\mathrm{FTS}})] * (1 - k_{\mathrm{N}}) \tag{8.21}$$

where $\max(A_{\mathrm{FTS}})$ and $\min(A_{\mathrm{FTS}})$ are the maximum and minimum values of abnormal scores in the training data, respectively; k_{A} and k_{N} are the strict coefficients of $\mathrm{TH_A}$ and $\mathrm{TH_N}$, respectively. The larger the values of k_{A} and k_{N}, the higher the credibility of the SA and SN samples obtained. Generally, the values of k_{A} and k_{N} can be selected from [0, 1].

In Eq. (8.20), the maximum FTS loss $\max(A_{\mathrm{FTS}})$ of normal training samples is set as the fundamental term of $\mathrm{TH_A}$. To avoid being too strict, a second term has been added as a relaxation term. In Eq. (8.21), the minimum FTS loss $\min(A_{\mathrm{FTS}})$ of normal training samples is set as the fundamental term of $\mathrm{TH_N}$. To avoid being too strict, a second term has been added as a relaxation term.

8.4.2 Experimental Results and Analysis

To verify the effectiveness of introducing FTS loss, multiple experiments were conducted. These experiments used four datasets: UCSD Pedestrian dataset (including both subsets Ped1 and Ped2, counted as two datasets) (Mahadevan et al. 2010), CUHK Avenue dataset (Lu et al. 2013), and ShanghaiTech (SH) dataset (Luo et al. 2021). The experiments use frame level AUC to evaluate anomaly detection performance. Below are the results and analysis of four of these experiments.

1. **Abnormal Detection Score**

Firstly, a video with thousands of frames is selected, and a frame by frame detection is performed using the FTS loss method. The calculated anomaly score curve is shown in Fig. 8.6. The content captured in this video from the starting frame to Frame 600 is relatively stable, and the scenes are all normal (with an ideal anomaly score of 0). At around Frame 600 (and also around Frame 800), someone running (from right) into the scene is considered abnormal (with an ideal anomaly score of 1, represented by a (green) shaded bar in the figure). The actual detected anomaly score is represented by a (red) curve, which remains small from the beginning of the video until Frame 600 (and from Frame 600 to Frame 800), and it shows the clear peaks in both instances (around Frame 600 and around Frame 800) of anomaly. It can be seen that there is a significant difference between abnormal scores and normal scores, which can provide a basis for anomaly detection.

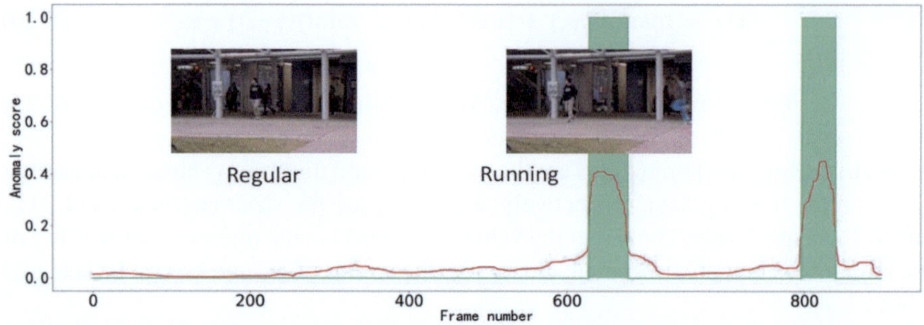

Fig. 8.6 Changes in anomaly scores during anomaly detection process (Sun et al. 2023)

2. **Feature Space Visualization**

Further detailed analysis of FTS loss can be achieved through visualization in the feature space. Figure 8.7 shows the trajectories of two video features in the feature space. The results obtained from training the model without using FTS loss are shown in Fig. 8.7a, where the distribution of feature point trajectories in the feature space is relatively random. This indicates that the temporal regularity of the video cannot be accurately maintained in the feature space. Figure 8.7b shows the results obtained from training the model using FTS loss. The distribution of feature point trajectories in the feature space is relatively orderly, and there is a large degree of separation between different (groups of) features. In other words, the temporal regularity of the video is well maintained in the feature space.

3. **Visualization of Detection Results**

An example of visualizing the detection results obtained by combining the FTS loss method is shown in Fig. 8.8. Among them, the circled part in the original image of Fig. 8.8a indicates the abnormal region (a person on bicycle), Fig. 8.8b is the corresponding FTS loss map, Fig. 8.8c is the corresponding FTS heat map, Fig. 8.8d is the corresponding GE loss map, and Fig. 8.8e is the corresponding GE heat map.

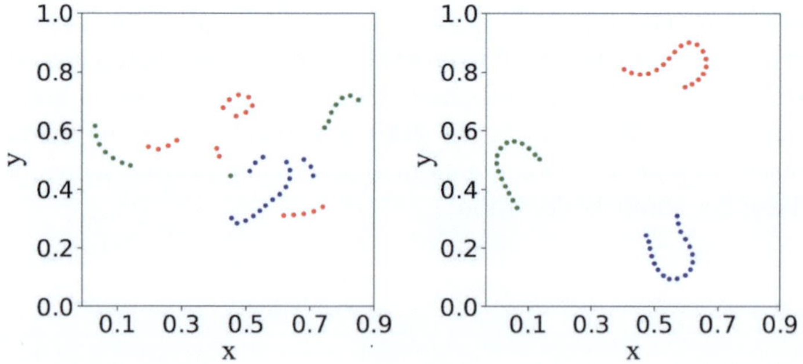

Fig. 8.7 Visualization of feature space (distribution of feature points) (Sun et al. 2023)

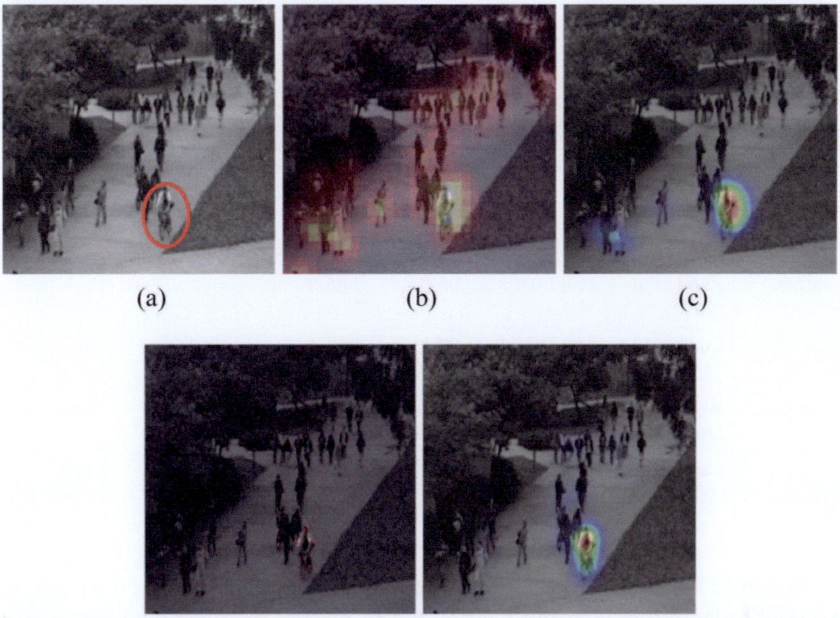

(a) (b) (c)

(d) (e)

Fig. 8.8 Visualization of test results (loss maps and heat maps) (Sun et al. 2023)

From these figures, it can be seen that FTS loss maps can indeed be used for detecting and locating anomalies, and the effect is even more obvious than GE loss maps.

4. **Anomaly Detection Performance**

The method combining FTS loss (Sun et al. 2023) was compared with some other methods (including probability-based methods, integration-based methods, and generative error-based methods) in terms of anomaly detection performance, and the results are shown in Table 8.4 (bold numbers indicate the best, italic numbers indicate the second best). The method combining FTS loss is optimal on one dataset and suboptimal on three datasets. In addition, the detection speed of this method far exceeds other methods.

8.5 Depth Generative Model for Feature Space Temporal Smoothing

The depth generative model used for feature space temporal-smoothing is an Unet based model, also known as the **Temporal-Smoothed Unet** (TS-Unet) model (Wang et al. 2021a). This model adds temporal-smoothed constraints to the feature space of the deep generative model, allowing the model to capture structural information

Table 8.4 Comparison of anomaly detection performance (AUC)

Detection Methods (Ref.)		UCSD Ped1	UCSD Ped2	CUHK Avenue	Shanghai Tech	Speed (FPS)
Probability	Tang et al. (2020)	*84.7*	96.3	85.1	*71.5*	*30*
Integrated	Ji et al. (2020)	83.5	98.1	78.3	–	–
	Wang et al. (2021b)	**85.8**	**99.0**	**92.1**	69.7	4
Generative error	Zhou et al. (2020)	83.9	96.0	86.0	–	–
	Luo et al. (2021)	–	92.2	83.5	69.6	10
	Wang et al. (2021a)	–	97.8	88.4	–	12
	Sun et al. (2023)	83.5	*98.3*	*91.1*	**72.9**	**117**

on the manifold distribution of normal samples, thereby enabling the deep generative model to learn the manifold distribution of normal samples more accurately. In anomaly detection, using more accurate structural information on the manifold distribution to calculate prediction errors can achieve better detection results.

Video data can be seen as a continuously changing spatiotemporal entity, with video frame images changing continuously along the time axis and exhibiting local smoothness. In the feature space of the generative model, the features of time continuous video frames should also have local smoothness, so as to better reflect the local structural relationships of the scenery.

The losses calculated in the model include generative loss and temporal smoothing loss.

8.5.1 Generative Losses

The generative loss used for constraints in the TS-Unet model includes four terms: ① Pixel intensity loss L_{int}; ② Pixel gradient loss L_{grad}; ③ Optical flow loss L_{flow}; ④ Generative adversarial loss L_{adv}. For a given video clip C_t, let I represent future frames in the video and let J represent future frames predicted by the model, the four losses can be calculated separately as follows:

$$L_{\text{int}}^t(I_t,\ J_t) = \|I_t - J_t\|_2 \tag{8.22}$$

$$L_{\text{grad}}^t(I_t,\ J_t) = \sum_{i,j} \|\nabla_x I_t - \nabla_x J_t\|_1 + \left\|\nabla_y I_t - \nabla_y J_t\right\|_1 \tag{8.23}$$

$$L^t_{\text{flow}}(I_t,\ J_t, I_{t-1}) = \|F(I_t - I_{t-1}) - F(J_t - I_{t-1})\|_1 \tag{8.24}$$

$$L^t_{\text{adv}}(J_t) = \frac{1}{2}\sum_{x,y}\left[\mathscr{D}(J_t)_{x,y} - 1\right]^2 \tag{8.25}$$

where ∇ represents the gradient operator; $\mathscr{F}$ represents the Flow-net (Dosovitskiy et al. 2015) used for generating optical flow maps; $\mathscr{D}$ represents a discriminator for generating adversarial arguments. The training loss of $\mathscr{D}$ is defined as

$$L^t_{\mathscr{D}}(I_t, J_t) = \frac{1}{2}\sum_{i,j}\left[\mathscr{D}(I_t)_{i,j} - 1\right]^2 + \frac{1}{2}\sum_{i,j}\left[\mathscr{D}(J_t)_{i,j} - 1\right]^2 \tag{8.26}$$

For each video clip C_t, the total generative loss of the TS-Unet model is represented as a weighted sum (where each W represents the corresponding weight):

$$L^t_{\text{global}} = W_{\text{int}}L^t_{\text{int}}(I_t, J_t) + W_{\text{grad}}L^t_{\text{grad}}(I_t, J_t) + W_{\text{flow}}L^t_{\text{flow}}(I_t, J_t) + W_{\text{adv}}L^t_{\text{adv}}(J_t) \tag{8.27}$$

If considering a total of T video clips, the total generative loss of the TS-Unet model on them is

$$L_{\text{global}} = \sum_{t=1}^{T} L^t_{\text{global}} \tag{8.28}$$

Similarly, the total generative loss of discriminator **D** on T video clips is

$$L_D = \sum_{t=1}^{T} L^t_D \tag{8.29}$$

8.5.2 Temporal Smoothing Loss

In order to fully capture the continuous and smooth structural information of video frame content over time, in addition to utilize the generative loss of the generative space, it is also necessary to utilize the temporal smoothing loss of the feature space (*i.e.* considering the smooth changes of video frame features in the feature space that are continuous over time). For a video sequence, the TS-Unet model calculates the Euclidean distance between the features of every two adjacent temporal video frames, and accumulates the Euclidean distances between all feature pairs in the sequence as a measure of the non-smoothness of the feature sequence, which is called **temporal-smoothed loss**. By minimizing the temporal roughness of the feature sequence, it is possible to obtain features that represent smooth changes in the feature space, thereby enabling the model to learn the temporal smoothness information of the video.

If $\{f_1, f_2, \ldots, f_T\}$ is used to represent the features of T video clips $\{C_1, C_2, \ldots, C_T\}$ in the feature space, then the temporal-smoothed loss L_{temp} is

$$L_{\text{temp}} = \sum_{t=1}^{T-1} \|f_{t+1} - f_t\|_2 \tag{8.30}$$

8.5.3 *Training and Testing*

By utilizing generative loss and temporal-smoothed loss, the model can be trained and tested. The training loss is the weighted sum of the generative loss and the temporal-smoothed loss (W_{temp} is the weight for L_{temp}):

$$L_{\text{training}} = L_{\text{global}} + W_{\text{temp}} L_{\text{temp}} \tag{8.31}$$

During testing, in order to reduce the impact of scene content changes on generative errors, frame level generative errors (corresponding to pixel intensity loss) in video frames can be used to determine anomalies. For each video clip C_t, the frame block level generation error $e(t)$ is defined as

$$e(t) = \max\left[\text{mean}_b\left(\sum_p \left\|I_{i,j,t} - J_{i,j,t}\right\|_2\right)\right] \tag{8.32}$$

where p represents the number of channels (here 3) in the video frame image; mean_b represents the mean filtering function for template size b; max(****) represents the maximum pooling function.

After obtaining the generative error at the frame block level, the generative error of all video frames can be normalized to the [0, 1] interval as follows:

$$e_{\text{norm}}(t) = \frac{e(t) - \min(e)}{\max(e) - \min(e)} \tag{8.33}$$

8.5.4 Experimental Results and Analysis

Some experiments on the above model have been conducted, and the results have been analyzed.

1. **Experimental Setup**

The two datasets used are UCSD Ped2 dataset (Mahadevan et al. 2010) and CUHK Avenue dataset (Lu et al. 2013). Some of their profiles are shown in Table 8.5. Examples of normal and abnormal samples (within the rectangular box) among them are shown in Table 8.6.

During testing, abnormal events are detected on a frame by frame basis, and the performance of the algorithm is evaluated based on the **Receiver Operating Characteristic** (ROC) curve, with the **Area Under Curve** (AUC) as the indicator. The higher the AUC value, the better the anomaly detection performance of the algorithm.

2. **Experiments and Results**

Below are three experiments and their results.

Table 8.5 Overview of UCSD Ped2 and CUHK Avenue datasets

Datasets	Training clips	Testing clips	Normal events	Abnormal events
UCSD Ped2	16	12	Pedestrians walking on the campus sidewalk	Cycling, skateboarding, etc. on the sidewalk
CUHK Avenue	16	21	Pedestrians walking on the sidewalk next to the building	Running, cycling, throwing things

Table 8.6 Examples of normal and abnormal samples (Wang et al. 2021a)

Datasets	Normal samples	Abnormal samples
UCSD Ped2		
CUHK Avenue		

(1) The impact of temporal smoothing on anomaly detection performance

The temporal-smoothed loss curves and anomaly detection performance AUC curves were calculated for Unet and TS-Unet at different training iterations, as shown in Fig. 8.9. In Fig. 8.9a, b, the horizontal axis represents the number of iterations, and the vertical axis represents the temporal-smoothed loss. In Fig. 8.9c, d, the horizontal axis represents the number of iterations, and the vertical axis represents ROC-AUC. The results on the UCSD Ped2 dataset are shown in Fig. 8.9a, c, while the results on the CUHK Avenue dataset are shown in Fig. 8.9b, d.

As shown in Fig. 8.9, the temporal smoothing constraint of the feature space better preserves the temporal smoothing structural properties of the video, significantly reduces the temporal-smoothed loss of the model feature space, and improves the performance of anomaly detection.

(2) The performance of TS-Unet model compared to some other related models

The TS-Unet model was compared with several other related models. The models taken for comparison include GMFC-VAE (Fan et al. 2020), IPR AD (Tang et al. 2020), and ST Cascade (Li et al. 2021a). The comparison results are shown in Table 8.7 (bold numbers indicate the best). As shown in the table, the TS-Unet model achieved the best results on both datasets.

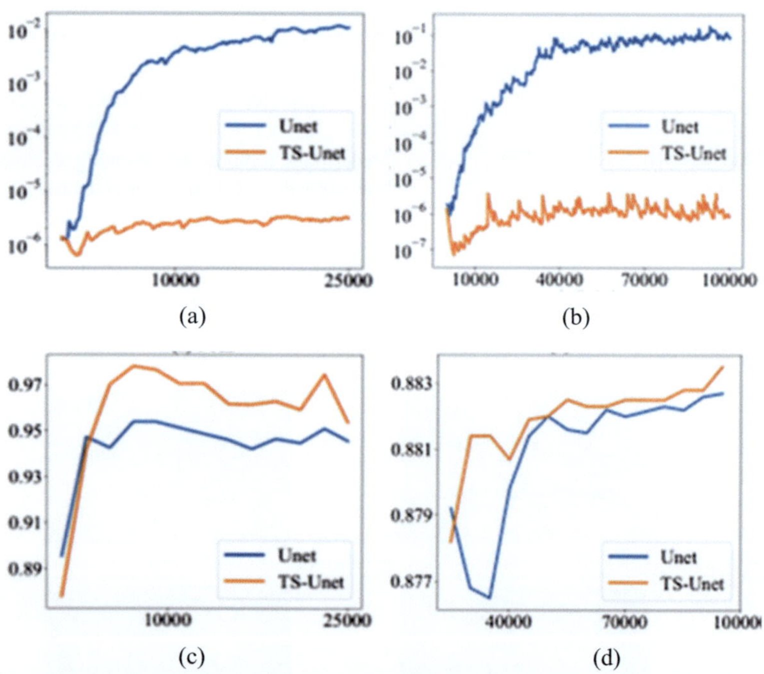

Fig. 8.9 Temporal-smoothed loss variation curves and anomaly detection performance AUC curves of Unet and TS-Unet (Wang et al. 2021a)

Table 8.7 Performance of TS Unet model compared to some other related models (Wang et al. 2021a)

Models	UCSD Ped2	CUHK Avenue
GMFC-VA	92.2	83.4
IPR-AD	96.3	85.1
ST-Cascade	92.9	83.5
TS-Unet	**97.81**	**88.38**

Table 8.8 Experimental results of four models (Wang et al. 2021a)

Datasets	AE	TS-AE	LSTM-AE	TS- LSTM-AE
UCSD Ped2	67.19	**81.28**	76.51	**82.25**
CUHK Avenue	74.12	**79.01**	79.18	**81.62**
Average	70.66	**80.15**	77.85	**81.94**

(3) Universality of temporal smoothing constraints in feature space

To demonstrate the universality of feature space temporal smoothing constraints, experiments were conducted by adding temporal smoothing constraints to two **Semi-Supervised Depth Generative Models** (SSDGM). These two models are called AE (Hasan et al. 2016) and LSTM-AE (Chong and Tay 2017), respectively. The AE model uses the AE network as a generative model, first reconstructing normal video frames to learn the manifold distribution of normal samples, and then detecting anomalies based on reconstruction errors. LSTM-AE is an improved model for AE. LSTM-AE adds an LSTM layer to the feature space of AE, allowing the network to learn not only the manifold distribution of normal samples, but also the transfer rules of normal sample features. During the anomaly detection process, LSTM-AE can identify samples that do not follow the manifold distribution and normal feature transfer rules as anomalies. The models with feature space temporal smoothing constraints added to these two models are referred to as TS-AE and TS-LSTM-AE, respectively.

The experimental results for the above four models are shown in Table 8.8 (bold numbers indicate the best). As shown in the table, temporal smoothing constraints have improved the anomaly detection performance of both AE and LSTM-AE models. From a universal perspective, temporal smoothing constraints have the potential to improve the performance of other models.

8.6 A Deep Generative Model Adapted to Scene Content

The **Semi-Supervised Deep Generative Model** (SSDGM) performs anomaly detection by using generative error maps. In the generative error map, errors mainly appear in the foreground target region of the scene. The main reason for this is that the model is easy to learn static content in the scene, but difficult to learn dynamic and diverse foreground target content in the scene. In addition, if there are abnormal events in the video frame images, the generative error of abnormal regions will be much larger than that of normal regions. The reason for this is that the model has already learned prior knowledge of normal events, but has not learned prior knowledge of abnormal events.

Due to the above issues, semi-supervised deep generative models sometimes cannot adapt well to changes in scene content. On the one hand, different videos have different numbers of foreground targets, resulting in varying baseline generative errors. This leads to a relatively large intra class variance in the generative errors of normal video frame images. On the other hand, when calculating the mean of the generative error maps, the generative errors of abnormal and normal regions may be averaged, reducing the discriminability of the generative errors between the two regions (*i.e.*, the inter class variance of the generative errors is relatively small).

Many semi-supervised deep generative models use the method of normalizing video clips to solve the above problems. Firstly, divide the long video into different short video clips, and assume that there is little change in the scene content within each short video clip. Then, within each video clip, normalize the mean of the generative error map of the video frames to the maximum-minimum values. Finally, a unified anomaly detection threshold to detect anomalies in all video clips is obtained and can be used for anomaly detection. Using this method, the generative error of each frame image is compared only with the generative error of other frame images in the same video clip. When the generative error of one frame image is significantly higher than that of other frame images in the same video clip, this frame image is judged as an abnormal frame image. However, anomaly detection must be performed in every video clip (even if the video clip does not contain any abnormal events). Due to the fact that in most cases the frame images are normal, the solution of normalizing each video clip will undoubtedly bring a large number of false alarms.

For solving the above mentioned problems, one of the solutions is that the model should be adaptive to changes in scene content.

8.6.1 Overall Workflow

The following introduces a **Scene Content Adaptive SSDGM** (SCA-SSDGM) that can adapt to changes in scene content (Wang et al. 2020a). Its flow charts during the training and testing phases are shown in Fig. 8.10 and Fig. 8.11, respectively.

During the training phase, SCA-SDGM uses frame level generative error training to comprehensively learn the knowledge of the entire scene. In the testing phase, SCA-SDGM adopted a **block-level post-processing** method, and using frame block level generated errors to detect anomalies. The post-processing method for frame blocks includes three steps: ① Calculate the average size of foreground targets on normal samples in the training set using frame difference method; ② Calculate the generated block level error at each position on the test frame image based on the average size; ③ Determine whether the video is abnormal based on the maximum

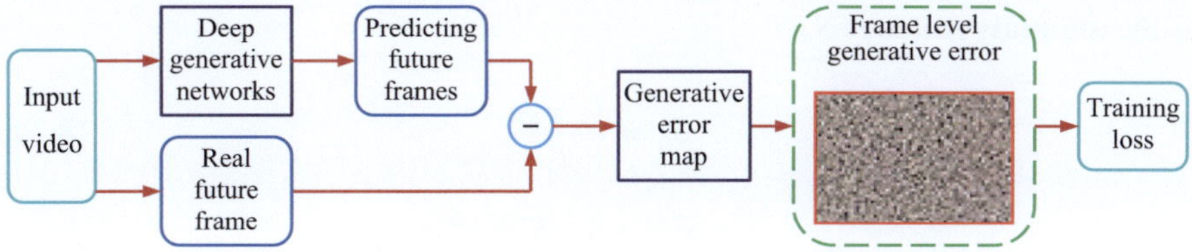

Fig. 8.10 Flow chart of SCA-SDGM training

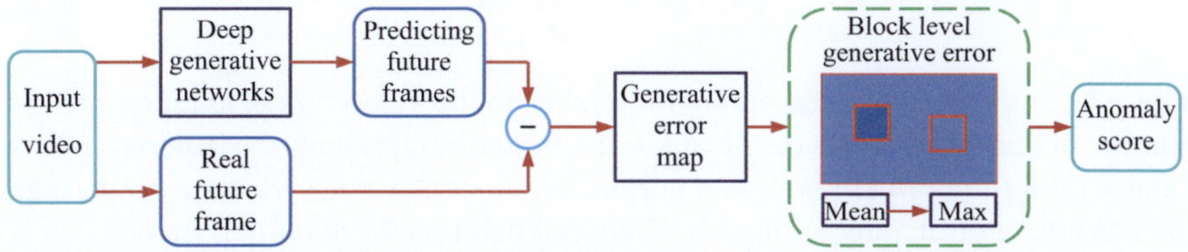

Fig. 8.11 Flow chart of SCA-SDGM testing (Wang et al. 2020a)

block level generative error on the test frame image. The first step above only requires a single operation and does not need to be repeated. The second and third steps can be achieved through a mean filtering operation (mean) and a max pooling operation (max), respectively. SCA-SDGM detects anomalies by using the largest block level generative error on the frame image, which reduces the impact of scene content changes on the value ranges of the basic generative error of the frame image, thereby reducing the intra class variance of the generative error of normal frame images. On the other hand, SCA-SDGM avoids averaging the generative errors of abnormal regions with those of normal regions, thereby increasing the inter class variance of the generative errors of both abnormal frames and normal frames.

8.6.2 *Specific Characteristics of the Model*

The model still uses the terms defined in Eqs. (8.26) to (8.29) in Sub-Sect. 8.5.1 when calculating the generative loss during training. Their weighted sum was also used in calculating the total generative loss (see Eq. (8.31)).

The main characteristics of the model are: frame block processing, frame block size adaptation, and anomaly score normalization. Below are their separate introductions.

1. **Frame Block Processing**

When comparing the generative errors between abnormal frames and normal frames to check for determining abnormal frames, it is necessary to consider the (relative) strength of the generative errors of frames. The saliency of the generative error I_a of abnormal frames relative to the generative error I_n of normal frames can be defined as the **anomaly saliency** S_a:

$$S_{\mathrm{a}} = \frac{I_{\mathrm{a}} - I_{\mathrm{n}}}{I_{\mathrm{n}}} \tag{8.34}$$

$$I_{\mathrm{a}} = \frac{\sum_{j=1}^{m} e'_j - \sum_{i=1}^{M-m} e_i}{M} \tag{8.35}$$

$$I_{\mathrm{n}} = \frac{\sum_{i=1}^{M} e_i}{M} \tag{8.36}$$

where M represents the total number of pixels on the video frame; m represents the number of abnormal pixels on the abnormal frame; e_i represents the generative error value of the i-th normal pixel on a normal frame or abnormal frame; $e_j{}'$ represents the generative error value of the j-th abnormal pixel on the abnormal frame.

In adjacent video frame images, it can be assumed that the generative error of normal regions in abnormal frames is approximately equal to the generative error of corresponding regions in normal frames. At this point, by substituting Eqs. (8.35) and (8.36) into Eqs. (8.34), (8.34) can be written as:

$$S_{\mathrm{a}} = \frac{\sum_{j=1}^{m} e'_j - \sum_{i=1}^{M-m} e_i}{\sum_{i=1}^{M} e_i} \tag{8.37}$$

As shown in Eq. (8.37), the significance of abnormal frames is negatively correlated to $\sum_{i=1}^{M} e_i$, which represents the generative error of normal regions in abnormal frames. This indicates that when using generative error to detect anomalies, the higher the generative error of the normal region counted in a video frame, the lower the significance of the abnormal frame.

Therefore, by reducing the proportion of generative errors in normal regions of video frames in the generative errors used for anomaly detection, the **anomaly saliency** of abnormal frames can be improved. The post-processing method for frame blocks was proposed for this purpose. This method detects anomalies by replacing frame level generative errors with (frame) block level generation errors. Specifically, it performs a two-step operation: Firstly, place a sliding window of a given size on the generative error map (this sliding window is also used for every frame in the video) to calculate the generative error at the block level at each spatial position; Secondly, select the maximum value of the generative error at all block levels on a video frame as an indicator to determine whether the video frame is abnormal. Referring to Fig. 8.11, these two operations can be represented as the average (mean) operation (implemented by convolution) and the maximum operation (implemented by max pooling), respectively:

$$e_{B_k}(t) = \frac{1}{h \times w} \sum_{i=1}^{h} \sum_{j=1}^{w} B_{k,i,j} \quad k = 1, 2, \ldots, K \tag{8.38}$$

$$e_B(t) = \max\left[e_{B_1}(t),\ e_{B_2}(t),\ \cdots,\ e_{B_K}(t)\right] \tag{8.39}$$

where $e_{Bk}(t)$ represents the block level generative error at the position B_k of the k-th block of a video frame; h and w respectively represent the height and width of the block; K represents the total number of frame blocks; $e_B(t)$ represents the maximum value of block level generative errors among all frames in a video frame.

The above two operations can also be combined and written together:

$$e_B(t) = \max\left\{\text{mean}_{B_k}\left[\text{GE}_{\text{map}}(I_t, J_t)\right]\right\} \tag{8.40}$$

where $\text{GE}_{\text{map}}(I_t, J_t)$ represents the generative error map between I_t and J_t; $\text{mean}_{Bk}(\cdot)$ represents 2-D mean filtering (template size B_k), and $\max(\cdot)$ represents max pooling.

2. **Adaptive Frame Block Size**

The selection of frame block size needs to consider the characteristics of abnormal regions and ideally correspond to the size of foreground targets in the image. If the frame block size is close to the size of the abnormal region, the frame block used for anomaly detection will contain as many abnormal pixels as possible and only as few normal pixels as possible, which will maximize the anomaly saliency of the frame block level generative error of the abnormal frame.

Considering that foreground targets in images obtained from different scenes may have different sizes, SCA-SSDGM needs to extract the sizes of each foreground target from normal video frames in the training set (such as using frame difference method), and then use their mean to determine the size of the sliding window. This can make the frame block size adapted to different scenes.

3. **Normalization of Abnormal Scores**

The generative error values obtained from different videos may be distributed in different interval ranges. Therefore, the maximum-minimum normalization method can be used to normalize each video frame (or video clip) one by one. However, this frame by frame normalization strategy may result in high abnormal scores in each video frame, and forcing the algorithm to extract abnormal events from normal video samples can also lead to a high false alarm rate. Due to the use of frame block post-processing in SCA-SDGM, the anomaly saliency of abnormal frames is improved, the inter class variance is increased, and the problems caused by different levels of normal generative errors are alleviated. In addition, it reduces the impact of the number of foreground targets on the basic generative error level of video frames, and diminishes the intra class variance of the basic generation error of normal video clips. To overcome these issues, a unified normalization strategy can be adopted.

This unified normalization method specifically normalizes the generative errors of all video frames to the [0, 1] interval as follows after obtaining the generative errors at the frame block level:

$$e_{\text{norm}}(t) = \frac{e_B(t) - \min(e_B)}{\max(e_B) - \min(e_B)} \tag{8.41}$$

where $\max(e_B)$and $\min(e_B)$ are the maximum and minimum values of the frame block level generative error e_B for all video frames, respectively. Due to the inclusion of multiple generative losses in SCA-SDGM, there will be multiple corresponding abnormal scores. At this point, the weighted sum of multiple abnormal scores can be used to calculate the final abnormal score:

$$e_{\text{globa}}(t) = \sum_i W_i e_i(t) \tag{8.42}$$

where $e_i(t)$ is the i-th abnormal score of the t-th frame; W_i is the weight of $e_i(t)$.

8.6.3 Experimental Results and Analysis

Many datasets can be used in the experiments, such as: UCSD Pedestrian dataset (including both subsets Ped1 and Ped2, counted as two datasets) (Mahadevan et al. 2010), CUHK Avenue dataset (Lu et al. 2013), Subway Exit dataset (Adam et al. 2008), and ShanghaiTech (SH) dataset (Luo et al. 2021). In the following, some results with the first three datasets are presented. The corresponding experimental settings of several characteristics introduced in the previous sub-section are as follows.

1. **Frame Block Processing Experiments**

Three experiments were conducted on frame block processing, all utilizing the CUHK Avenue, UCSD Ped1, and UCSD Ped2 datasets.

(1) Frame block processing enhances the saliency of anomalies

The experiment calculated the anomaly saliencies of the generative error at both the frame level and the frame block level. Equation (8.34) is used in calculation, where the mean of all abnormal frame generative errors is taken as I_a, and the mean of all normal frame generative errors is taken as I_n. The results are shown in Table 8.9 (bold numbers indicate the best).

As shown in Table 8.9, the anomaly saliency obtained from frame block level processing is significantly improved as compared to frame level processing, which is advantageous for anomaly detection.

(2) Robustness of frame block processing to changes in foreground target density

Table 8.9 Comparison of anomaly saliencies of frame level and frame block level generative errors (Wang et al. 2020a)

	UCSD Ped1	UCSD Ped2	CUHK Avenue
Frame level	1.1580	0.7475	2.6341
Frame block level	**2.5239**	**2.4162**	**3.4552**

The basic generative error in the video is closely related to the density or number of foreground targets. The experiment compared the correlation between frame level and frame block level generative errors with foreground target density. The results are shown in Table 8.10 (bold number indicate the best).

As shown in Table 8.10, the correlation between frame block level generative error and foreground target density is smaller than that between frame level generative error and foreground target density. Because the generative errors in different videos have a positive correlation with the density of foreground targets, a small correlation will make the level of basic generative errors relatively stable.

Secondly, the experiment compared the different ratios of basic generative errors at the frame level and frame block level in scenes with different foreground target densities. Specifically, three pairs of videos with different foreground target densities were selected, and the relative basic generative error ratios obtained from each pair were calculated. The experimental results obtained using the UCSD Ped2 dataset are shown in Table 8.11 (bold numbers indicate the best). Each video clip in this dataset is relatively short, and the number of foreground targets in each frame image is relatively consistent.

As shown in Table 8.11, when the foreground target density is different, the ratio of frame block level generative errors is relatively smaller than that of frame level generative errors. Because this ratio reflects the degree to which the generative error is affected by changes in foreground target density, the closer the ratio is to 1, the better. Therefore, it can be inferred that frame block level processing is less affected by the number of foreground targets than frame level processing.

(3) Improvement of anomaly detection performance through frame block processing

The **Area Under Curve** (AUC) of **Receiver Operating Characteristic** (ROC) was used as the evaluation indicator to experimentally compare the anomaly detection performance during frame level processing and frame block level processing. The obtained ROC curves are shown in Fig. 8.12, where the horizontal axis represents

Table 8.10 Correlation of generative errors between frame level and frame block level with foreground target density (Wang et al. 2020a)

	UCSD Ped1	UCSD Ped2	CUHK Avenue
Frame level	0.9698	0.9847	0.7512
Frame block level	**0.8808**	**0.8625**	**0.6398**

Table 8.11 Ratio of generative errors at different foreground target densities (Wang et al. 2020a)

	Number of foreground targets (low/ high density)		
	10/25	15/25	10/30
Frame level	2.0822	2.1739	2.6305
Frame block level	**1.2875**	**1.5104**	**1.6264**

False Positive Rate (FPR) or **false alarm rate**, and the vertical axis represents **True Positive Rate** (TPR) or **recall**. Figure 8.12a–c, correspond to the results of using the UCSD Ped1, UCSD Ped2, and CUHK Avenue datasets, respectively. The obtained AUC index values are shown in Table 8.12 (bold numbers indicate the best).

As shown in Fig. 8.12 and Table 8.12, the frame block level processing significantly improves anomaly detection performance compared to the frame level processing.

2. **Frame Block Size Adaptive Experiments**

The selection of frame block size affects the performance of anomaly detection. When generative error maps are size of 256 × 256, experiments were conducted with different frame block sizes, and the results (performance AUC varying with frame block size) are shown in Table 8.13 (bold numbers indicate the best).

As shown in Table 8.13, different frame block sizes have different impacts on detection performance for different databases, and the optimal frame block size for performance varies (but is close to their respective foreground target sizes). This indicates that the frame block size needs to be selected based on content changes in data. Therefore, frame block size adaptation should be an effective method.

3. **Abnormal Score Normalization Experiments**

Sub-Sect. 8.6.2 introduces the use of a unified normalization strategy instead of a frame by frame normalization strategy in abnormal score normalization. Below is an experimental comparison of two strategies.

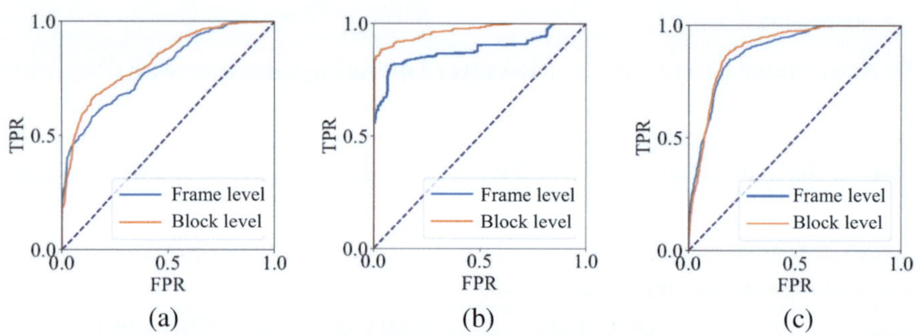

Fig. 8.12 ROC curves of frame level and frame block level anomaly detection performance (Wang et al. 2020a)

Table 8.12 Comparison of anomaly detection performance (AUC) at frame level and frame block level (Wang et al. 2020a)

	UCSD Ped1	UCSD Ped2	CUHK Avenue
Frame level	79.66	88.46	88.85
Frame block level	**82.88**	**96.78**	**89.82**

Table 8.13 Effects of different frame block sizes on anomaly detection performance (AUC) (Wang et al. 2020a)

Frame block sizes	UCSD Ped1	UCSD Ped2	CUHK Avenue
10 × 10	82.8	90.6	**90.2**
20 × 20	83.0	96.7	89.7
30 × 30	82.9	**96.8**	89.8
40 × 40	**83.4**	93.8	89.8
50 × 50	83.2	93.8	89.7
60 × 60	82.9	92.5	89.8

In video anomaly detection tasks, two application scenarios can be considered. The first scenario is when it is already known that the video contains anomalies, and only the time of occurrence of the anomalies in the video needs to be located. The second scenario is that it is not known whether the video contains anomalies, and it is necessary to determine whether the video contains anomalies and locate the time of occurrence of the anomalies. Because each test video clip in the dataset contains anomalies, these clips can be used to represent the first scenario. For the second scenario, it is possible to consider using all training and testing video clips in the dataset simultaneously (all training videos are normal videos, and all testing videos contain anomalies).

In the experiment, two scenarios were tested separately. The results obtained from using two strategies of frame normalization are shown in Table 8.14 (bold numbers indicate the best).

As shown in Table 8.14, the anomaly detection performance using the unified normalization strategy on "training + testing data" is superior to that on "testing data". The anomaly detection performance on "testing data" using frame by frame normalization strategy is better than that on "training + test data". In other words, when the training data is added to the evaluation data, the abnormal score obtained by using the unified normalization strategy increases, while the abnormal score obtained by using the frame by frame normalization strategy decreases.

The reason here is that the frame by frame normalization strategy normalizes the abnormal scores of each video clip to the [0, 1] interval, which can generate many false alarms in video clips without anomalies. It can be seen that frame by frame

Table 8.14 Effects of frame normalization and unified normalization on anomaly detection performance (AUC) (Wang et al. 2020a)

Evaluation data	Frame normalization			Unified normalization		
	UCSD Ped1	UCSD Ped2	CUHK Avenue	UCSD Ped1	UCSD Ped2	CUHK Avenue
Testing data	**0.833**	**0.987**	**0.872**	0.829	0.968	0.898
Training + testing data	0.676	0.755	0.744	**0.940**	**0.976**	**0.938**

normalization strategy is not suitable for videos containing a large number of normal samples. In addition, the unified frame normalization strategy is more suitable for practical applications where most video clips are normal video clips, and is also more suitable for use in the work of using generative errors to determine anomalies.

8.7 Master-Auxiliary Aggregation Strategy

Many anomaly detection methods based on different working principles and network structures have been proposed, such as: ① Anomaly detection based on deep generative error (such as (Hasan et al. 2016; Liu et al. 2018; Nogas et al. 2020)), in which deep generative models are first used to learn the manifold distribution of normal samples, and then the samples with large generative errors are identified as anomalies; ② Anomaly detection based on deep distance detection for anomalies (such as (Oza and Patel 2019; Wu et al. 2019; Jiang and Li 2021)), a deep neural network is first used to learn the one-class hyperplane of normal samples, and then the samples that fall outside the one-class hyperplane are judged as anomalies; ③ Anomaly detection based on deep probability detection for anomalies (such as (Lee et al. 2018; Sabokrou et al. 2018; Ravanbakhsh et al. 2019; Tang et al. 2020)), a **Generative Adversarial Network** (GAN) is first used to learn the distribution probability density of normal samples, and then the samples with low distribution probability density are identified as anomalies.

The following introduces a technique that utilizes the **Master-Auxiliary Aggregation Strategy** (MAAS) and combines different anomaly detectors (Wang et al. 2021b). MAAS first uses an anomaly detector based on pixel value generative errors as the master detector to provide basic anomaly detection capabilities, and then use some other detectors as auxiliary detectors to provide high-precision decisions with diversity and complementarity.

8.7.1 Basic Framework and Flowchart

For an anomaly detector, the stricter the threshold for anomaly detection, the higher the confidence and detection accuracy of the anomaly decision. Based on this, MAAS sets two strict thresholds for each auxiliary detector: a strict normal threshold and a strict abnormal threshold. Here, the strict normal threshold is used to extract strong normal samples from the corresponding auxiliary detector to achieve high-precision decision-making. The strict anomaly threshold is used to extract strong abnormal samples from corresponding auxiliary detectors to achieve high-precision decision-making. In addition, MAAS extends the strong normal decisions and strong abnormal decisions obtained from the auxiliary detector based on the temporal continuity of the event occurrence: all video frames between strong abnormal frames with sufficiently short time intervals are extended to strong abnormal frames, and all video frames between strong normal frames with sufficiently short time intervals are extended to strong normal frames. Next, MAAS counts the number of frames in each video that are judged as strong normal and strong abnormal frames on all auxiliary detectors. Finally, MAAS calculates the ratio of strong abnormal number to strong normal number for each video frame, fuses the decisions of the auxiliary detector into soft weights, and weights the abnormal scores of the master detector to obtain a heterogeneous aggregation detector.

The flowchart of the master-auxiliary aggregation strategy is shown in Fig. 8.13. The figure includes four functional modules: ① Strong normal and strong abnormal sample detection, where each auxiliary detector detects strong normal frames and strong abnormal frames in the video using strong normal thresholds and strong abnormal thresholds, respectively; ② Obtaining statistics of strong normal frame rates and strong abnormal frame rates, which refers to the counting of the numbers of strong normal frames and strong abnormal frames determined by each auxiliary detector (also taking into account the frames interpolated based on the temporal continuity of events); ③ Calculation of soft weights, that is, calculating the frame to frame ratio of strong abnormal and strong normal for a video frame as the soft weight for that video frame; ④ Soft weighting, multiplying the soft weights from the auxiliary detector with the corresponding abnormal scores from the master detector to obtain the abnormal scores output by the detector aggregation.

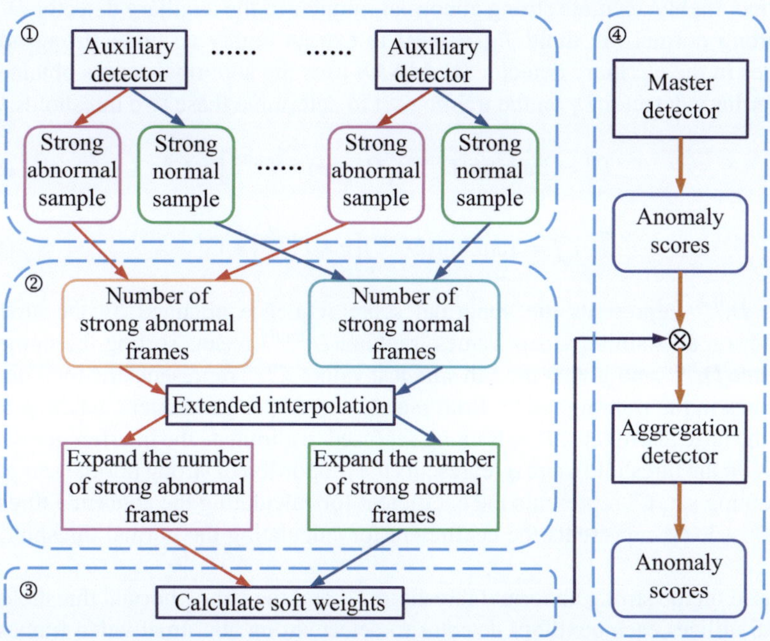

Fig. 8.13 Flowchart of the master-auxiliary aggregation strategy (Wang et al. 2021b)

The master-auxiliary aggregation strategy provides a framework for combining different detectors. In Sect. 8.5.1, four types of generative loss calculations were discussed, namely Eqs. (8.26) to (8.29). Thinking these four types of generative losses, namely pixel intensity loss, pixel gradient loss, optical flow loss, and adversarial loss, it can be considered that four anomaly detectors can be constructed based on them, namely the pixel intensity-based detector D_{int}, the pixel gradient-based detector D_{grad}, the optical flow-based detector D_{flow}, and the adversarial discrimination-based detector D_{adv}. In the following discussion, the pixel intensity-based detector will be used as the master detector D_{m}, while the other three detectors will be used as auxiliary detectors D_i, $i = 1, 2, 3$.

8.7.2 Master-Auxiliary Aggregation Modules

Referring to Fig. 8.13, the following introduces the four modules in the master-auxiliary aggregation.

1. **Strong Normal and Strong Abnormal Sample Detection**

MAAS sets two thresholds for each auxiliary detector: a strong abnormal threshold T_i^{a} and a strong normal threshold T_i^{n}. The strong abnormal threshold T_i^{a} is used to extract highly accurate strong abnormal samples in the auxiliary detector D_i, and the strong normal threshold T_{in} is used to extract highly accurate strong normal samples in the auxiliary detector D_i. MAAS uses the abnormal scores obtained by the auxiliary detector D_i on the training set to determine these two thresholds:

$$T_i^{\mathrm{a}} = \mathrm{ranking}(D_i^{\mathrm{train}})\left[(1-p) * T^{\mathrm{train}}\right] * C^{\mathrm{a}} \tag{8.43}$$

$$T_i^{\mathrm{n}} = \mathrm{ranking}(D_i^{\mathrm{train}})\left[q * T^{\mathrm{train}}\right] * C^{\mathrm{n}} \tag{8.44}$$

where D_i^{train} represents the abnormal score sequence obtained by the auxiliary detector on all training video frames; ranking(D_i^{train}) means sorting the numerical sequence D_i^{train} and giving the i-th smallest value; T^{train} represents the total number of frames in the training video. Both p and q are hyper-parameters, where p represents the false alarm rate in the training set (used to eliminate the interference of false alarms on the threshold), and q represents the proportion of strong normal samples in the training set. C^{a} represents the coefficient for calculating the abnormal threshold T_i^{a}, $C^{\mathrm{a}} > 1$, C^{n} represents the coefficient for calculating the normal threshold T_i^{n}, $C^{\mathrm{n}} < 1$。

Based on the strong abnormal threshold T_i^{a} and the strong normal threshold T_i^{n}, MAAS utilizes each auxiliary detector to detect strong abnormal video frames and strong normal video frames:

$$S_i^{\mathrm{a}}(t) = \begin{cases} 1 & d_i(t) \geq T_i^{\mathrm{a}} \\ 0 & \text{otherwise} \end{cases} \tag{8.45}$$

$$S_i^{\mathrm{n}}(t) = \begin{cases} 1 & d_i(t) \leq T_i^{\mathrm{n}} \\ 0 & \text{otherwise} \end{cases} \tag{8.46}$$

where $S_i^{\mathrm{a}}(t)$ and $S_i^{\mathrm{n}}(t)$ represent the strong abnormal decision functions and strong normal decision functions of the auxiliary detector D_i for the test video frame I_t, respectively; $d_i(t)$ represents the abnormal score of the auxiliary detector D_i on the test video frame I_t.

2. **Statistics of Strong Normal and Strong Abnormal Frame Numbers**

After all auxiliary detectors have completed the strong abnormal decisions and strong normal decisions for the test video frame I_t, MAAS calculates the numbers of strong abnormal frames $V[S_i^{\mathrm{a}}(t)]$ and strong normal frames $V[S_i^{\mathrm{n}}(t)]$, given by the three auxiliary detectors:

$$V[S_i^{\mathrm{a}}(t)] = \sum_{i=1}^{3} S_i^{\mathrm{a}}(t) \tag{8.47}$$

$$V[S_i^{\mathrm{n}}(t)] = \sum_{i=1}^{3} S_i^{\mathrm{n}}(t) \tag{8.48}$$

Equations (8.47) and (8.48) count the numbers of frames directly identified as strong abnormal frames and strong normal frames, respectively. In practice, the occurrence of normal or abnormal events has a certain degree of temporal continuity. If the time interval between two strong abnormal frames is short enough (which can be represented by a hyper-parameter), then it can be considered that these two strong abnormal frames belong to the same abnormal event, and the video frames between them should also be abnormal frames. Similarly, if the time interval between two strong normal frames is short enough (which can be represented by a hyper-parameter), the video frames between them should also be normal frames. For this purpose, MAAS also infers the video frames between two strong abnormal frames with sufficiently short time intervals as strong abnormal frames, and counts the number into the strong abnormal frame rate. MAAS also infers the video frames between two strong normal frames with sufficiently short time intervals as strong normal frames, and counts the number into the strong normal frame rate. The above operations are equivalent to an extension (expansion) interpolation operation, and the result of the operation is to obtain the expanded strong abnormal frame rate $V[S_i^{\mathrm{a}}(t)]$ and the expanded strong normal frame rate $V[S_i^{\mathrm{n}}(t)]$, respectively.

3. **Calculate Soft Weights**

By using the video frame I_t to obtain the extended strong abnormal frame rate $Vi[S_i^{\mathrm{a}}(t)]$ and the extended strong normal frame rate $Vi[S_i^{\mathrm{n}}(t)]$ on the auxiliary detector, a soft weight $W(t)$ can be obtained by calculating the ratio of strong abnormal frame and strong normal frame for the video frame I_t:

$$W(t) = \frac{1 + r \times V^*[S_i^{\mathrm{a}}(t)]}{1 + r \times V^*[S_i^{\mathrm{n}}(t)]} \tag{8.49}$$

where r is a hyper-parameter that adjusts the impact of the decision of the auxiliary detectors on the final aggregation detector.

4. **Soft Weighting**

Multiplying the soft weight obtained from the auxiliary detector of video frame I_t with the abnormal score calculated in the master detector yields the final abnormal score of the video frame in the aggregation detector:

$$D_{\mathrm{agg}}(t) = D_{\mathrm{m}}(t) \times W(t) \tag{8.50}$$

8.7.3 Experimental Results and Analysis

The following analyzes two experiments related to aggregation strategies and methods. The experiments utilized the following datasets: UCSD Pedestrian dataset (including both subsets Ped1 and Ped2, counted as two datasets) (Mahadevan et al. 2010), CUHK Avenue dataset (Lu et al. 2013), Subway Exit dataset (Adam et al. 2008), and ShanghaiTech (SH) dataset (Luo et al. 2021).

1. **Selection of Master and Auxiliary Detectors**

In MAAS, a total of four detectors are involved: D_{int} detector based on pixel intensity, D_{grad} detector based on pixel gradient, D_{flow} detector based on optical flow, and D_{adv} detector based on adversarial discrimination. If one of them is selected as the master detector and the other three are used as auxiliary detectors, there can be four combinations. The experimental results for the four combinations are shown in Table 8.15 (bold numbers indicate the best).

For each combination in Table 8.15, the previous row shows the results of using only one detector, while the next row shows the results of detector aggregation with that detector as the master detector and three other detectors as auxiliary detectors.

From Table 8.15, two points can be seen: ① For each combination, the effect of using detector aggregation is better than using a single detector alone, indicating that aggregating detectors can indeed improve the performance; ② The results obtained by using different detectors as the master detector are different, among which D_{int} has the best effect as the master detector. The possible reasons for this latter point include: ① Pixel intensity attribute is the most important basic attribute of video data; ② Many depths generative error detectors based on pixel intensity have achieved good performance in anomaly detection (Liu et al. 2018). The aggregation strategy adopted

Table 8.15 Effects of different master and auxiliary detector combinations (AUC) (Wang et al. 2021b)

Detectors	UCSD Ped1	UCSD Ped2	CUHK Avenue	Subway Exit	Shanghai Tech	Mean values
*D*int	82.88	96.78	89.82	95.72	67.58	86.56
*D*int as master detector	**85.79**	**99.04**	**92.13**	**96.46**	**69.7**	**88.62**
*D*grad	77.80	96.89	84.20	96.15	68.27	84.66
*D*grad as master detector	**84.69**	**98.14**	**90.7**	**96.86**	**68.42**	**87.76**
*D*flow	86.66	98.00	86.07	94.62	68.98	86.87
*D*flow as master detector	**86.79**	**98.04**	**90.11**	**96.34**	**70.62**	**88.38**
*D*adv	53.19	57.59	84.41	91.31	61.37	69.57
*D*adv as master detector	**80.55**	**94.16**	**88.36**	**95.75**	**65.66**	**84.90**

by MAAS distinguishes between master and auxiliary detectors, which have unequal positions in the aggregation and need to be treated differently.

2. **Comparison of Aggregation Methods**

The common methods for aggregating different detectors can be divided into three categories: ① Weighted sum method (such as (Ouyang and Sanchez 2021)), ② Sorting method (such as (Sabokrou et al. 2015)), and ③ Cascade method (such as (Li et al. 2021a)).

The weighted sum method uses the weighted sum of abnormal scores from multiple detectors to detect anomalies, which has the advantage of being simple and convenient. It can aggregate both homogeneous and heterogeneous detectors. The disadvantages include: ① It is difficult to set appropriate weighting for different detectors; ② Due to the mixing of decisions from multiple detectors with unknown performance, incorrect decisions in one detector may interfere with correct decisions in other detectors.

The sorting method sorts the abnormal scores of different detectors, and then uses the maximum, minimum, or median as the final abnormal score. The sorting method is suitable for aggregating homogeneous detectors, but not for aggregating heterogeneous detectors. Two reasons here are: ① The abnormal scores of heterogeneous detectors have different semantics and numerical ranges, and are not comparable to each other; ② Even if the abnormal scores of each detector are normalized, different detectors have different optimal anomaly detection thresholds, making the aggregation difficult.

Table 8.16 Performance (AUC) comparison between MAAS and three types of aggregation strategies (Wang et al. 2021b)

Aggregation methods	UCSD Ped1	UCSD Ped2	CUHK Avenue	Subway Exit	Shanghai Tech	Mean values
Weighted sum	82.55	98.33	88.55	96.03	69.09	86.91
Sorting (max)	82.81	91.23	89.89	95.62	69.6	85.83
Sorting (min)	55.96	96.13	84.90	93.68	61.80	78.49
Sorting (median)	84.76	95.61	89.26	96.17	69.27	87.01
Cascade	74.59	92.65	84.67	94.82	62.61	81.87
MAAS	**85.79**	**99.04**	**92.13**	**96.46**	**69.7**	**88.62**

The cascade method uses multiple detectors in cascade, and different detectors make their own abnormal decisions in the cascade order, until the last detector makes the final decision on all undecided samples. Cascade method can be used to aggregate heterogeneous detectors, but its main drawback is that if the detectors at the front make incorrect decisions, the detectors following cannot correct these errors, and as the number of cascaded detectors increases, errors will accumulate.

The four detectors used in MAAS were aggregated according to the three aggregation strategies mentioned above. When using sorting, they can be further divided into three subclasses based on maximum, minimum, and median values, thus forming a total of five different aggregation combinations. They were experimentally compared with MAAS, and the performance indicator remains AUC. The results are shown in Table 8.16 (bold numbers indicate the best).

As shown in Table 8.16, the aggregation strategy adopted by MAAS has certain advantages compared to the aggregation strategies in existing anomaly detection methods. The reasons include: ① By extending interpolation, MAAS efficiently utilizes the high accuracy decisions in the auxiliary detector; ② Through the soft weighting step, MAAS improves the robustness of the aggregated detector; ③ By setting threshold constraints, MAAS reduces erroneous decisions fused into the final anomaly detectors.

References

Adam A, Rivlin E, Shimshoni I, *et al.* Robust real-time unusual event detection using multiple fixed-location monitors. IEEE Trans-PAMI, 30(3): 555–560 (2008).

Balakrishnan T S, Jayalakshmi D, Geetha P, *et al.* Accurate recognition of human abnormal behaviours using adaptive 3D residual attention network with gated recurrent units (GRU) in the video sequences. Computer Methods in Biomechanics and Biomedical Engineering-Imaging and Visualization, 12(1), https://doi.org/10.1080/21681163.2024.2429402 (2024).

Chong Y S, Tay Y H. Abnormal event detection in videos using spatiotemporal Autoencoder. Lecture Notes in Computer Science: vol.10262, 189–196 (2017).

Cong Y, Yuan J S, Liu J. Abnormal event detection in crowded scenes using sparse representation. Pattern Recognition, 46(7): 1851–1864 (2013).

Debbarma T, Pal T, Saha A, *et al.* HCNNet: A hybrid convolutional neural network for abnormal human driver behaviour detection. Sadhana-Academy Proceedings in Engineering Science, 50(1): 9. https://doi.org/10.1007/s12046-024-02656-z (2025).

Dosovitskiy A. *et al.* FlowNet: Learning optical flow with convolutional networks. Proc. ICCV, 2758–2766 (2015).

Fan Y, Wen G, Li D, *et al.* Video anomaly detection and localization via Gaussian mixture fully convolutional variational autoencoder. Computer Vision and Image Understanding, 195: 102920 (2020).

Hasan M, Choi J, Neumann J, *et al.* Learning temporal regularity in video sequences Proc. CVPR, 733–742 (2016).

Huang P, Jiang H M, Wang S X, *et al.* Enhancing human behavior recognition with dynamic graph convolutional networks and multi-scale position attention. International Journal of Intelligent Computing and Cybernetics, https://doi.org/10.1108/IJICC-09-2024-0414 (2024).

Huang J, Quan W, Li X W. Visual anomaly detection algorithms: Development and Frontier review. Journal of Visual Communication and Image Representation, 112: https://doi.org/10.1016/j.jvcir.2025.104585 (2025).

Ji X, Li B, Zhu Y. TAM-Net: Temporal enhanced appearance-to-motion generative network for video anomaly detection. Proc. IJCNN, 1–8. (2020)

Ji G L, Qi X S, Wang J Q. Review of deep learning-based video anomaly detection. Pattern Recognition and Artificial Intelligence, 37(2): 128–143 (2024).

Jiang W X, Li G. One-class neural network for video anomaly detection and localization. Journal of Electronic Measurement and Instrumentation, 35(07): 60–65 (2021).

Jin D W, Hu Y Y, Chen B H, *et al.* TIAN: A time series imaging association network for human abnormal behavior detection. Information Fusion, 118: 102906. https://doi.org/10.1016/j.inffus.2024.102906 (2025).

Lee S, Kim H G, Ro Y M. STAN: Spatio-temporal adversarial networks for abnormal event detection, Proc. ICASSP, 1323–1327 (2018).

Li N, Chang F, Liu C. Spatial-temporal cascade autoencoder for video anomaly detection in crowded scenes. IEEE Trans. Multimedia, 23: 203–215 (2021a).

Li X L, Ji G L, Zhao B. Convolutional auto-encoder patch learning based video anomaly event detection and localization. Journal of Data Acquisition and Processing, 36(3): 489–497 (2021b).

Lin C X, Ma T, Wu F, *et al.* Application of temporal action detection technology in abnormal event detection of surveillance video. IEEE Access, 13: 26958–26972. https://doi.org/10.1109/ACCESS.2025.3533552 (2025).

Liu W, Luo W, Lian D, *et al.* Future frame prediction for anomaly detection: A new baseline. Proc. CVPR, 6536–6545 (2018).

Liu D Y, Li Y, Zhou Z, *et al.* Weakly supervised video anomaly detection based on spatiotemporal dependence and feature fusion. Journal of Data Acquisition and Processing, 39(1): 204–214 (2024a).

Liu Y M, Sang H F. Human abnormal behavior recognition based on keyframes localization. Journal of Electronic Measurement and Instrumentation, 38(3): 104–111 (2024b).

Lu C, Shi J, Jia J. Abnormal event detection at 150 FPS in MATLAB. Proc. ICCV, 2720–2727 (2013).

Luo W, Liu W, Lian D, *et al.* Video anomaly detection with sparse coding inspired deep neural networks. IEEE Trans-PAMI, 43(3): 1070–1084 (2021).

Lyu J H, Zhao M H, Hu J, *et al.* Bidirectional skip-frame prediction for video anomaly detection with intra-domain disparity-driven attention. Pattern Recognition, 170: https://doi.org/10.1016/j.patcog.2025.112010 (2026).

Ma Y L, Shi H M, Wang Y, *et al.* TIAN: Research on abnormal behavior detection technology in controlled areas based on human body parts trajectory tracking. Journal of instrumentation, 20(5): P05032. https://doi.org/10.1088/1748-0221/20/05/P05032 (2025).

Mahadevan V, Li W, Bhalodia V, *et al.* Anomaly detection in crowded scenes. Proc. CVPR, 1975–1981 (2010).

Mao G J, Wu X Z, Xing S L. Research on visual anomaly detection based on multi-scale normalizing flow. Acta Automatica Sinica, 50(3): 640–648 (2024).

Murakami N, Hiramatsu N, Kobayashi H, et al. Subspace-based embedded feature reduction for fast anomaly detection. In: Petersen J, Dahl V A (Eds.): SCIA 2025, LNCS 15726, 210–223 (2025).

Nogas J, Khan S S, Mihailidis A. DeepFall: Non-invasive fall detection with deep spatiotemporal convolutional autoencoders. Journal of Healthcare Informatics Research, 4(1): 50–70 (2020).

Ouyang Y, Sanchez V. Video anomaly detection by estimating likelihood of representations. Proc. ICPR, 8984–8991 (2021).

Oza P, Patel V M. One-class convolutional neural network. IEEE Signal Processing Letters, 26(2): 277–281 (2019).

Ravanbakhsh M, Sangineto E, Nabi M, *et al.* Training adversarial discriminators for cross-channel abnormal event detection in crowds. Proc. WACV, V.2: 1896–1904 (2019).

Sabokrou M, Fathy M, Hoseini M, *et al.* Real-time anomaly detection and localization in crowded scenes. Proc, CVPRW, 2015: 56–62 (2015).

Sabokrou M, Khalooei M, Fathy M, *et al.* Adversarially learned one-class classifier for novelty detection. Proc. CVPR, 3379–3388 (2018).

Sun L, Wang Z G, Zhang Y-J, *et al.* A feature-trajectory-smoothed high speed model for video anomaly detection. Sensors, 23(3): #1612 (https://doi.org/10.3390/s23031612) (2023).

Sun C, Wu Y W, Jia Y D. Context modeling and reasoning for video abnormal event detection. Chinese Journal of Computers, 47(10): 2368–2386 (2024).

Tang Y, Zhao L, Zhang S, *et al.* Integrating prediction and reconstruction for anomaly detection. PRL, 129: 123–130 (2020).

Wang Z G, Yang Z L, Zhang Y-J. A promotion method for generation error-based video anomaly detection. PRL, 140: 88–94 (2020a).

Wang Z G, Zhang Y-J. Anomaly detection in surveillance videos: A survey. Journal of Tsinghua University (Science and Technology), 60(6):518–529 (2020b).

Wang Z G, Yang Z L, Zhang Y-J, *et al.* Ts-Unet: A temporal smoothed Unet for video anomaly detection. Proc. ICIG (LNCS 11890), 789–798 (2021a).

Wang Z G, Zhang Y-J, Wang G J, *et al.* Master-auxiliary aggregation strategy for video anomaly detection. IEEE SPL, 28: 1794–1798 (2021b).

Wang Z G. Researches on Semi-Supervised and Deep Generative Model-Based Surveillance Video Anomaly Detection Algorithms (Dissertation). Beijing, Tsinghua University (2022).

Wu P, Liu J, Shen F. A deep one-class neural network for anomalous event detection in complex scenes. IEEE Trans-NNLS, 31(7): 1–14 (2019).

Yuan J, Zhang Y-J. Application of sparse denoising auto encoder network with gradient difference information for abnormal action detection. Acta Automatica Sinica, 43(4): 604–610 (2017).

Zhang W L, Qi H, Li S. Application of spatial temporal graph convolutional networks in human abnormal behavior recognition. Computer Engineering and Applications, 58(12): 122–131 (2022).

Zhao R Y, Hua F, Wei B Y, *et al.* A review of abnormal crowd behavior recognition technology based on computer vision. Applied Sciences-Basel, 14(21), https://doi.org/10.3390/app14219758 (2024).

Zhou J T, Zhang L, Fang Z, *et al.* Attention-driven loss for anomaly detection in video surveillance. IEEE Trans-CSVT, 30, 4639–4647 (2020).

Zhu X R, Qian X Y, Shi Y Z, *et al.* Video anomaly detection with long-and-short-term time series correlations. Journal of Image and Graphics, 29(7): 1998–2010 (2024).

Index

Y.-J. Zhang, *Spatiotemporal Image Understanding*,
https://doi.org/10.1007/978-981-95-7130-7

MIX
Papier aus verantwortungsvollen Quellen
Paper from responsible sources
FSC® C105338
FSC
www.fsc.org

If you have any concerns about our products,
you can contact us on
ProductSafety@springernature.com

In case Publisher is established outside the EU,
the EU authorized representative is:
Springer Nature Customer Service Center GmbH
Europaplatz 3, 69115 Heidelberg, Germany

Printed by Libri Plureos GmbH
in Hamburg, Germany